A Portrait in Four Movements

A Portrait in
Four Movements

The Chicago Symphony under
Barenboim, Boulez, Haitink, and Muti

ANDREW PATNER

Edited by John R. Schmidt and Douglas W. Shadle

With a Foreword by Alex Ross

The University of Chicago Press

Chicago and London

The University of Chicago Press, Chicago 60637

The University of Chicago Press, Ltd., London

© 2019 by The University of Chicago

All rights reserved. No part of this book may be used or reproduced in
any manner whatsoever without written permission, except in the case
of brief quotations in critical articles and reviews. For more information,
contact the University of Chicago Press, 1427 E. 60th St., Chicago, IL 60637.

Published 2019

Printed in the United States of America

28 27 26 25 24 23 22 21 20 19   1 2 3 4 5

ISBN-13: 978-0-226-60991-1 (cloth)

ISBN-13: 978-0-226-61008-5 (e-book)

DOI: https://doi.org/10.7208/chicago/9780226610085.001.0001

Frontispiece: Drawing of Andrew Patner, by Tom Bachtell

Library of Congress Cataloging-in-Publication Data

Names: Patner, Andrew, 1959–2015, author. | Schmidt, John R., 1947– editor. |
Shadle Douglas W., editor.

Title: A portrait in four movements : the Chicago Symphony under
Barenboim, Boulez, Haitink, and Muti / Andrew Patner ; edited by
John R. Schmidt and Douglas W. Shadle ; with a foreword by Alex Ross.

Description: Chicago ; London : The University of Chicago Press, 2019. |
Includes bibliographical references and index.

Identifiers: LCCN 2018042359 | ISBN 9780226609911 (cloth : alk. paper) |
ISBN 9780226610085 (ebook)

Subjects: LCSH: Chicago Symphony Orchestra—History . | Conductors
(Music)—Interviews. | Barenboim, Daniel, 1942– | Boulez, Pierre, 1925–2016. |
Haitink, Bernard, 1929– | Muti, Riccardo. | Concerts—Illinois—Chicago.

Classification: LCC ML28.C4 C424 2019 | DDC 784.206/077311—dc23

LC record available at https://lccn.loc.gov/2018042359

♾ This paper meets the requirements of ANSI/NISO Z39.48–1992
(Permanence of Paper).

Contents

Afterword: Riccardo Muti Remembers Andrew Patner

Foreword

[ALEX ROSS]

Andrew Patner, the beloved Chicago critic, author, and radio personality, combined two traits that are rarely found in one person. He was, first of all, brilliant—near-omniscient, all-remembering, lavishly cultured. He was also generous—selfless and tireless in his efforts on behalf of friends, acquaintances, and perfect strangers. These traits intersected in Andrew's immense spirit of curiosity. His urge to be of service increased his store of knowledge. I have never met anyone who was more avidly open to the world around him. One anecdote illustrates the governing principle of his life. Walking the streets of Chicago, he made a habit of offering directions to people who looked lost. Once, he approached an older couple who seemed particularly befuddled. They turned out to be Philip Roth and Claire Bloom.

Andrew was born on Beethoven's baptismal day, in 1959, in Chicago. His roots were in the city's Jewish community and in its activist circles. His mother, Irene, worked for the ACLU and for the arts-education initiative Urban Gateways; his father, Marshall, was a public-interest lawyer who, Andrew proudly recalled, won the 1969 case *Gregory v. the City of Chicago* before the Supreme Court, arguing for Dick Gregory's right to protest segregation. Early in his career,

Andrew seemed destined for a career in political reporting; he wrote for the *Wall Street Journal* and published a book about the radical columnist I. F. Stone. But he stepped away from the *Journal* while caring for a childhood friend who was dying of AIDS; the plague years of the 1980s and 1990s dominated his attention. When he resumed writing regularly, he devoted himself largely to culture, with the Chicago Symphony at the heart of his concerns. Yet the monastic, art-for-art's-sake attitude endemic to so much of the classical world was entirely foreign to him. Making music was always one more form of activism, one more act of conscience.

I knew Andrew for the final ten years or so of his life. In that period, he became increasingly indispensable to my work and life. We lived in different cities, and our friendship was largely an electronic one. I had many delightful dinners and coffees with him and his longtime partner, the *New Yorker* illustrator Tom Bachtell, but for the most part our relationship consisted of email messages—a vast number of them. We exchanged at least three or four emails a day, sometimes dozens. It is often said that human interaction in the digital age is shallower, more insubstantial than in prior eras. In general, I suspect this to be true, but not with Andrew presiding. He was a voracious user of social media, and he had the effect of enlarging and enriching these platforms, endowing them with wit, depth, rigor, and heart. In our daily exchanges, Andrew and I spoke of criticism and journalism, of the classical music business, of culture and politics, of personal matters. These thousands of messages linger on my computer, and they are a bottomless fund of invaluable information and delightful trivia. Once, for some reason, we got onto the subject of musicians' driving habits. Andrew proceeded to provide his "driving survey of Grand Maestri I Have Known." Some excerpts:

Muti—Total comfort. Like driving with my Father, but in nicer cars.
Boulez—Fright level one. Car and racing fanatic. Like driving with
one of my (all male, first) cousins. Only maestro to use the
phrase, "Don' worree. I never loss a passenger yet!"

Solti—Fright level three. Lunatic. As with all else, relied on his
"guardian angel" to see him through.

Discretion prevents me from quoting more, but one internationally
celebrated conductor, a "two-handed talker," attains Fright Level Five.

I was a colleague of Andrew's in the curious world of music criticism, and I learned a great deal from him about the practice of my
profession. He offered, first of all, corrections, particularly in any
matter pertaining to Chicago—and with Andrew there was no matter that did not in some way or other pertain to Chicago. In one *New
Yorker* article, I made the appalling mistake of referring to Orchestra Hall, in Chicago, as Symphony Hall. Into my inbox popped an
email titled "Great article, Alex—one factual caveat, though." He
went on to say, "There has never been nor is there now a 'Symphony
Hall' in Chicago"—a superbly Patneresque locution, suggesting that
even if my article had appeared a century earlier it still would have
been erroneous. He would challenge me if I was praising an artist he
deemed dubious or discounting one he treasured. On certain points
we never reached agreement; a favorite way to pass a morning was to
reopen an old debate. (Driving habits aside, he resisted any criticism
of Pierre Boulez.) But these quarrels became more infrequent, largely
because I had absorbed a portion of Andrew's almost limitless wis-
dom. I kept coming round to his point of view.

This collection enshrines his lifelong, passionate, not uncriti-
cal devotion to the Chicago Symphony, giving particular attention
to four conductors who have led the ensemble in recent decades:
Barenboim, Boulez, Haitink, and Muti. These formidable figures saw
Andrew as an intellectual equal and entrusted him with insights that
appear nowhere else. His interviews collectively constitute a history
of recent trends in the art of conducting. More than anecdotal, they
interrogate major personalities on crucial questions of performance
history and practice, especially at the nexus of American and European traditions. His reviews and commentaries, meanwhile, give a
nuanced portrait of Chicago's musical culture, told from the stand-

point of a singularly privileged and perceptive observer. At the 2015 celebration of Andrew's life—a heartbreaking but magnificent occasion that drew around a thousand people to Orchestra Hall—Muti was heard to say: "Every time a person like Andrew disappears, it will be very difficult to replace him." It is, in fact, impossible, but this book allows his voice to linger.

Preface

[JOHN R. SCHMIDT]

Andrew Patner published over 1,400 reviews as a critic for the *Chicago Sun-Times* from 1991 to his sudden death, at age fifty-five, in early 2015. He wrote about theater, opera, ballet, solo recitals, chamber music, pop, jazz, cabaret, and an eclectic variety of other performances in venues throughout the city. But most of all he wrote about the Chicago Symphony Orchestra, an institution that is central to Chicago's musical life, and about the conductors who led the orchestra in those years.

Few critics of Andrew's caliber have ever covered the performances of a single great orchestra over a comparable period. For over two decades he attended at least one concert of almost every Chicago Symphony program (sometimes he went back for a second) and wrote about most of them, first as one of several reviewers for the *Sun-Times* and then as chief classical music critic from 2006. His responses to performances were further informed by his personal relationships with conductors, guest soloists, and orchestra members, who often talked to him about what had happened in rehearsals. He brought to those concerts a rare and intense musical attentiveness, vast musical knowledge, passionate engagement, and an ability to put what he had experienced into vivid prose.

Starting in 1998, Andrew added to his print reviews something no other critic had ever done: regular radio interviews with the CSO's lead conductors. On a weekly program on WFMT, Chicago's classical music station, he hosted:

- Daniel Barenboim, music director from 1991, shortly before Andrew began reviewing its concerts, until he left that position in 2006;
- Pierre Boulez, who conducted as a regular guest from 1992 to 1995, served as principal guest conductor from 1995 to 2006, was named conductor emeritus in 2006, and eventually relinquished his role as a guest conductor after poor health forced him to stop at the end of 2012;
- Bernard Haitink, principal conductor from 2006 to 2010 and a regular guest thereafter;
- Riccardo Muti, who returned to the orchestra in 2007 for the first time in thirty-two years, was named the new music director in 2008, and assumed that position in 2010.

These programs were not interviews in any conventional sense but conversations with both parties clearly enjoying themselves. (The reporter would have constantly inserted "[*Laughs*]" and "[*Both laugh*]" into the text of any official transcripts.) Barenboim and Haitink each appeared twice, while Boulez appeared three times. Broadcast conversations with Muti, by contrast, became regular parts of the maestro's visits to Chicago until two weeks before Andrew's death, which Muti called "a tragic loss for the cultural life of Chicago."

The combination of Andrew's reviews of the Chicago Symphony with his conversations with each of its major conductors provides a sustained portrait of an orchestra operating at the highest level of musical excellence that is unique in musical literature. This collection is intended to make that portrait available in permanent form.

In selecting and editing the reviews, I generally focused on major works, particularly those that also became the subject of broadcast conversations. The differing emphases of the conductors in their programming created a natural mix of composers and works covered in the interviews. Haitink focused on the core Germanic repertoire, while Boulez provided an eclectic variety of twentieth- and twenty-first-century composers. Barenboim and Muti cut across musical periods and created a Wagner-Verdi split in their respective operatic choices. To ease reading, I cut repetitious passages, excised references to works falling outside the broader narrative, and eliminated extraneous details such as notices of future concert dates and venues.

Reviews are identified by the date of publication in the *Sun-Times*—typically a day after the concert. Unless otherwise indicated, all concerts in Chicago were at Symphony Center. Andrew frequently traveled with the orchestra, and the reviews of concerts elsewhere identify their location. The chapters on Barenboim and Boulez contain substantial gaps until Andrew became chief critic for the *Sun-Times*. A brief gap in his coverage also occurred in the fall of 2013, when he was renegotiating his contract with the *Sun-Times*. WFMT invited him to discuss a much-anticipated concert performance of Verdi's *Macbeth* with Riccardo Muti that fall, so excerpts from that discussion appear here instead.

In editing the radio transcripts, I set out to make them readable by cutting extraneous material, adding punctuation and transitional words, and correcting obvious errors. Even so, I attempted to retain both the character of each speaker's unique speech patterns and the flavor of these relaxed conversations, in which both Andrew and his guests participated with equal verve. The radio interviews are identified by the date of broadcast on WFMT, though they were often taped a few days earlier. The reviews and interviews are set out chronologically so that a conductor's comments about the music at upcoming concerts are followed by Andrew's reports on the result. The headings to both the reviews and the radio transcripts have been added to facilitate narrative flow, and each section is best approached as a single unit.

Douglas Shadle has framed Andrew's account of recent decades with an introductory history of the Chicago Symphony up to Barenboim's arrival and some comments on the role in the orchestra's continuing musical life of each of the four conductors whose work is brought to life in Andrew's reviews and conversations. Doug's extraordinary knowledge of American orchestral history and his own love of the Chicago Symphony make him the ideal scholar to provide that commentary.

Beyond the portrait of a great orchestra and its conductors, I hope the volume will give readers a sense of the personality that led Alex Ross to describe Andrew when he died as "one of the wisest, wittiest, most generous, most avid, most altogether vital people in the world of the arts." Alex's foreword gives us a wonderful picture of that vital personality and their long friendship. As for myself, I met Andrew when a friend introduced us at the intermission of a Chicago Symphony concert around the time he began writing for the *Sun-Times*, and there is no one I would rather look across the room today and see, ready as always to talk and laugh. We cannot bring back the sound of his engaging laughter. But his distinctive voice, in print and on the radio, is here talking, as he most liked to do, about the music he loved.

Introduction

The First Century: A Sketch

[DOUGLAS W. SHADLE]

The Chicago Symphony Orchestra is one of the world's finest musical ensembles. As a teenager in the early 1990s, I fell in love with the distinct sound of the orchestra's brass section. Much to my family's aggravation, our stereo frequently blasted Reiner's Strauss and Bartók. I also appreciated the clarity and nuance that Solti brought to even the most famous music, particularly the Beethoven symphonies. The beautifully produced recording of the Ninth Symphony featuring Jessye Norman was my first introduction to the extraordinary work of Margaret Hillis, the founder and first director of the Chicago Symphony Chorus, whose award-winning collaborations with Solti left an indelible mark on my imagination. The Chicago Symphony became my touchstone.

Classical music lovers have no published history of the orchestra along the lines of Howard Shanet's riveting treatment of the New York Philharmonic or Donald Rosenberg's deep account of the Cleveland Orchestra. Former CSO principal flutist Donald Peck's insider take and sports columnist William Barry Furlong's deep dive into a single season are the best available accounts. This book is different. We make no claim that it rivals the historical depth or gossipy intrigue found in these other books. But we think something is still missing from these traditional stories: the *music*. Books that describe the history of an orchestra usually pull readers into a world behind the scenes. We want to put music first.

Fortunately, we have special materials at our fingertips: the discerning reviews and radio interviews of *Sun-Times* critic Andrew Patner. The vivid imagination and profound insight that leap off the page in Andrew's work capture the orchestra's musical magic—the same magic that casts its spell over each of us—in ways that no traditional narrative ever could. And the questions he posed to each conductor probed their attitudes toward both specific works and the broader meanings of classical music.

Andrew's writings and interviews often reference the orchestra's history. For that reason, we thought readers should have a snapshot of the developments that led to its status as a global musical powerhouse. Many of the issues that shape contemporary public discussions about orchestras—financial viability, high-flying conductors, union disputes, programming variety, attracting new audiences, and so on—in fact coalesced in the late nineteenth century, when the first truly permanent orchestras began to dot the country's landscape. Over time, Chicago audiences came to expect certain qualities from the orchestra that distinguished it from its peers around the globe— sonic brilliance in the brass section, deep connections to the city, and an emphasis on Central European repertoire of the late nineteenth century. The successful union of such local and global concerns over the long term propelled the orchestra into the preeminent place it now holds.

The orchestra has thrived, moreover, because of its exceptional artistic stability. Only ten conductors have served as music director since its founding in 1891, compared to the fifteen who've led the Boston Symphony and the twenty who've directed the New York Philharmonic during the same period. Although players might disagree about the extent to which a conductor shapes an orchestra's sound, or vice versa, there is no question that long-term relationships generate a high level of comfortability, respect, and understanding that continuous personnel disruptions at the top tend to destroy.

Finally, as in several large cities, Chicago's major newspapers maintained a robust critical tradition of writing about the orchestra that stretches back well over a century. Prominent critics have included George P. Upton, W. L. Hubbard, Felix Borowski, Claudia Cassidy, Robert Marsh, and Tom Willis. More than merely documenting the orchestra's activities and reviewing its concerts, these critics provided rich contexts for understanding how the orchestra's work fit into the larger enterprise of classical music around the world. Andrew's intellectual investment in the orchestra and its future marked him as one of the best in this tradition, and the collection of his work in this volume proves that he was an orchestra critic par excellence.

Beethoven or Bust

The Chicago Symphony's first conductor, Theodore Thomas (dir. 1891–1905), was a dyed-in-the-wool classicist. "The man who does not understand Beethoven and has not been under his spell," he once quipped, "has not lived half his life."[1] He believed that an orchestra's mission was to educate audiences *through* music. His career also had all the highlights we've come to expect in the lives of noteworthy conductors. In a tale foreshadowing Toscanini and Bernstein, he appeared in New York at a moment's notice to replace his teacher, Carl Anschütz, for a performance of Donizetti's *Lucrezia Borgia* in 1859, when he was only twenty-four. This successful debut led to increasingly important engagements with New York's standing orchestras, but Thomas remained unsatisfied leading musicians he had not assembled himself. So he decided to become an entrepreneur—to conduct, manage, and invest in an orchestra on his own terms. That is, he wanted to be a dictator. And his gamble paid off, for he monopolized the country's orchestral landscape over the next forty years.

From an organizational perspective, American orchestras in the 1800s looked almost nothing like those today, save for the shared repertoire of European classics. From its founding in 1842, the New York Philharmonic was a cooperative venture in which the musicians

FIGURE 1. Theodore Thomas in Cincinnati, 1902. Reproduced with permission,
Chicago Symphony Orchestra Rosenthal Archives.

made decisions democratically and shared the season's earnings
among themselves as a dividend. At various points later in the century, Chicago musicians (notably Hans Balatka) attempted to create
their own professional orchestras using a different business model
that required membership subscriptions. In sharp contrast, Thomas
conceived of the orchestra in profit-seeking terms and approached
his artistic choices with sound business acumen. He founded his own
orchestra, the Theodore Thomas Orchestra, in 1863 and first experi-
mented with matinee concerts in New York City—not too heavy, not
too light. Next, he added a series of "symphony soirees" with meatier
fare. To keep his musicians in good musical shape (and well paid), he

then scheduled light concerts—what we now call "pops"—during the summer. And when he thought New Yorkers might tire of his orchestra, he took it on tour around the country, building what became known as the "Thomas Highway."

Thomas's orchestra made him famous. He joined the Brooklyn Philharmonic as music director in 1873 and would take over the New York Philharmonic three years later. He also inaugurated the Cincinnati May Festival, which he and his orchestra would accompany every other year between 1873 and 1904. In a move foreshadowing the cutthroat process of hiring a conductor today, the Cincinnati College of Music poached Thomas away from New York for a time. Brooklyn begged him to stay, and he agreed on the selfish condition that he could skip most of the rehearsals. One writer for the *New York Dispatch* wrote, "We predict that, at no very distant time, Mr. Thomas will have more than enough of dull, village-like Cincinnati, and that he will be thankful to return to the city where he obtained his fame." Certainly spoken like a true New Yorker.

Thomas did not last at the conservatory for much longer than a year, but he had already begun a new affair with another Midwestern "village." Beginning in 1877, Thomas brought his personal orchestra to Chicago every July to entertain audiences with a series of concerts that drew from the group's standard repertoire of both serious and lighter works. The ensemble performed well over three hundred concerts over the course of the next thirteen years and single-handedly introduced the city to great orchestral music. All the while, Thomas continued to direct both the New York Philharmonic and the Brooklyn Philharmonic during the winter and toured with his own orchestra in between the two series. Thomas's hectic schedule matched that of any top-flight conductor today.

New York, Thomas's permanent home, eventually earned the envy of other cities. A Boston investment banker named Henry Lee Higginson leveled an artistic challenge to the august New York Philharmonic in 1881 by establishing a full-time orchestra, the Boston Symphony, based on a model of corporate sponsorship. Higginson himself would finance any deficits and permanently endow the en-

semble. New York's wealthy beau monde, which included Vander-
bilts, Carnegies, and Morgans, balked on promises to offer Thomas
a similar arrangement, leaving him to settle with the democratic
Philharmonic and the pressures of managing his own players and
finances. Charles Norman Fay, a Chicago utilities executive, had
other designs. Fay met Thomas at Delmonico's steak house in New
York just before Christmas in 1890, and the two men signed paper-
work that would finally make Thomas the ruler of his own orchestra without the worries of overseeing the business. It was an offer
he couldn't refuse. "I would go to hell if they gave me a permanent
orchestra," he told Fay.

Thomas's decision to leave New York for Chicago caused quite a
stir. As with any high-profile orchestral departure, rumors about his
successor spread like wildfire. Some wondered if Tchaikovsky, who
was set to inaugurate Carnegie Hall in 1891, might be a willing candidate. Others hoped for an American, but the city would have to
wait for Bernstein for that dream to come true. Thomas's support-
ers, meanwhile, showed their gratitude at his farewell concert with
flowers, a laurel wreath, and hundreds of waving handkerchiefs.
George William Curtis, a member of the city's musical old guard,
toasted Thomas at a send-off dinner, saying, "To the genius, the un-
tiring enthusiasm, the intelligence, the energy, the masterly skill of
that youth, more than any other single force, we owe the remarkable musical interest and cultivation, and the musical preeminence
of New York today." Now Chicago had him.

Thomas's Chicago tenure did not get off to a good start. First came
the union dispute. Before his first season began, Chicago musicians
came to suspect that Thomas's new contract allowed him to boycott
local players. The Chicago branch of the National League of Musicians
(forerunner of today's American Federation of Musicians) went so far
as to draft a resolution censuring Thomas for his behavior but suddenly dropped it when no one could find any tangible proof. Newspapers in Boston and New York gleefully reported on the faux controversy while Thomas claimed that the accusations were patently
absurd. Given carte blanche over programming decisions, Thomas

also aimed too high during his first season, leading some critics to guess that the orchestra's "severe" character would lead to its early demise. Low attendance led to crushing deficits for the orchestra's benefactors during the first two seasons, and Thomas mismanaged the budget for music at the 1893 World's Columbian Exposition to the tune of a quarter million dollars, or nearly $6 million today. The orchestra was already in dire straits.

Recovering from these losses would prove difficult, but rather than giving up and returning to New York (or retiring from the business altogether), Thomas doubled down. He appealed to the city's pride in a characteristically forthright open letter to the *Tribune*, written in January 1894: "It is this scorn of mediocrity and this indomitable determination to have the *best*, and maintain only the highest standard in all its enterprises, which makes the greatness of this city." The dire situation changed rapidly as the city responded. Subscriptions began to soar under new manager Anna Millar's watchful eye. Thomas appointed fresh players to key positions and began to take the orchestra on eastern tours over the next several years. Along with the celebrated architect Daniel Burnham, he also oversaw the construction of Orchestra Hall as a more intimate (and cheaper) replacement of the cavernous Auditorium Theater. And he even allowed a guest conductor to lead the orchestra for the first time—Richard Strauss, director of the Royal Opera in Berlin.

By the time Thomas died, a matter of weeks after Orchestra's Hall inaugural concert in December 1904, he had laid the groundwork for the orchestra's long-term success. Personnel remained relatively stable during his final years, and the ensemble had acquired the well-drilled timbre that had made Thomas famous. Though acoustically challenging—a problem that would continue to plague audiences— Orchestra Hall became the group's permanent home. Rose Fay Thomas donated his extensive collection of fully marked scores to the orchestra library. And he had passed the baton to his trusty assistant, violist Frederick Stock, whose rapport among players and audiences was unquestioned. If, as Thomas once claimed, "a symphony shows the culture of a community," Chicago was poised to stand second to none in its ongoing rivalry with cities whose orchestras had taken years if not decades longer to flourish.

The Power of Modesty

Frederick Stock (dir. 1905-42) stood on the CSO podium for nearly four decades, though his formidably active tenure proved to be far less tumultuous than Thomas's. With little drama, the trustees picked him over the likes of Felix Mottl, Hans Richter, and Felix Weingart-ner—all famous Europeans—as Thomas's first successor. The ad-ministration then paid special attention to the financial levers that were its proper domain: what types of concerts to schedule when, how long tours should be sustained, and how assets like Orchestra Hall could help place the orchestra on a solid fiscal footing. Their oversight let Stock focus on what he could do best: expanding the repertoire, drilling the orchestra, creating a network of alluring guest artists, and educating a new generation of listeners. Perhaps the only real complaint critics ever leveled at him was the lugubri-ousness of the memorial concerts he led in the middle of each win-ter season to honor the anniversary of Thomas's passing. As early as 1907, Edward Elgar told the musicians, "I have never been in Japan or South Africa. Maybe they have better orchestras there, but in Europe they have none better than the Theodore Thomas Orchestra."[2] By the time Stock died, in 1942, the orchestra was unquestionably one of the world's best.

Stock's first ten seasons were remarkable for their unremark-ability, save perhaps when the board banned women from wearing hats at evening concerts or when Stock had to fire a veteran cel-list for threatening to fight a critic outside his home after the critic published a nasty review. Trustee Philo Adams Otis's account of the 1911-12 season reads, "The season came and went quietly and calmly, without disturbing influences, [and] with no serious finan-cial issues to meet."[3] By that time, orchestra management had be-come especially adept at raising funds through subscriptions and donations and had wiped out nearly half of the immense mortgage

FIGURE 2. Frederick Stock. Photo by G. Nelidoff. Reproduced with permission, Chicago Symphony Orchestra Rosenthal Archives.

on Orchestra Hall. Outside of any artistic endeavors, the orchestra found itself embroiled in controversy when the trustees decided to rename it since the ensemble had been operating officially as "The Theodore Thomas Orchestra." Management decided on "The Chicago Symphony Orchestra (Founded by Theodore Thomas)" to preempt potential competitors from taking the Chicago Symphony Orchestra name while still honoring Thomas. Thomas's widow was furious and claimed that her husband's name might as well be scrubbed from the annals of Chicago history. She obviously did not get her way.

Stock, meanwhile, had begun a new artistic program by dedicating one concert per season exclusively to American composers — a risky maneuver that, under Thomas, had led to perplexed audiences and disastrous reviews. Decidedly unlike Thomas, Stock was a talented composer and understood the challenges composers faced when finding outlets for their music. They inevitably required the goodwill of performers, who often preferred to spend their time perfecting well-worn pieces rather than risking the possibility of sounding bad after rushing to learn a new one. To his credit, Stock knew how to steer people with tact and grace. To sell his American concert idea to the public and the press, he typically included a special draw—a famous guest soloist, an invitation for the composer to conduct, or a nod to civic pride with a program featuring Chicagoans. Over time, Stock integrated American works into the regular concert series without drawing undue attention to them, and he is still remembered as one of the first true champions of American composers.

The Great War proved to be the first major disruption in the harmonious whirring of the Chicago Symphony's engines. To show solidarity with American allies, Stock regularly opened and closed concerts with patriotic tunes like "America" and "The Star-Spangled Banner." By the 1917–18 season, he also programmed an American orchestral work on each concert. But these patriotic signals did not appease everyone. The clear majority of the country's orchestral musicians, including those in the CSO, were German-speaking immigrants or first-generation citizens. Considering the heavily Germanic standard repertoire, nativist agitators in Chicago openly questioned the orchestra's loyalty, leading one of the trustees to make a public declaration of its unfettered support of the war effort "from conductor to kettledrum." Firebrands nevertheless demanded that Stock be investigated on the suspicion of being an "enemy alien"—a charge he vigorously denied since he had applied for citizenship long before the war. Public speculation about his naturalization status became so distracting that he took a voluntary leave of absence to spare the orchestra the negative publicity. But his citizenship papers finally came through just as the war was ending, making the whole affair a moot point.

With Stock back at the helm, the CSO directed fresh attention to meaningful educational experiences for patrons. Thomas believed that mere exposure to great music was an education all its own. In one apocryphal story, a critic told him that his audiences didn't like Wagner's music very much, to which he replied, "Then we will play him until they do!" Stock had a subtler idea, one that would have been laughable for Thomas: children's concerts. The idea made good business sense because it cultivated new demand for the orchestra's artistry. But Stock also genuinely adored children and was a natural teacher who joyfully interacted with them from the stage. The series far exceeded anyone's wildest expectations and numbered well over 200 performances by 1942, nearly all of which Stock directed himself. A generation later, the charismatic Leonard Bernstein would lead roughly a quarter of that number with the New York Philharmonic.

With seemingly endless stores of energy, Stock also inaugurated another educational institution: the Civic Orchestra of Chicago, a training ground for young musicians that prepared them for entry into the rigors of professional life. The idea was simultaneously a patriotic response to complaints about "Teutonic" musicians during the war years and an ingenious tactic designed to create a self-sustaining personnel pipeline for the CSO. It was also a surprising display of liberality, for the orchestra accepted women and even boasted a woman concertmaster by its fourth season. Over the next twenty years, the Civic Orchestra became a beloved, integral component of the city's musical landscape and provided orchestras all over the country with some of their finest players.

Though he was at the height of his artistic powers, the final years of Stock's tenure were far from the easiest. Union wage standoffs plagued the seasons just before the Great Depression, which only exacerbated the orchestra's ongoing economic difficulties. Stagnant wages led to persistent union commotion, and the situation became so grim that the musicians eventually agreed to cut the size of the orchestra, to reduce the number of concerts in the season, and to take a temporary wage decrease to save the ensemble. Stock then crafted unusual techniques to pull the orchestra out of the financial abyss. In the summer of 1934, for example, the musicians engaged in a

friendly rivalry with the Detroit Symphony that culminated in a soft-
ball game umpired by Cubs legend Mordecai "Three Finger" Brown.
And in 1936, the orchestra revitalized the concert space of Ravinia
Park, which reawakened its languishing summer concert series and
became the orchestra's permanent summer home.

But a different kind of competition arose as the financial difficulties of the Depression lingered. With seemingly endless government resources at its disposal, the Chicago-based Illinois Symphony
Orchestra, an arm of the Federal Music Project, wooed audiences
away from the CSO with a charismatic leader, Izler Solomon, and exciting programs. In turn, the wily Stock employed every trick in the
book to win back the city. He invited an all-star cast of guest musicians that included Jascha Heifetz and Paul Hindemith, promised
more world premieres than ever, pursued recordings as a new source
of revenue, and even hosted raucous fund-raising parties, the most
colossal of which was held at the old Chicago Stadium and featured
performances by jazz greats Fletcher Henderson, Tommy Dorsey, and
Paul Whiteman.

Fortunately, these efforts paid off and the CSO pushed into the
war years with a robust balance sheet. The orchestra's golden anniversary season in 1940–41 became one of its most successful, including the world premiere of Igor Stravinsky's now canonical *Symphony
in C*. When Stock passed not long after the opening of the 1942 season, the orchestra had returned to its rightful place as the center of
the city's musical life. The *Sun* printed a tribute by University of Chicago Chancellor Robert Maynard Hutchins, who said that Stock's
thirty-seven years with the Chicago Symphony Orchestra "made him
and it synonymous."

The Age of Anxiety

Though the orchestra had achieved an enviable financial footing by
1942, Stock's death ushered in new levels of volatility that had become all too familiar in other major orchestras. Throughout the Stock
era, most conductors attempted to commodify their celebrity status

and routinely tested the marketplace as free agents (to use a professional sports metaphor). The prospect of hiring these free agents brought along the potential for behind-the-scenes meddling by artist managers and for sharp public criticism from the press. The most active meddler by far was Arthur Judson, who in the 1930s simultaneously managed the Philadelphia Orchestra and the New York Philharmonic and consulted with several other organizations on personnel matters. Closer to home, *Tribune* critic Claudia Cassidy, known to some as "Acidy Cassidy," took it upon herself to wield tremendous influence over public opinion about the orchestra during her tenure from 1942 to 1965. Now more than ever, artistic or financial choices could have disastrous consequences if they did not please the right people. The orchestra's age of innocence was over, as Stock's three successive replacements all fell headlong into this web of intrigue.

The orchestra first hired Désiré Defauw (dir. 1943–46), a refugee who had narrowly escaped the Nazi onslaught of Belgium in 1940. Soon after directing the NBC Symphony under Toscanini's auspices, Defauw became engaged as a frequent guest conductor of the Boston Symphony Orchestra. Critics remarked that his renditions were "perfect"—almost *too* perfect, they complained. When Defauw debuted in Chicago, in January 1943, Cassidy left the concert unimpressed, remarking that "his treatment of the winds turned that Debussy fog [*Nuages*] into a far less lovely frog."[4] Perhaps underestimating Cassidy's influence, the orchestra's management hired Defauw as music director only a month later. She immediately led a savage campaign to discredit Defauw and persisted for four grueling years. Displaying a true gift for language, she claimed that he "mauled" Mozart, created a "raucous distortion" of Ravel, and led otherwise "drably dull" performances throughout his tenure. She had originally preferred Stock's assistant, Hans Lange, but later championed Artur Rodziński, the fiery leader of the New York Philharmonic who had occasionally led the CSO at Ravinia Park. She would soon have her way. Over a matter of days in February 1947, Rodziński angrily resigned from the Philharmonic, Defauw quietly left the CSO, and the beleaguered Chicago trustees signed Rodziński to replace him.

Rodziński's one-year stint was no less cataclysmic. He had taken the reins in New York at the very moment Defauw had begun in Chicago. One of Cassidy's New York counterparts, the inimitable Virgil Thomson, lavished the virtuosic leader with his approval. Rather than fleeing from the press, Rodziński became disgusted with the Philharmonic's meddling manager, Arthur Judson, and resigned after the board refused a "him or me" ultimatum. Cassidy was thrilled to catch Rodziński and called his debut with the CSO "deeply satisfying."[5] As a true theater lover, she fawned over his fully staged performances of Wagner's *Tristan und Isolde*. But the trustees abruptly fired the temperamental conductor mid-season, finding his plans to spend huge sums of money on opera, demands for a long-term contract, and secret maneuvering to move the orchestra back to Auditorium Theater completely unacceptable. The dismissal predictably incensed Cassidy, who led a smear campaign against the trustees, and angered a large audience base that was crucial for raising funds to wipe out annual deficits. Some citizens even asked the city council to intervene. But the trustees held their ground, citing irreconcilable differences, and decided to hire a series of guest conductors for the next two seasons instead. According to hornist Philip Farkas, the subscribers became so impassioned about the issue that police had to guard the aisles in Orchestra Hall to prevent fistfights between the factions. Rodziński left amid wild cheers from the audience after the final concert of the season, while Cassidy felt the orchestra's potential for true greatness had been squashed by a clique of stubborn philistines.

Rafael Kubelik (dir. 1950–53), one of the guests in the second season after Rodziński's departure, agreed to be the orchestra's new permanent conductor. Kubelik had fled Central Europe following the iron-fisted 1948 Communist takeover of Czechoslovakia and accepted the Chicago position over an offer from the BBC Symphony. Cassidy, who had called Kubelik's guest debut "superficial," argued in favor of hiring the much more experienced George Szell despite her mild distaste for his conducting.[6] Predictably, she launched countless barbs in Kubelik's direction, much as she had in Defauw's, calling his programs "jumbled" and emphasizing his inability to interpret the standard repertoire with the same insight he brought to contemporary works. "Dull Bach, Befuddled Brahms," read one of her best headlines.[7] Writers outside Chicago, such as New York's Howard Taubman, became suspicious of the controversy since Kubelik's records on the Mercury label were outstanding. But Cassidy and her *Tribune* colleague Seymour Raven (who would later become the CSO's general manager) ultimately felt that Kubelik was too wet behind the ears to manage the orchestra's complex programming needs and too artistically eclectic to serve the community effectively. The trustees felt likewise and let Kubelik go on mutually agreeable terms in 1953. He received mostly warm receptions when he returned as a guest over the next several decades of a distinguished career that blossomed elsewhere.

The First Golden Age

The orchestra found its next great steward in Fritz Reiner (dir. 1953–62), a notoriously dictatorial leader who drove the ensemble into its first true golden age of international acclaim. More than just a free agent, Reiner was an all-star. Sensing the potential to mold the orchestra to his vision—and to fatten his wallet with the orchestra's sound financial standing—Reiner felt the CSO presented a prime opportunity to seal his legacy. The combination of Reiner's idiosyncratic artistic goals, rare ability to secure (or cull!) personnel, and savviness with new media led to the happy consequence of a truly unique orchestral sound that remains accessible to new generations of classical music lovers through a series of celebrated recordings.

Like Thomas, Reiner had already developed a reputation as a builder and had risen to the top of the food chain as director of the Metropolitan Opera after extended tenures in Cincinnati and Pittsburgh. Outside of any personal quibbles, Cassidy's chief gripe with Defauw and Kubelik was that they were unable to realize the orchestra's full sonic potential. World-class players, she argued, required a world-class leader, or else the orchestra would never again rise above

FIGURE 3. Fritz Reiner and the newest members of the orchestra in the fall of 1953.
From left to right: Nathan Snader, violin; Juan Cuneo, violin; Joseph Golan, violin;
Alan Fuchs, horn; Ray Still, oboe; Sheppard Lehnhoff, viola; and János Starker, cello.
Reproduced with permission, Chicago Symphony Orchestra Rosenthal Archives.

"provincialism"—a persistent fear in Chicago. Assuming he would
have more time, Kubelik had fired musicians he found unacceptable
and had reseated others to build on their individual strengths. The
orchestra had not faced such hands-on personnel management since
the Stock era and resented Kubelik for the moves, but critics generally felt the timbre of the orchestra had improved dramatically during his final season. Reiner then took over where Kubelik left off.

Cassidy loved the results. Following Reiner's first concert in 1954,
she welcomed the orchestra back: "So for all the pinpoint brilliance
you can hear coming round the season's bend, something more important is there, too. The return of that special quality, the orchestra's
tone. It is a fruity tone, and it carries an undertow. When it turned
languorous in the Berlioz, or began to surge and swirl in the Strauss,
or took on damask sheen in the Brahms, why then some of us felt we

had come home."[8] And Reiner continued to impress. Upon returning from his mid-season vacation, Cassidy welcomed him with style: "We have had other fine music these last weeks in Orchestra Hall, so how was this different? [. . .] It was the light cast on the music. You know how some evenings you walk out and the air is so fresh, the sky so luminous, the lights in the skyscrapers so gleaming, that everything seems crystalline, as if it would be forever fresh. That was the way the orchestra sounded."[9] It was Reiner's sound. According to all who worked with him, he carefully crafted it in each rehearsal by taking everything apart and putting the pieces back together again just so.

Reiner's discerning ear and careful score preparation were especially suited to recording, and critics had considered him a premier interpreter on record long before he joined the CSO. Reiner recorded extensively with Columbia as director of the Pittsburgh Symphony but switched to RCA when he joined the Met. He continued with RCA in Chicago and took the market by storm with the release of Strauss's *Also Sprach Zarathustra*, which became widely regarded as a masterpiece of the era after its stereo re-release in 1960. Reiner recorded well over one hundred works with the CSO. As a TV fan (he loved *Trash or Treasure* and Groucho Marx in *You Bet Your Life*), the maestro also welcomed the opportunity to work with WGN-TV to broadcast the orchestra. "Writers for comedy and musical shows are running out of material," he once told the *Tribune*, "whereas music, particularly good classical music, is inexhaustible; people want to hear it again and again."[10] Unfortunately, technical limitations hampered the project, and Reiner quickly tired of the extra duties despite an avalanche of enthusiastic fan mail.

Although Reiner had carried the orchestra to new artistic heights on stage, on record, and over the air, his final years ended with a whimper. It all began with a proposed European tour in 1959 that he single-handedly canceled at the eleventh hour because of illness. The once infatuated Cassidy quickly launched another of her smear campaigns, complaining that Reiner had withdrawn from the city's social life and increasingly programmed uninspiring repertoire. The lost income further infuriated the musicians, who organized a "players' committee" in response. The committee intended to bypass the local union branch and sought direct representation in negotiations with management. The tired and ill Reiner wanted to stay away from the clash and resigned before the start of the 1962 season, preferring to linger for one more year as musical advisor with a few guest appearances. As biographer Philip Hart has explained, Reiner told his social circle, "They have my music; they cannot have my body."[11] The administrators who joined Cassidy in scorning Reiner's aloofness pined for Stock, who had unquestionably made Chicago his home.

A French Interlude

The troubles plaguing Reiner's final years left the orchestra in a situation much like the one it faced after Stock's sudden death. Lingering wage disputes nearly led to the first cancellation of summer concerts at Ravinia since the mid-1930s, and Reiner's laser-like focus on recordings had allowed educational programs like the children's series and the Civic Orchestra to languish. The next director would need to pick up the pieces. Several candidates emerged, notably Georg Solti, director at Covent Garden, and recent CSO guests Hans Rosbaud, Erich Leinsdorf, and Jean Martinon. Solti rejected an offer outright and later recalled in his memoirs that Claudia Cassidy had noticed him smiling during a performance of Mozart's *Marriage of Figaro* when "it would have surprised me less," she wrote, "to see him cut his throat."[12] He wanted nothing to do with the orchestra so long as she reviewed concerts for the *Tribune*. Cassidy enjoyed Leinsdorf, but he bolted for the Boston Symphony before a deal with Chicago could be sealed. That left Rosbaud and Martinon.

Director of the Southwest German Radio Symphony Orchestra, Rosbaud debuted with the CSO in the 1958–59 season to critical acclaim. Known in Europe as an advocate of new music, he introduced the city to an eclectic repertoire of locally unknown modern works by Max Reger, Albert Roussel, and members of the Second Viennese School. Over the next several seasons, he also showed audiences the breadth of his repertoire, which included local favorites like Bruckner and Mahler. They luxuriated in every minute of it, as did the orchestra, which gave him its traditional fanfare of appreciation, or "Tusch," at the close of his 1961 appearances. After Reiner announced his resignation, the orchestra invited Rosbaud to a lengthy autumn residency in 1962, portending a potential offer to be the ensemble's next director. His appearances, especially a concert of Stravinsky's *Le sacre de printemps*, elicited some of Cassidy's most ebullient praise:

> Stravinsky himself made a recording so transparent in texture that detail stands out as if you had X-ray eyes in a jungle. Pierre Monteux, who conducted the premiere, gave us an exposition of the score in 1948. Two years later Leonard Bernstein turned into Nijinsky's "Faun" as he identified himself emotionally with a paroxysmal, orgiastic, and strangely beautiful performance. Rosbaud gave us a blueprint. Not the kind that lies inert on the drafting table, but the kind that sets skyscrapers soaring, flings bridges into space, and sends the imagination spinning into orbit.[13]

But Rosbaud became ill and died suddenly of a heart ailment just weeks after his appearances. Pierre Boulez and Bernard Haitink would later describe Rosbaud as a conductor's conductor because he made music speak with his arms rather than words, and trumpeter Bud Herseth named him as the greatest conductor he'd ever encountered.

With Rosbaud's sudden death, choosing Martinon (dir. 1963–68) to be Reiner's permanent successful became a fait accompli. Director of the Concerts Lamoureux in Paris and a talented composer, Martinon was virtually unknown to American audiences until 1957, when he conducted the Boston Symphony Orchestra as a guest. Cyrus Durgin of the *Boston Globe* found that he had a thorough technique without being pedantic, a careful eye for detail without being dry, and a passionate temperament without being an exhibitionist. These qualities enchanted Cassidy at his Ravinia debut in 1960, and by his final

FIGURE 4. Jean Martinon and principal players of the orchestra backstage prior
to a performance of Frank Martin's *Concerto for Seven Wind Instruments, Timpani,
Percussion, and String Orchestra* on February 10, 1966. From left to right: Clark Brody,
clarinet; Willard Elliot, bassoon; Donald Peck, flute; Dale Clevenger, horn; Martinon;
Ray Still, oboe; Adolph Herseth, trumpet; Donald Koss, timpani; and Jay Friedman,
trombone. Photo by Terry's Photography. Reproduced with permission,
Chicago Symphony Orchestra Rosenthal Archives.

guest appearance with the CSO in spring 1962, she was enthralled:
"Admiration for the Frenchman, which had taken off like a jet last
week, rose to a new level of esteem at last night's farewell, when his
mutual affinity with the orchestra had widened and deepened."[14]
Cassidy and the orchestra had found their man.

But fortune—and Cassidy—could be fickle. When Leinsdorf returned to Chicago the following season with the Boston Symphony,
she predicted that the conductor and orchestra would be "hopelessly
incompatible." Leinsdorf, she sneered, "confused compassion with
sentimentality, and the apocalyptical with a great noise." Martinon
remained her favorite. After a performance of Bartók's *Concerto for
Orchestra*, one of Reiner's signature pieces, she said that Martinon

brought "the brilliance, the sudden savagery, the involuntary out-cry, the fiercely contemporary voice so sharply and incisively of our time" that Reiner had exposed at the height of his tenure. Then she changed her mind. By May 1964, she was complaining that Marti-non's programs and performances "are worse than embarrassing, they are a bore." She gave up completely in the next season, claiming after the opening concert that he would have been fired had he been a guest. And the barbs continued to fly until she left her post as *Tribune* music critic the following April.[15] (Some attributed Cassidy's change of heart to the orchestra's decision to fire general manager Seymour Raven, a former colleague at the *Tribune*, but she had started grum-bling well before this incident.)

Martinon remained for two more tumultuous seasons, and the criticisms continued to mount. With Cassidy out of the picture, he gritted through the more judicious reports of Tom Willis, her *Tribune* successor, Earl Calloway, a savvy new critic for the African Ameri-can *Defender*, and Robert Marsh, one of Andrew Patner's long-time predecessors at the *Sun-Times*. They all agreed on the nature of Mar-tinon's problems—namely that his mind was elsewhere. As a gifted composer, he focused too much energy on his own large-scale works, which Chicago audiences typically enjoyed but critics elsewhere found lacking. He was also contracted for a relatively small num-ber of weeks in Chicago, and some felt that he gave more polished performances on tour and in guest roles than with the orchestra at home. Meanwhile, he had attempted to fire principal oboist Ray Still, in part because Cassidy published damning fan mail complaining of wretched woodwind intonation and in part because Still had chal-lenged Martinon in rehearsals. His unsuccessful effort created a rift among many of the players that lasted for years. Compounding these problems, audiences disliked the results of the multi-million-dollar renovation of Orchestra Hall that had left its acoustics drier than ever. Willis described the situation as "general confusion" in Decem-ber 1966, and it became a foregone conclusion that Martinon's five-year contract would not be renewed.[16]

The Second Golden Age

Chicago found itself with a vacancy the size of a black hole, leaving board president Louis Sudler and manager John Edwards searching for a way to patch things up. The 1967–68 season was an unusually exciting time across the country, for Chicago, Boston, and New York all had director openings. As Cassidy had predicted, Leinsdorf was out in Boston. The high-flying Bernstein left New York to pursue a true freelance career. And while rumors swirled around who would take what seat, every astute observer predicted that Chicago would pick Sir Georg Solti, former president Eric Oldberg's first target before Martinon's disastrous term. Unlike Defauw or Martinon, Solti brought the possibility of recovering the famed Central European warmth and expressiveness that had come to define the orchestra's sound under Thomas, Stock, and Reiner. In fact, his recent recordings of Wagner's *Ring* cycle with the Vienna Philharmonic had sealed his reputation as an authoritative interpreter of the late-nineteenth-century repertoire Chicagoans craved but were denied under Martinon.

By the late 1960s, American orchestras had reached a financial tipping point that made musical directorships less appealing to conductors accustomed to European government largesse. Unions in major orchestras had finally negotiated for fifty-two-week seasons, which drove up wages and sharply increased the potential workload on permanent directors, who could get away with inviting only so many guests before charges of disloyalty would be hurled their way. Although Solti initially balked at the offer because he felt he was too busy at Covent Garden, the prospect of focusing renewed energy on great symphonic repertoire with a world-class collection of players (and without Cassidy's interference) ultimately swayed him. With the summer season under the separate aegis of the Ravinia Festival, which had hired Seiji Ozawa as its first music director during Martinon's tenure, the CSO offered a built-in solution for the busy Solti, who maintained resident commitments elsewhere and wanted to stay fresh when appearing in Chicago. And as part of his contract

FIGURE 5. Adolph Herseth and Sir Georg Solti rehearse Karel Husa's Trumpet Concerto on March 3, 1988, at the Perth Concert Hall prior to the orchestra's first concert in Australia (photo by Jim Steere). Reproduced with permission, Chicago Symphony Orchestra Rosenthal Archives.

negotiations, he offered to share the load with Carlo Maria Giulini, who had been one of Edwards's other choices for the head position but became the orchestra's first principal guest conductor instead.

Solti quickly returned the orchestra to the glory days of Reiner. The majority of Solti's early principal players dated from the Reiner era, granting him the ability to mold a cohesive unit to his artistic vision. Peter Gorner, one of the *Tribune's* newer critics, felt that "the Solti sound" had "arrived" by December of his first season: "The sound, like the man, is lean and lithe, devoid of fluff or bluff. It exudes virility, vitality, and verismo. Its lyrical side is lined with inner tension and nothing goes slack. But drama is the name of the game as it thrusts, coasts, and stabs its way to the heart of the matter."[17] By the 1980s, critics like John von Rhein began to complain that the orchestra had perhaps become *too* virtuosic, trading soul for brilliance, but von Rhein conceded that Orchestra Hall was partially culpable. "That the Bruckner was splendidly performed was not the question," he once explained, "It was. Solti worked with a combination of de-monic energy and rare expansiveness to build a symphonic cathedral whose every musical detail cohered with true architectural strength. [. . .] But Orchestra Hall and its dry acoustics conspired to rob that sound of a certain essential quality: resonance, and, ultimately, spirituality."[18] With great music at their disposal, however, most listeners didn't care.

Solti's lofty vision translated into unparalleled international success. At the time of his appointment, he brought a well-earned reputation as a master recording artist, and he drastically increased the orchestra's activity on record and radio, which had foundered under Martinon. His recordings with the CSO ultimately won twenty-five Grammy awards, catapulting the orchestra into the highest echelon. (Several of these recordings, incidentally, featured the work of Margaret Hillis, another Reiner holdover.) Perhaps more important, Solti's contract required that he lead national and international tours. These wildly successful trips outside Chicago effectively eliminated any notion that Chicago was a "provincial" orchestra. Audiences everywhere, but especially in New York, raved about the ensemble. In his memoirs, Solti recalled a concert in Carnegie Hall that generated seemingly endless applause. Such responses were commonplace. Writing for the *Christian Science Monitor*, critic Miles Kastendieck once claimed that Solti and the CSO had "conquered New York." In a reciprocal effect, guest conductors often felt deflated after they returned to their home orchestras, as if they had to settle for a Chevy after driving a Rolls Royce. Even the great Leonard Bernstein, who conducted the orchestra in Shostakovich's Seventh Symphony in 1988, found himself in tears, hugging everyone on stage after an unforgettable performance of a piece he had long championed.

Not all of Chicago's patricians (or critic Robert Marsh, for that matter) appreciated Solti's sparse contracts, which typically required him to be in residence anywhere from eight to twelve weeks over the course of the season. But Solti was a strategist who molded the situation to his advantage with minimal fallout. The appearance of his telegenic wife (a self-proclaimed "very mediocre musician") and young children at CSO events, for example, endeared him to the com-

FIGURE 6. Former music directors Rafael Kubelík and Sir Georg Solti along with new ninth music director Daniel Barenboim at the rededication of the Theodore Thomas memorial—*The Spirit of Music*—on October 18, 1991. Photo by Terry's Photography. Reproduced with permission, Chicago Symphony Orchestra Rosenthal Archives.

munity, though he insisted on keeping a home base in London for stability and his children's well-being. On the artistic front, he appointed high-quality principal guest conductors (Giulini and Claudio Abbado) whose approaches were different enough that they complemented his work and cultivated a stable of leading short-term guests like Leonard Slatkin and Erich Leinsdorf. Contemporary music was one of Solti's admitted weaknesses, and at the start of his tenure he shifted the task of expanding the orchestra's repertoire onto composer Bruno Maderna, who led short annual residencies until his sudden death in 1973. Maderna's passing left a substantial void in the orchestra's coverage of contemporary music, though Solti himself led well-received premieres by Karel Husa, Ellen Taaffe Zwilich, and Witold Lutosławski. John Corigliano joined the orchestra as composer-in-residence under the auspices of the Meet the Composer program in 1986, ensuring that contemporary music would maintain a steady presence at Orchestra Hall.

This kaleidoscopic approach to orchestra direction and programming came to define the American landscape during Solti's tenure, and, under his leadership, the diversity it entailed ultimately placed his orchestra atop the world's roster of great musical institutions. He left his position in 1991 with a sterling reputation around the globe. Chicagoans will remember him for recovering Thomas's Germanic idealism, Stock's charm and affability, and Reiner's precision while placing his own virtuosic sheen on the orchestra. This was the Chicago Symphony he handed off to his successor, Daniel Barenboim, and this was the Chicago Symphony that Andrew Patner began to cover during his distinguished career.

I

Daniel Barenboim

(1991–2006)

Daniel Barenboim was no stranger to the Chicago Symphony when he took the reins in 1991. He made his Orchestra Hall debut as a pianist in 1958, soloed with the group repeatedly in the 1960s, and directed his first subscription concert in 1970. After his conducting debut, *Tribune* critic Peter Gorner remarked that the orchestra "could not have sounded more glorious," while his colleague Tom Willis gushed, "Mr. Barenboim can conduct anything he likes and count on my listening."[1] The profundity of Barenboim's readings were strengths in the late Germanic repertoire Chicago craved, but his aura faded before he became director as some listeners disliked the restlessness of his interpretations across the stylistic spectrum. Noting a distinct lack of precision, John von Rhein of the *Tribune* complained that he "seemed willing to sacrifice just about everything to surface dynamism, sweep, and lyrical underlining." This approach was far different from the disciplined, crisp, and clean Solti sound. By 1981, though, listeners had acclimated to Barenboim's unorthodox approach, with von Rhein observing that he "substitutes a fervent spontaneity for the clockwork virtuoso response that sometimes passes for making music."[2] His infrequent guest appearances over the next several years, especially when he directed Mozart or Beethoven from the keyboard, reminded the city of his idiosyncratic style and sparkle.

Barenboim's positive aura shattered abruptly in 1987, when Solti announced his retirement. In a moment reminiscent of Claudia Cassidy's notorious attacks on several of the orchestra's conductors, writers for the city's major newspapers led a fierce campaign against Barenboim. Robert Marsh of the *Sun-Times* insisted that the orchestra should hire a distinguished American like Leonard Slatkin or James Levine, but the board and orchestra president Henry Fogel really considered only two choices: Barenboim and Claudio Abbado, Solti's former principal guest. Marsh and von Rhein openly supported Abbado while panning Barenboim's appearances. "If this is the future of the CSO," von Rhein groused, "this reviewer wants no part of it."[3] Barenboim, who had directed the Orchestre de Paris since 1975, also raised the ire of those who felt he might be spread too thin after he accepted a position leading the Opéra-Bastille in 1988. To everyone's surprise, however, the leader of the Opéra fired the outspoken maestro just weeks before executive director Henry Fogel named him as Solti's successor. Fogel faced immense backlash in the press, while the players, who had supported Barenboim far more than the critics, welcomed his charisma on the podium and relaxed rehearsal demeanor despite his occasional erratic interpretations.

The dust didn't exactly settle in Chicago as controversy continued to follow the new director. In one of his first press conferences, he assured reporters that he planned to direct tremendous energy toward integrating the city's arts institutions, revitalizing the Civic Orchestra, and scheduling chamber concerts as part of the CSO season. He also supported the orchestra's engagement with contemporary music by continuing the composer-in-residence program with Shulamit Ran and Augusta Read Thomas and by enlisting the eminent Pierre Boulez as principal guest conductor. Despite these positive steps, critics wondered if Barenboim would ultimately fulfill his promises. In the summer before he began, he signed a ten-year contract with the Deutsche Staatsoper, guaranteeing that his schedule would remain as limited as Solti's. Then the orchestra went on strike, delaying his first season by several weeks. Barenboim stayed out of the fray, but the dispute gave relations between management and the musicians a sharp edge at the very outset of his tenure. The rift was slow to heal.

Like others of its caliber, the CSO faced significant financial pressures during Barenboim's tenure, such as declining audiences, rising guest artist fees, and the requirement of maintaining world-class compensation for the players. Management also announced in 1993 that it was embarking on a much needed $105-million renovation of Orchestra Hall. The acoustical changes generated substantial improvements, the stage itself and backstage accommodations for musicians were enhanced, and patrons heartily approved of other amenities like expanded lobbies and restrooms. Criticism of Barenboim's performances nevertheless continued in certain quarters. After a Mahler performance, for example, one CSO player claimed that he "ripped the engine out, took it apart, and then couldn't figure out how to put it back together again."[4] Making matters worse, nationwide contractions in the recording industry and shrinking grant funding did not spare the CSO.

The orchestra hired Deborah Rutter (then known as Deborah R. Card) to steer the ship after Henry Fogel became president and CEO of the American Symphony Orchestra League in 2003. With the help of long-time artistic administrator Martha Gilmer, who oversaw the immense tasks of the orchestra's programming and scheduling, she initiated innovative ventures designed to attract new audiences, such as "Friday Night at the Movies" and "Afterworks Masterworks." Rutter's internal controls on spending also led to a balanced budget by Barenboim's departure in 2006. During a period that saw orchestras in Houston, Baltimore, and Pittsburgh on the brink of financial collapse, the CSO emerged as a model of sound fiscal management.[5]

The maestro, meanwhile, proved to be a successful builder in his own right. He earned immediate critical acclaim as a dynamic leader of the Civic Orchestra, which had weakened under Solti, and took aspiring local conductors under his wing. More importantly, he set about finding replacements for critical positions vacated by retirements—an issue that Solti had treated with less personal investment.

Two of his first significant hires offered a tremendous boost to the violins: Robert Chen as co-concertmaster (later sole concertmaster) and Yuan-Qing Yu as assistant concertmaster. He also addressed the departures of veteran wind principals—flutist Donald Peck, oboist Ray Still, and bassoonist Willard Elliot, all of whom had joined under Fritz Reiner and Jean Martinon. Barenboim replaced them with terrific young players who made his woodwinds the envy of directors everywhere: Mathieu Dufour, Alex Klein, and David McGill. But his hardest assignment was replacing principal trumpet Bud Herseth, who had been hired by Artur Rodziński as principal trumpet in 1948 and retired in 2001. Barenboim finally found virtuoso Chris Martin in 2005. Though the process was slow and arduous, Barenboim had built an orchestra that could be fully responsive to his artistic vision—and one that remained as strong as any in the world.

: :

The portrait that emerges in the following pages reveals Barenboim's progression as a molder of the orchestra and finally its champion. Early in his tenure, Patner tended to agree with John von Rhein that the conductor's performances could be turbulent, both in quality and interpretation—the latter a consequence of his devotion to the mystical spontaneity associated with famed Romanian conductor Sergiu Celibidache. Over time, however, the orchestra defied natural odds as it felt one lightning strike after another, first with signature pieces of the late nineteenth century and then with Barenboim's stable of contemporary works and prized soloists, particularly pianist Radu Lupu. A trip to Argentina allowed Barenboim to return to his boyhood home as the leader of a great ensemble. Patner increasingly enjoyed these fresh experiences and reminisced with Barenboim about them at the end of his tenure.

By 2006, the orchestra sounded noticeably different than it had under Solti—softer around the edges and less driven. Patner's coverage was spotty near the end of Barenboim's tenure, but his friend Alex Ross's New Yorker commentary on the maestro's final concerts captured the city's general feeling: "I had an adverse reaction when

FIGURE 1.1. Daniel Barenboim, 2005 Chicago Symphony Orchestra European tour. Photo by Todd Rosenberg. Used with permission.

I first heard the great Chicago orchestra under Barenboim, a decade ago. There was a crude and chaotic quality to the sound. [...] Now he no longer pushes so hard, for his personality has melded with the orchestra's. His musicianship is old-fashioned; he doesn't go in for glossy perfection, instead favoring sinewy textures, earthy rhythms, freely singing lines." Building enough trust between maestro and orchestra to change artistic directions requires real effort, and Barenboim worked for it. After his final concert, Ross noted, the audience applauded for fifteen minutes as he congratulated every one of the players: "Barenboim could not have made a more graceful exit."[6]

DOUGLAS W. SHADLE

Early Weaknesses and Emerging Strengths

Lazy Mozart, Strong Carter and Brahms

Chicago Sun-Times, **May 13, 1994** Wednesday's Orchestra Hall concert—Barenboim's last before a tour to New York and Europe, and his last of the season — seemed a kind of temporary valedictory, summing up many of the music director's strengths and weaknesses. It opened with a genre in which Barenboim is a definite hit with audiences: a piano concerto casting him as conductor and soloist.

In January's performances of Mozart's popular F Major Concerto, K. 459, Barenboim piloted his Steinway concert grand as if it were a performance racing car. Wednesday, the analogy could have been made to a gas-guzzling Cadillac. His playing was automatic, lazy and unexciting.

With the aid of conductor Pierre Boulez and composer-in-residence Shulamit Ran, Barenboim has succeeded in introducing a steady diet of 20th century and contemporary music to subscription audiences.

The reprise of Elliott Carter's *Partita*, which received its world premiere here in February, showed the level of commitment he can get from the orchestra. They played this rhythmically complex 18-minute score with the same attention and skill they bring to Mahler and Bruckner.

Brahms always brings out the best in Barenboim. His slow tempo choices, which can be wrong-headed in other works, acted as clarifying agents in the majestic Fourth Symphony. Every phrase was presented as a piece of the larger whole, and he injected the well-known passacaglia finale with drama and suspense. He rewarded the cheering crowd with a jaunty tour-style encore of Brahms' Hungarian Dance in G minor.

At Best as Beethoven Soloist-Conductor

Chicago Sun-Times, October 27, 1997 Georg Solti died last month on the cusp of his 85th birthday. He was scheduled to celebrate that milestone Saturday by conducting what would have been his 1,000th concert with the orchestra that he indelibly placed on the world cultural map.

Daniel Barenboim, Solti's successor as CSO music director, took the podium for the all-Beethoven program instead, serving as soloist as well in the composer's Third Piano Concerto. Saturday's program had a celebratory, even triumphant, air befitting the life of this most optimistic and forceful of the great conductors.

Beethoven was an essential part of the 28-year Solti/CSO legacy, and the Seventh Symphony was closely associated not only with the late music director laureate but with Barenboim's rival for succession, former principal guest conductor Claudio Abbado.

With the eyes of the gala benefit crowd upon him, Barenboim offered one of his most convincing performances of a large-scale classical orchestral work. Dispensing with pauses between the movements, he offered a reading that was fully aware of the dynamism of the Solti and Abbado approaches while bringing out the lyrical inner voices and solo passages he favors.

Most impressive was his work as soloist-conductor in the C minor concerto. This is what Barenboim does best. His luxurious romantic playing is so deeply felt that it persuades both players and audience of its old-fashioned agenda.

Celebrating a Great Trumpeter

Adolph Herseth's 50th Anniversary

Chicago Sun-Times, June 9, 1998   Sunday afternoon at Symphony Center, a full house gathered to pay tribute to Adolph "Bud" Herseth, the trumpet-besotted boy from Bertha, Minn., whose only experience had been "college band, dance band, Navy band" when Artur Rodziński hired him 50 years ago to be the principal trumpet of the Chicago Symphony Orchestra. It is, as Herseth is fond of pointing out, the only job he's ever had and, despite a 77th birthday next month, a job he has no intention of leaving anytime soon.

Herseth's credentials as a soloist and technician have never been in question. But it is his loyalty to the role of an orchestral player and his devotion as a mentor to generations of brass players worldwide that Herseth has always regarded as his greatest accomplishments.

The Bible says that the angel Gabriel will blow a trumpet to announce the Day of Judgment; accordingly, the orchestra billed Sunday's international trumpet reunion as "Gabriel's Children." Players had flown in from as far away as Japan, former Chicago colleagues came out of retirement, and jazz trumpeter Arturo Sandoval even offered a double high C.

Herseth played proud papa in the Haydn Trumpet Concerto, offering both sharply etched calls and dreamy, slow cantilena lines.

Music Director Daniel Barenboim has called the straight-talking Herseth the "conscience of the orchestra" and its "moral musical center." Barenboim's offering of a repeat performance of Beethoven's "Emperor" piano concerto (heard Saturday night) as a part of Sunday's program made clear the high regard he has for his senior colleague.

As wonderful as the Beethoven was, and as much as Herseth had wanted a work from the standard repertoire on the program ("That's what I do," he explained), the crowd was eager for the various brass summits to be scaled. And they were not disappointed.

Doc Severinsen[7] may be as sparkly in his dress as Herseth is staid, but the two were an eloquent and hilarious match in "Side by Side," trading jazz and popular riffs. And when Herseth offered two of his favorite classical excerpts from Mussorgsky and Scriabin, Severinsen shot back a few bars of Mahler of his own.

Taking on Signature Pieces

More Elegant and Restrained "Ein Heldenleben"

Chicago Sun-Times, **December 18, 1998** This week's Chicago Symphony Orchestra concerts under music director Daniel Barenboim take the peculiar inwardness of musical heroism as their theme and argue its case with loving eloquence.

Richard Strauss wrote his autobiographical Op. 40 tone poem *Ein Heldenleben* ("A Hero's Life") in 1898 when he was not even at the midpoint of a lengthy and productive career. Having tackled Dons

Juan and Quixote, Nietzsche's Zarathustra and Germany's Till Eulen-
spiegel, the composer told the novelist Romain Rolland, "I do not see
why I should not compose a symphony about myself; I find myself
quite as interesting as Napoleon or Alexander."

Barenboim led an interpretation more elegant and restrained by
half than his previous outings with a work that has become a staple,
even a signature, of his repertoire. Avoiding the arbitrary tempos of
his past readings, Barenboim sculpted a performance that matched
the work's story. Concertmaster Samuel Magad thrives in this piece's
understated romanticism and his refined solos met with strong
applause.

Herseth Triumphs in Mahler Fifth

Chicago Sun-Times, **March 8, 2000** Saturday night, now-and-forever
Chicago Symphony Orchestra principal trumpet Adolph "Bud" Her-
seth flubbed some notes in the orchestra's otherwise exquisite per-
formance of Bruckner's Fourth Symphony at Carnegie Hall. And in
Monday's *New York Times*, a reviewer suggested that the 78-year-old
Herseth might start thinking about retirement.

So Monday night, in the third and last performance of the orchestra's Carnegie residency, all eyes and ears were on Herseth in Mahler's
Symphony No. 5, a signature work for this trumpet god in his 52 seasons with the Chicago Symphony.

One Chicago wag suggested that the crusty Herseth had pasted
a photo of the New York critic to his music stand. Whatever the explanation, and even with music director Daniel Barenboim picking
an almost intolerably slow pace for the Mahler, Herseth showed that
when the chips are down, his chops can't be touched. From the symphony's opening solo trumpet calls to his leadership of the various
chorales and fugues to his daring rides-above-the-tempest-tossed
passages of *Sturm und Drang*, the orchestra's unofficial captain was
in full command.

The Carnegie audience demanded not one but two solo bows, the latter coming when, in a move reminiscent of the *To Tell the Truth* quiz show, the trumpet section began to stand as a group and then took their seats, leaving Herseth alone for his deserved ovation.

Lightning Strikes with Radu Lupu in Berlin

Everyone Knew It Was Something Extraordinary

Chicago Sun-Times, **April 24, 2000** On paper, the pair of programs that Daniel Barenboim and the Chicago Symphony Orchestra brought to the Berlin Easter week *Festtage* ("Festival Days") this weekend did not seem particularly adventurous. Nor was anyone predicting any musical fireworks with the presence of two outstanding but cerebral pianists as soloists in those staples of the classical repertoire, the Brahms piano concertos.

But such is the nature of live performance when you are dealing with artists of the highest level. Lightning can strike at unexpected moments. And it did with Saturday afternoon's performance of the D-minor Concerto No. 1, Op. 15 with the Romanian-born Radu Lupu as soloist.

Somehow from Lupu's first entrance the already tightly focused capacity audience at Berlin's modern landmark Philharmonie shared a sense that something extraordinary was about to unfold. In a piece that thousands of listeners know practically by heart, Lupu's complete command of the modulations of tempo and spirit animated the work so that one actually wondered after each beloved passage what was going to come next.

Barenboim sometimes can turn his orchestral Brahms into a heavy cousin of Wagner with perversely slow tempos and overly personal crescendos and diminuendos. On Friday, when the Milanese virtuoso Maurizio Pollini was the soloist in the B-Major Second Concerto, Op. 83, the result was a sort of musical civil war with rapid, rhythmically daring piano passages alternating with almost funereal orchestral stretches.

On Saturday, however, Lupu lifted Barenboim along with him,

and Barenboim led the orchestra in a partnership that appeared almost to be one of second nature. With a few Bachlike gestures, Lupu cued Barenboim to a solution to the deceptively tricky fugal passages of the third movement. That an accomplishment this rare can sound almost effortless is another miracle of musical art.

Boulez's *Notations for Orchestra* were given almost pointillistic detail and attention with the vaunted acoustics of Hans Scharoun's 1963 concert hall allowing one to hear every subtle interplay between the many instrumental threads that make up these inviting miniatures. An extremely spry Boulez literally leapt over a guardrail to take the first of a series of solo and joint bows demanded by the uncharacteristically effusive Berlin audience.

On Saturday, after Lupu's historic triumph, a performance of Stravinsky's *Le Sacre du printemps* ("The Rite of Spring") might have seemed like overkill or at least a jarring shift of orientation. But Barenboim gave the best reading of the work's demanding, pulsating first half that this listener has heard from him.

And what a showcase for the CSO! Is there another orchestra that has a quartet of principal wind players that can match flutist Mathieu Dufour, oboist Alex Klein, clarinetist Larry Combs and bassoonist David McGill in both individual excellence and collective unity? Between the world-famous Berlin Philharmonic and the parade of international orchestras that passes through this city, Berliners certainly have the opportunity to make comparisons. Their wild cheers for these players, and for such stalwarts as horn players Dale Clevenger and Daniel Gingrich and cellist John Sharp in the Brahms works, concertmaster Samuel Magad, alto flute player Richard Graef, E-flat clarinetist John Bruce Yeh and timpani player Donald Koss, among others, made it clear that they rightly value Chicago's players as among the best in the world.

Returning Home to Argentina

A Happy Conductor Plays Falla in Buenos Aires

Chicago Sun-Times, **October 12, 2000** Fifty years ago, a seven-year-old native of this historic Latin American city took the stage of the legendary Teatro Colón and gave his first full-length professional piano recital to audience cheers and critical hosannas. The self-confident, smiling little boy with a shock of thick black hair might have been just another prodigy or he might even have gone on to have a respectable career exclusively as a pianist.

But the little boy's father, Enrique Barenboim, the Buenos Aires-born son of Russian Jewish immigrants, had bigger plans for his son Daniel. From the boy's earliest childhood and on through his late teenage years, Enrique, with the support of his wife, Aida, steered his son toward a broad-based life in music that would bring him to the heights of keyboard stardom and make him one of the most prominent orchestra and opera conductors of his time.

Enrique and Aida were both piano teachers and the Barenboims were well-integrated into the cosmopolitan artistic and intellectual culture of what was then very much a world capital. Both parents encouraged their son to have as normal a childhood as possible for someone of his unusual musical gifts, one that included playing soccer in the streets around their apartment house with other neighborhood children.

In August, the 57-year-old Barenboim returned as a soloist to the Teatro Colón to mark the half century since his acclaimed debut. And now he is here, his hair thinned and turned white, with the Chicago Symphony Orchestra after almost a decade as the CSO's music director, to lead three concerts at the Colón as the final leg of the CSO's first-ever tour of South America.

At a press conference Monday night, after the end of the Jewish holiday of Yom Kippur, Barenboim told a large crowd of journalists of the significance that this visit has for him. "One of my earliest memories is of my father talking about how in 1923, at the age of 11, he heard the Vienna Philharmonic on its first tour to Buenos Aires at the Colón," said Barenboim, speaking in both Spanish and English. "And he talked about how this opened up a whole world of sound and excitement."

"The Chicago Symphony has played a major, major role in my development as a conductor from when I first led the orchestra 30 years ago in 1970," he said. "And even then, I had dreams of leading them here in the city where I was born.

"When I was invited to become music director, and as the years of partnership have grown between me and the orchestra, I watched as every major orchestra in the world came here, dozens of them, and never the CSO. I knew that we had to remedy this.

"And now, nearly 80 years after my father first had that formative experience hearing the Vienna Philharmonic here, I am profoundly happy to be here with the orchestra."

Although the Barenboims would emigrate to Israel in 1952, just before Daniel turned 10, he made many important contacts here as a boy. Argentina had a long history of encouraging immigration and welcoming exiles into an active participation in Argentinian life. Barenboim spoke of his father taking him to play for and talk with Romanian conductor Sergiu Celibidache, after he had escaped war-torn Europe and was living in Buenos Aires.

This began a lifelong devotion to Celibidache's mystical approach to music and his almost maniacal devotion to spontaneity. "In later life, I recalled these early meetings with Celibidache and told him that, given his approach, I was his best student because I had never studied with him!" Barenboim said with a hearty laugh.

Two questions, one on the internationalization of current works and one on the CSO's playing of Latin music, allowed Barenboim to elaborate on his musical philosophy.

"Cultural nationalism as a force that can lead to fascism, and political nationalism, is over in music, is over in the arts," he said. "But a cultural nationalism that allows us to smell Czechoslovakia in current performances of Dvořák or Janáček, to smell France in music of Debussy or Ravel, that should still be alive.

"What an orchestra such as ours can demonstrate is that musicians on the highest level, wherever they come from, can play French music, Spanish music, German music, exactly as it should sound. Music itself has none of these national or political connotations, only we and our perceptions do."

Barenboim insisted that he did not program Falla's *The Three-Cornered Hat* because it was Latin music of a Spanish composer who had lived his later years and died in Argentina.

"I came to this great score because it really is a great score," he said. "It stands up to the other great ballet scores of its time by Stravinsky, Bartók, and Debussy because of its innovation and its inclusion of many kinds of music and styles. We actually prepared it to take with us to Germany (earlier this year), and now it has entered our repertoire. And we are bringing it to you, just as we are bringing Mahler and Bruckner, because it is great music, and not because you should hear a 'Latin' conductor or the sound of Al Capone in our playing, but because you should hear great music played by a great orchestra."

Reaching New Heights at Home and Abroad

Playing Better Than It Has in Years

Chicago Sun-Times, October 7, 2002 You had to gape a bit last week when the CSO opened the 112th season at New York's historic Carnegie Hall. In what single concert venue other than Carnegie's Isaac Stern Auditorium could you possibly see Paul Newman and Joanne Woodward, financiers Henry Kravis and Felix Rohatyn, the legendary retired *New York Times* music critic Harold C. Schonberg (a spry, cigarette-fancying 90), Hollywood mogul Barry Diller and his wife, designer Diane von Furstenberg, Danny Glover, New York Philharmonic music director Lorin Maazel and Caroline Kennedy?

But even among the glitterati, the CSO's three-evening residency had a more serious agenda. The orchestra, which has been in the world's top rank for decades, is playing better than it has in years and

Daniel Barenboim and his players wanted to show America's cultural capital the kind of serious work that they can do in a real residency.

When Barenboim puts his mind to it he can construct fascinating programs. And over the course of these three performances he made a certain logical and emotional argument that went beyond the mere sonic showing off that the CSO is certainly capable of.

Wednesday night's gala reprised the orchestra's first hometown subscription week program with a bill of Spanish music by Manuel de Falla and Maurice Ravel, with Barenboim taking the keyboard slot as well as the conductor's role in Falla's *Nights in the Gardens of Spain*.

A week of settling in with this music in Chicago allowed the orchestra to shine in the wide palette of colors that Barenboim had in mind. Even Ravel's hoary *Pavane for a Dead Princess* had a grace and elegance one rarely encounters (no doubt assisted by the hall's ability to carry a pianissimo to the farthest seat). New York critics have been gunning for the CSO since its first Carnegie appearance in 1898 (these were its 109th, 110th, and 111th performances here), but after a stunning, even suspenseful, *Bolero*, *Newsday*'s Justin Davidson, this year's winner of the Pulitzer Prize in criticism, wrote, "Barenboim has shaped an orchestra that can drive itself." The cheering crowd drew idiomatic encores of two entr'actes from Bizet's *Carmen* and the old Brazilian dance hit "Tico Tico."

Thursday night's concert started at the dawn of German romanticism and traveled to its dissolution in the world of atonality. Two and a half years ago, Barenboim and the CSO teamed with Romanian-born pianist Radu Lupu for a performance of Brahms's First Piano Concerto in D minor, Op. 15 in Berlin that was one of the most thrilling events in the orchestra's recent history. One of Carnegie's few flaws is that its stage is not friendly to pianists playing concertos with large orchestras, so no one, least of all Lupu, who complained in rehearsals that he could not hear himself play, expected lightning to strike twice. Yet somehow it did, with a warhorse being transformed into a cantering stallion.

For most conductors, playing Schoenberg's 1909 *Five Pieces for Orchestra*, Op. 16 from memory might seem like showboating. But

Barenboim's doing so here was a way of serving notice that this still-daring and complex music is in his bones and that he wanted the players to treat it as they would any other core repertoire.

By the time the printed program concluded with Wagner's Overture to *Tannhäuser*, even veteran New York concertgoers were shaking their heads at the unity, power and lyricism of the CSO's sound. Barenboim's trademark Wagner encore of the Overture to Act Three of *Die Meistersinger von Nürnberg* was sublime.

Japan—Something Special Is Happening

Chicago Sun-Times, **November 1, 2003** Welcoming the Chicago Symphony Orchestra to its fifth tour of Japan, U.S. Ambassador Howard Baker told an audience of diplomats and other dignitaries in the salon of his Tokyo residence last week that at least since Alexis de Tocqueville the world has envied what Americans have been able to do through voluntary activities in the arts, sciences and commerce.

Coincidentally, but not unimportantly, the former U.S. senator and White House chief of staff echoed remarks that Chicago Symphony music director Daniel Barenboim made earlier this month at the orchestra's annual meeting in Chicago: While we live in a time of difficult communication between the world's leaders and misunderstandings among peoples, the rest of the world is in awe when it can hear and see what American cultural organizations accomplish through their own initiative and without government control.

In an era when funding and other support for the arts is reaching crisis proportions even in European capitals, it is particularly interesting to follow the Chicago Symphony on tour in Japan, a country that tends to follow the American philosophy of self-reliance but also one that demonstrates what can happen when the fine arts are given a position of respect and cultural value.

After three sold-out concerts in Tokyo's 2,300-seat Bunka Kaikan concert hall, another in Osaka's 2,700-seat Festival Hall and another Wednesday night in Fukoaka's acoustically splendid new 1,781-seat Symphony Hall, it is apparent both that the orchestra is playing at the top of its game and that few audiences know how to appreciate such work as well as the Japanese.

Taking their seats early and listening in rapturous silence—even in Osaka's massive auditorium, one of the widest I have ever seen (you could almost hear the audience listening during the quietest moments of Gustav Mahler's 80-minute Ninth Symphony)—the Japanese patrons wait for the last notes of the last chords to die away before they begin to create what seem like waves of clapping. Opening night in Tokyo brought forth seven curtain calls over seven minutes that would probably still be going on if Barenboim had not led concertmaster Robert Chen off of the stage with him. Similar ovations in Tokyo and Fukuoka led to encores of Sibelius, Mendelssohn and Gluck (with titles for each selection given by Barenboim—in Japanese).

Even after the orchestra has left the stage, the Japanese concert experience hasn't ended. Where else are musicians such as principal trombone and tuba Jay Friedman and Gene Pokorny liable to be mobbed by a crowd of autograph seekers that literally runs toward them as they exit the stage door?

And even a pair of Chicago ears can tell that something special is happening at this stage of the often-complex Barenboim-Chicago Symphony partnership. Particularly in the Romantic repertoire of Mahler, Bruckner, Wagner and Tchaikovsky that is the focus of this tour, performances have featured a warmth and cohesiveness in the strings and a gentleness and almost mystical intuition in the wind playing that underscores the quiet beauty of pieces that are too often thought of as sonic juggernauts. It is almost as if there is a dialogue going on not only between the players but between the pieces both within individual concerts and from concert to concert and venue to venue.

Showing His Strength in Berg and Mozart

Chicago Sun-Times, **June 12, 2004** This program ranging over 150 years tied together those two periods where Vienna stood as the indisputable center of the musical world, from masterpieces of Mozart and Schubert to one of the most captivating works of Schoenberg's brilliant disciple Alban Berg. It is all music where the strongest points of the Barenboim-Chicago partnership come through: a lightness and flexibility of touch, a deep sense of communication between podium and players and virtuosic playing solely at the service of the scores being presented.

For Berg's *Seven Early Songs*, Barenboim called on his frequent Berlin Staatsoper collaborator, the German soprano Dorothea Roeschmann. She makes a natural partner for Barenboim, with her clear and beautiful sound, a complete absence of pretension, an intuitive understanding of lyrics and great intelligence that enables her to move across genres and centuries. These 1905–08 miniatures of the Second Viennese School (orchestrated by the composer in 1928) were heard in perfect presentations of this simultaneously challenging and inviting cycle.

Of course no one plays a Mozart piano concerto like Barenboim—at once luxuriously taking full advantage of the modern Steinway grand piano and displaying an innate connection to the composer's spirit of play and that sense of deep knowledge of the world that lurks behind Mozart's apparent gaiety. When he is both pianist and conductor, the same qualities are present on the slightly wider canvas of the small orchestra.

If there has ever been any doubt about where Barenboim stands with the orchestra's players, watch their faces during and after the C Major Concerto No. 25, K. 503. That this rich work has found its place in the repertory only in the last 50 years reminds you that there are indeed new things under the sun.

Thursday's performance can be seen as a reminder and a reflection of Barenboim's tenure in Chicago: intense, unfinished, vaguely dissonant and ultimately radiant. Barenboim's elegant and elastic encore of the F Major andante movement of Mozart's C Major Piano Sonata, K. 330, added two other words to the list that are inseparable from any attempts to describe this great artist: spontaneous and unpredictable.

A Conversation among Geniuses

Two Restless Geniuses Together

Chicago Sun-Times, **May 26, 2005** Four of the most exciting nights in
Orchestra Hall's modern history took place in June 1983 when James
Levine led the Chicago Symphony Orchestra in a live recording project of the five Beethoven piano concertos with Alfred Brendel as soloist. Add Tuesday night—when Levine returned to partner another
first-rate pianist, Chicago Symphony music director Daniel Barenboim, in a special one-night-only benefit for the musicians' pension
fund—to this roster of magic and magnificence.

There was a lot of history on the Armour Stage Tuesday, the kind
of history that is both very much alive and that sets one to wondering about the future. It is sometimes forgotten that one of the things
that made the Solti era at the Chicago Symphony was that Levine was
in charge at Ravinia.

As this all-Brahms program—the D Major Second Symphony and
the B-Flat Major Second Piano Concerto—reminded us, Levine and
Barenboim, as different as they are, have many complementary aspects. They both are products of the Central and East European Jewish migration to the Americas. They both were piano prodigies. They
both live for and in music. They each are non-European Jews who
made great names for themselves conducting Wagner at Bayreuth;
for a decade they had adjacent dressing rooms and compared notes
daily there each summer. Barenboim might be seen as taking a more
mystical approach to music, but he is a master at achieving practical results. Levine is a "music as it is on the page" man, but as in the
transparency and lightness that he found in even the weightiest passages of Brahms, he can create magical performances.

In the concerto, the contrasting approaches of these different yet
always intuitive men came together as if two hands were clasping.
Barenboim's seemingly superhuman athleticism in the great allegro movements had Levine at times offering an almost evanescent
accompaniment. The sublime andante, as beautiful as one will ever

hear, turned into chamber music, with principal cello John Sharp an equal third partner.

After four minutes of roaring cheers from both audience and orchestra, Barenboim and Levine returned to the stage for an elegant, even poignant, conversation in music—the Schubert F minor Fantasy for piano, four hands. It was as if these two restless geniuses were saying, "What times we have had in Chicago. What times."

Going Out on Top

New Carter, Hair-Raising Mahler

Chicago Sun-Times, **November 7, 2005** Part valedictory, part celebration, part getting on with the business of keeping a great orchestra at the top of the musical heap, the Chicago Symphony Orchestra's last tour with Daniel Barenboim as its music director has taken it to Carnegie Hall with its collective eyes and spirit focused on the past, the present and the future.

As this city filled with 30,000 runners from around the world to take part in Sunday's New York Marathon, the orchestra and Barenboim conducted something of a marathon themselves with three concerts at the most storied musical venue in North America. Each featured one of the monumental works of the symphonic repertoire, along with other pieces ranging from Mozart wind concertos through one of Arnold Schoenberg's most complex 12-tone explorations to a new work by the indefatigable American composer Elliott Carter, whose 97th birthday is next month.

Throughout his music directorship, Barenboim has paid special attention to the wind and violin sections, areas where leadership focus sometimes was eclipsed in the past by the orchestra's legendary brass sections. The dividends paid off greatly in New York, where Carnegie's superb acoustics allowed listeners to hear the Chicago violins in all of their renewed glory in works as contrasting as Mozart's delicate E-flat Sinfonia Concertante for wind soloists and orchestra and Bruckner's mammoth Symphony No. 5 in B-flat Major.

The Mozart was a bittersweet affair as Alex Klein, an outstanding Barenboim hire as principal oboe in 1995, was the lead soloist, making only his second return to the orchestra since a neurological disorder, focal dystonia, forced his very early retirement from the orchestra two seasons ago. Klein, who now cannot play for more than an hour at a time, sounded divine.

The most varied program of the tour saw Mathieu Dufour, whom Barenboim hired as principal flute in 1999, as soloist in Mozart's G Major Flute Concerto, K. 313, as well as the New York premiere of Carter's *Soundings*, and Schubert's "Great" C Major Symphony, D. 944.

That Carter still composes within shouting distance of his 100th birthday and that he is capable of composing works as intricate and attractive as *Soundings* are remarkable accomplishments enough. But unlike many other composers today, Carter listens attentively to both performances of his works and the thoughts of those who play them, and in the weeks since its Orchestra Hall world premiere he expanded both an enchanting set of passages for three piccolos and one of the solo piano statements (the nine-minute work has Barenboim alternating as piano soloist and conductor—but never both at once) to make the work even more effective.

Of the many seats Barenboim has filled in the orchestra—more than one-third of the orchestra—none has been more challenging to fill (for him or for anyone who would have been in his position) than that of principal trumpet, a position which the 53-year reign of Adolph "Bud" Herseth cemented in the international public's mind as primus inter pares. After one unsuccessful appointment and several finalists who never quite crossed the finish line, Barenboim's appointment of the boyish Christopher Martin is clearly a winner.

As he did last month in Chicago, he led off a hair-raising account of Mahler's C-sharp minor Fifth Symphony, a work that is identified with the CSO perhaps more than any other.

Barenboim still has more distance from Mahler than he does from Bruckner and Schubert, but as he prepares to leave this great Mahler orchestra after 17 years, and with Martin picking up Herseth's mantle, they are surely meeting in a very happy middle. As one New York-based critic was heard saying afterward, "You schooled us tonight."

Looking Back at His Chicago Years

How He Decided What to Play; Favorite Musicians

WFMT Broadcast, February 2006

PATNER: You are performing the Schubert Symphonies Eight and Nine together. I wonder if you might talk a bit about Schubert the symphonist.

BARENBOIM: I believe many composers find a particular discipline to write their innermost thoughts about music or what can be said through music, and those works represent a kind of diary. In Beethoven's case it's clearly the string quartets and the piano sonatas, and not the symphonies. In Schubert's case it's not the symphonies, but in many ways the songs and maybe the chamber music. In Mozart's case it's the piano concertos, not the piano sonatas. So one cannot claim that Schubert symphonies really give us the clue to his greatness as a composer, but I think that for me the two B-flats, numbers Two and Five, and the "Unfinished" and the "Great" C major, numbers Eight and Nine, represent the pinnacle of his symphonic thought.

The "Unfinished" and the "Great" C major are a wonderful combination in one concert because they give such opposite impressions of Schubert as a composer. The C major, with its majestic energy and large canvasses, and the "Unfinished," which is one of the most intimate of all symphonies. I think it's very good for musicians in the orchestra to be faced with an all-Schubert program and to see the different characteristics of the music. There are only a few symphonies. There's hardly any other music that they know unless they play chamber music. It's an enrichment for the orchestral musical life to play, once in a while, a program of only one composer like Schubert.

PATNER: Do you think that any of the operas are worth much time?

BARENBOIM: I have looked. I cannot claim that I have studied them in great depth. My friend Claudio Abbado did *Fierrabras*[8] in Vienna. I can't help feeling of the operas that I have read and studied that the dramatic content is really not on a par with the music, and even the music is not vintage Schubert.

PATNER: And yet here is somebody who could achieve, in a two-minute or three-minute song, the height of drama and of musicality, and could do it in the symphonies to a great extent, but just somehow couldn't translate it.

BARENBOIM: But I wonder how successful Bruckner, or for that matter Mahler, would be if they were asked to just write a little intermezzo. Composers need either the huge canvas or they need this intimacy. Composers are rare that are equally at home in the large forms and in the small ones.

PATNER: Speaking of somebody who had success in many forms and who has been central to you, as he has been to music throughout history, that is Mozart. You said in many ways his ultimate expression of his inner personality and spirit is in his piano concertos.

BARENBOIM: The piano concertos are obviously opera without words. The D minor concerto, which Radu Lupu is playing with me, is *Don Giovanni* in miniature. The C major concerto, which Alfred Brendel is playing with me, is also very operatic in nature. It has the nature of an opera finale and could almost be the finale to Act One of *Don Giovanni*. I wanted in my last season here to do a little miniature survey of Mozart.

PATNER: Your collaboration with Radu Lupu has been a long one, personal and pianistic. How would you characterize Lupu and what he brings particularly to Schubert and Mozart?

BARENBOIM: He's a wonderful musician to start with. One does not say Radu Lupu the great virtuoso, as one would say of [Vladimir] Horowitz, but he plays the piano extraordinarily well. But the main quality is his ability to play in a way that it sounds as if he's making the music up at that moment. It's not that he's a pure and intuitive musician, not at all, but he has the real key to the balancing of the different elements of music—the harmony, the melody, the rhythm, the colors, all of that. By the way he studies the music, he arrives at a sort of skeleton which he then fills with body when he plays at the concert. This is what gives his performances the feeling of just inventing it on the spur of the moment.

PATNER: A few years ago when you had the Chicago Symphony in Berlin, you did Brahms First with him, and there was a feeling about twenty bars into his entry that this was going to be something remarkable, and it just soared and soared and soared, and he lifted everybody up with that.

BARENBOIM: He's also one of the few people I like to play four hands with. Playing four hands on one piano is a very difficult affair. It's not like two violins playing together, where one enhances the other and enriches it. To play four hands on one piano or on two pianos you have to play much lighter than you play when you play alone because otherwise you get this sort of wooden piano sound. He knows how to play two people on one piano and to play together on two pianos, and it's a joy to lighten, and lighten, and lighten. You take away more and more until you're sort of practically whispering, but the dialogue, like the dialogue of whispering, is much more exciting than the dialogue of two people shouting at each other.

PATNER: I get the sense, when I watch the two of you play four hands, that you're listening to each other with your fingers as much as you're listening to each other with your ears.

BARENBOIM: Yes, absolutely.

PATNER: Alfred Brendel is a fixture with almost all of the world's great orchestras.

BARENBOIM: I'm very much looking forward to playing the Mozart C major concerto, which I've heard him play on many occasions, although I've never conducted it with him. He has a particular sense of wit when he plays, and I think especially the last movement of this concerto lends itself very much to these "Brendel-isms."

PATNER: He gets branded with adjectives and people call him an intellectual pianist.

BARENBOIM: When Artur Schnabel[9] came on the scene he was criticized during his lifetime by half of the music lovers for being an intellectual and by the other half for being much too much of a Romantic. In the end all these perceptions are very misleading and speak more about the person who is uttering them than about the person they are trying to define or explain.

PATNER: An artist isn't about finding one thing and replicating that for the rest of his or her career. That person wouldn't be an artist if he did that.

BARENBOIM: In many ways the difficulty for critics, or, for that matter for a knowledgeable audience, is to go to a concert and to try and understand what the artist is trying to do and judge him by the degree of success he's achieving in what he himself has set out to do, not by comparing it with the way we think it should go.

PATNER: Throughout your career you have been interested in the music made in the twentieth century, and now the music that continues to be made in this, the twenty-first century.

BARENBOIM: I don't believe that contemporary music is one compartment. There is wonderful contemporary music and terrible contemporary music, and there is wonderful nineteenth-century music and terrible nineteenth-century music. I play the music that I have great interest in, whether it was composed in the eighteenth, nineteenth, or twenty-first century. I have obviously concentrated on certain contemporary composers in the same way that I have concentrated on certain composers of the nineteenth century. I have in fact played very little Mendelssohn, I have played no Meyerbeer, I have played no Bellini. For me the great masters of today are Pierre Boulez and Elliott Carter. And then you have younger composers like Isabel Mundry and our own Augusta Read Thomas. This is my last season in Chicago, and these are four commissions that I gave and that I will conduct, provided they are finished.

I have been often criticized for choosing the composers I was going to champion. But I was not choosing to champion or not to champion. I was playing music that I find interesting, important, or amusing to me.

PATNER: Last year with [James] Levine, Levine played the second Brahms symphony and you played the second Brahms concerto with him, and this year Zubin Mehta will conduct the first Brahms symphony and then you'll play the first Brahms concerto. Is there something special when you and Mehta are working together at this stage?

BARENBOIM: Mehta has been one of my closest friends for a very long time. We met in 1956, so next year is really fifty years of our friendship. We met at a conductors' class in Siena.

PATNER: Before or after your bar mitzvah?

BARENBOIM: It was just after.

PATNER: Because I'm thinking next year you'll be 63.

BARENBOIM: We have had a wonderful friendship over all these years, which of course is no guarantee that we make good music together. But it's a wonderful feeling to have a friend that you have liked and admired for so many years, that is in the same profession, shares the same passions, and has very similar tastes in so many things. We've had many disagreements, but we have never had a fight. Well, in the days when we were both single, we had a disagreement, a fight or whatever, about a girl. Two or three weeks after the incident, we were playing together in a room at La Scala, and somehow it all fell into proportion, much to the chagrin of the girl.

PATNER: If you're listening, Miss X.

BARENBOIM: But other than that I have not had a real disagreement. I'm delighted that he has found the time to come to Chicago to do this one concert with me.

Argentine Jokes; Changes in the Orchestra and in Him

WFMT *Broadcast,* June 2006

PATNER: It's my understanding that in your native city of Buenos
Aires, Argentina, there's the highest per capita number of
psychoanalysts. Now, I'm not going to attempt to psychoanalyze
you.

BARENBOIM: No, you're just trying to suggest that I'm in need of
psychiatric treatment. But before you start you have to explain
to our listeners that the reason for the quantity of psychoanalysts in Argentina is that the Argentinians take themselves very
seriously. The jokes about Argentinians are the same as the
jokes about the Poles in America or the Belgians in Europe, all
the things which are today not politically correct, but could be
very funny. All the jokes about the Argentinians are about their
preoccupation with themselves. Most of those jokes can't be
translated.

But, for instance, how does an Argentinian commit suicide?
He climbs up his ego and he jumps. Then there is the Argentinian who went to Paris and went up the Eiffel Tower to see how
Paris looked without him. And the Argentinians always are very
happy when there is thunder because they say God is photo-
graphing them.

I say this with a lot of affection because I feel partly Argentinian and very close to them. But it is true that there is something about the Argentinian mentality being extremely . . . not
egoistic, but egocentric, and not in a negative way. Not in the
sense that I am the belly button of the world, but in the sense of
only if I know myself do I know everything else and everybody
else. A greatly exaggerated preoccupation with the self.

I think it has to do with the history of Argentina. Argentina
will soon celebrate 200 years of its independence. It considers
itself the most European of all Latin American countries, and it
is. Not only the way it looks, but the way people think, the way
they dress, the way they behave. There was a terrific amount of

economic immigration to Argentina as opposed to political. It is
not people who went to Argentina because politically they were
in difficulties and had to run away, but immigration of Italians,
Jews, Arabs, English, Spanish, Turks, who went for the economic
possibilities.

Economic immigration has a completely different effect,
both on the people who immigrate and on the people who
receive them. If you arrive in Buenos Aires from Aleppo in
Syria, where a lot of the Jewish community in Argentina origi-
nated, not because you had to leave Aleppo and Syria and the
Middle East, but because you saw Argentina as the land of
opportunity, you look at Argentina differently than if you arrive
there because you have no choice. And the people there receive
you differently. This idea of cosmopolitanism rather than glob-
alization is a very healthy and very important state of affairs.
There is no clash of loyalties and no clash of culture.

When I left Argentina in 1952, the Jewish community was
the third largest community in the world after the United States
and the Soviet Union. There were 800,000 Jews in Argentina.
Now it's a lot less because many went to Cuba and are socialists.
Many went to Israel after the creation of the state of Israel—and
there are whole kibbutzim of Argentinians where it's absolutely
still an Argentinian way of life and they still put the same sauce
on the salad like in Buenos Aires, although it is already the third
generation.

PATNER: You are at the end of a long period in Chicago with this
orchestra. What do you think twenty years from now it's going
to mean to you?

BARENBOIM: I don't know, because I have very little interest in the
perception of things. I'm not interested in how things are perceived now, and I certainly am not interested about how we
perceive things from the past. I'm much more interested in the
content. The perception is only a commentary. It's not the text
itself. I think that our society has become enslaved by how it is
perceived.

PATNER: But I'm asking how you—

BARENBOIM: How will I perceive Chicago? But it's the same thing.
It's really unimportant. It's unimportant how I would feel twenty
years from now about where I am today.

PATNER: Then what does this association mean now for you?

BARENBOIM: I have conducted this orchestra for thirty-six years.
I think there are three people who were here before me. Otherwise I have seen everybody practically from the first day they
entered the orchestra, because I conducted not only for thirty-
six years, but every year, with an exception of four years in the
early eighties when for personal reasons, because of my first
wife's illness, I didn't come to America at all.

I have seen young people grow old and wise, others grow
wise and never age, and others grow simply old and not wise.
I am very attached to that. When we started in the seventies I
had a lot less experience than I have now. And they had more
experience because the orchestra was not young at all then. It's
much younger now. The combination of those factors—of me
having less experience and they having more experience—
I learned a lot of the repertoire with them. But then they learned
quite a lot of it on me, too. It was a very, very healthy give and
take.

One of my favorite memories is of conducting the first performance by the Chicago Symphony of *Pelleas und Melisande* of
[Arnold] Schoenberg in 1973. We were very close in our musical
idiom with a lot of the music. As the years went by, we developed in many ways in different directions. I'm not trying to
make a quality judgment, but musical education in America
became very different.

If you look at the strings, in the seventies they were still the
result to a great extent of Ivan Galamian's teachings, the great
Armenian teacher in New York.[10] But by 1980 or so the whole
generation of string players has been a product of his apostles
and not of him. And I don't believe the apostles do justice to the
master.

PATNER: Apostolic succession does not always work in the training
of artists.

BARENBOIM: And I think American society in general changed quite
a lot since then. The role of music, which has diminished worldwide, the role of music in the society, the real value of music in
the society, is catastrophic in America. I read an article in the
New York Times saying that all those who speak with a defeatist
attitude about the state of classical music in America should
revise their opinion because there is more music than there was
before.[11] Sure, quantity, no question about that.

But the place of music in the general culture of a human
being is much lower now than it was fifty years ago, not only in
America, but more so in America. Now eighty percent, I would
say, of the intellectuals, the people who are concerned with culture and the arts, philosophy and literature and painting, have
no connection to music whatsoever. It's not whether they like it
or they don't like it. They have no connection to it. And I have
felt it getting worse and worse even in the seventeen years that
I have been here.

An orchestra is, for better or for worse, a mirror of the
society. You have in an orchestra intelligent people, and you
have less intelligent people; you have generous people; you have
avaricious people; you have people with temperament, exactly
like in society, and it is a mirror of the society. At the same time,
we have managed to get really very high-quality musicians in
the orchestra. Over a third of them have come in the last seventeen years since I am here. And the level of individual excellence
is extraordinarily high.

PATNER: Many of them have come from different backgrounds, less
traditional symphonic orchestral backgrounds, different countries, different traditions. As a listener and observer, it's not
just that they've come, but that mix of people has energized
the whole organism of the orchestra.

BARENBOIM: We played the third act of [Richard Wagner's] *Parsi-
fal* last week, a work that was new to, I would say, 105 percent of

the orchestra. [PATNER *laughs*.] And in a very short time, I think
we achieved what I would call the creation of a collective lung in
the orchestra, because making music is not about following the
conductor or the conductor giving you clear instructions. Any
mediocre professional conductor can do that and any mediocre
professional musician, if he has the ability and the willingness,
can follow that. But the ability to be on the stage and everybody
breathe the music in the same way. In the end, the quality of a
great orchestra is a mixture of the individual excellence which
these people possess probably like no other orchestra in the
world, plus the ability not only to listen to each other, but also
to hear the music innerly in the same way.

When the conductor gives the upbeat and the whole orchestra hears innerly the first sound in exactly the same way, then
you get a right musical expression. If the conductor has not
been able to guide the different aesthetics that are inevitable
in any group of people, especially a high-quality one, even the
greatest individual excellence will not hide the fact that basically there is no communion.

[Eds: Unfortunately Andrew did not review this special concert, but John von Rhein's commentary in the *Tribune* described
Barenboim's "sensuous and diaphanous web of sound" and
claimed that "the orchestra's saturated brass and rich strings
would have put any Bayreuth pit band to shame."[12]]

PATNER: An interesting thing about those concerts last week that
only further underscores your point is that the third act of *Par-
sifal* followed the *Notations* of Boulez. To have on the same
program this great work of Wagner, with which you are long
associated, and you've come to share a sound in making that,
but also they've learned these Boulez pieces and you learned
together the largest piece of the set [no. 7], which was written
for you and the orchestra here in Chicago—to hear that same
level of unity of purpose and commitment was a wonderful
thing.

BARENBOIM: It shows what Boulez always maintained—that there are two problems with contemporary music. One is the quality of the performance, because very often there is not enough time and not enough understanding, and therefore people are just satisfied with being able to play the right notes at the right time. The other is the familiarity. You cannot pretend for pieces of the complexity and the virtuosity of *Notations* to become part of the repertoire, you should play them once every ten or fifteen years. Let's not talk about the Fifth Mahler which has been played so much, but just think how often even the Seventh Mahler has been played. The fact that we were able to play them with this naturalness and familiarity is a result of the fact that we have studied and restudied them periodically and played them often on tour as well. At the first rehearsal we had for those pieces, I just played through and made, at the most, two or three corrections in every piece, and I said, "On Thursday morning we will go more in detail." But on Thursday morning, the notes were all correct and we focused on how much softer, how much longer, or the transparency. When you play something for the first time, it's very difficult to have the same degree of freedom. And the seventh *Notation*, the longest one, is in parts very rigid, but in others very free music. We were able to achieve that in a very short amount of time. We did not even play them through on the morning of the concert. That was not necessary. I just did the places where I thought we could go further, and that was it.

PATNER: Some people don't realize that when a conductor and an orchestra have achieved a level of understanding and communication, a very good rehearsal might not include playing something through.

BARENBOIM: It's like a medical examination. If you have a problem in your stomach, a good doctor will make a thorough medical examination. But as your problem is being dealt with, they don't check your ears every time you come. Maybe as a result of the medical examination of your stomach they found that there is some connection with your teeth. And therefore you go to the dentist. But you don't go every time. You concentrate on the areas that need to be dealt with. When you rehearse a piece of the complexity of *Notations* and you rehearse the problem areas, you have to rehearse in such a way that the musician can draw conclusions from that for the rest of the music without you having to play all the rest of the music.

PATNER: Players have said to me over the years that you know a great deal about string instruments and about how to recommend a player might hold or finger an instrument. I have heard a number of string players say, "He showed us how to take a certain passage, and once I figured that out, then when I get to something similar, or even something that I thought was unrelated later in the work, I've already solved it."

BARENBOIM: Don't forget that a great orchestra musician is able to express himself completely through what he plays and at the same time listen to everybody. This is why I maintain that playing in an orchestra in an intelligent way is the best school for democracy, because you learn to express what you have to express, but simultaneously you listen to another voice. You play with your stand partner, if you play a string instrument, but you listen to the second clarinet, or the second horn, or the contrabassoon or whatever has some commentary to make.

It is very important when you play a piece that is new to the orchestra, and also when the piece is well known, to be able to take the key passages apart in the same way that you would take a car apart and then put it together again. The moment the musicians have been through that process, they learn by themselves who to listen to at this moment, who is a partner, who plays the same note, what to do, what to do with all those things, the minute they see how it is constructed.

You cannot expect a musician who plays the violin, the double bass, the clarinet or the trombone to study the whole score in such a way that he knows exactly how it is constructed. The time is not there, and it is not his function, provided the conductor sees it as his function to provide a guide to the ear of each and every individual player. Playing with a conductor is not playing with the stick or after the stick or whatever the case may be, but is basically the ability of the conductor to make everybody aware of everything that is going on at every specific moment of the piece of music.

PATNER: Do you feel that there is any unfinished business for you here in Chicago? Is there something that you wished maybe could have been completed or added to your legacy here?

BARENBOIM: I told you I'm not so interested in the past and I'm not interested in the perception, so the question of legacy is really— that's not the way I think. I think musically we have done a lot of things. Sure, there are areas of the repertoire which I would have liked to have touched more on with the orchestra.

PATNER: For example?

BARENBOIM: We did a very unusual and very good performance of the Sibelius Fifth Symphony. I would have liked to have done the Seventh as well. We played quite a lot of Bach and found our own way of playing Bach. I wish I could have done some of the Passions, but then I never did those.

I've heard the criticism that has been leveled at me that I am not interested in contemporary music per se, but only in a few contemporary composers. I take that as a compliment because I don't think that I have ever conducted anything out of a sense of duty. It's not my duty to present all kinds of contemporary music or all kinds of nineteenth-century music. It is my duty to present the music that is of interest to me and that I feel I have something to say in.

II

Pierre Boulez

(1991–2010)

The peerless French composer and conductor Pierre Boulez's long-standing relationship with the Chicago Symphony extends nearly as far back as Daniel Barenboim's. In fact, Boulez made his conducting debut with the orchestra in February 1969 with Barenboim as soloist. The pianist showcased Bartók's first concerto on a characteristically Boulezian program of music by Debussy, Webern, and Messiaen. A few months later, the New York Philharmonic named Boulez as Leonard Bernstein's successor—a bombshell decision since the field had included Colin Davis, Zubin Mehta, Seiji Ozawa, and even Barenboim himself. During Boulez's six-year tenure in New York (longer than about half of all Philharmonic directors), he shocked audiences by performing works by high modernists like George Crumb and Luciano Berio alongside Mendelssohn and Mozart. For several summers he also led members of the orchestra in a series of low-priced "Rug Concerts," a plan he developed with stage designer Peter Wexler that involved removing seats in Philharmonic Hall and replacing them with rugs and couches. His experimental, if at times stormy, tenure demanded the artistic, administrative, and community engagement skills required of a contemporary orchestra leader, but he later avoided the role in favor of guest appearances.

Boulez returned to Paris in 1977 to head IRCAM, a new contemporary music center established under the auspices of French President Georges Pompidou. IRCAM and Boulez became synonymous over the next fifteen years as he hosted the world's leading composers and directed the affiliated Ensemble Intercontemporain. Barenboim, meanwhile, had become the director of the Orchestre de Paris. The former collaborators were now two of the city's most powerful musical leaders, and they soon refreshed their partnership. Boulez made frequent guest appearances with Barenboim's orchestra, and Barenboim commissioned orchestrations of Boulez's first four *Notations*. (The CSO would later commission the next four, though only number VII was ever completed.) Just before the CSO decided to hire Barenboim, in 1989, Pierre Bergé, head of the Paris Opéra, fired him from the position of music director for the newly established Opéra-Bastille. Bergé's move angered Boulez, who resigned from his position as a national theater administrator and boycotted the institution in solidarity. It was only natural, then, that the composer would ease back into Chicago as the Barenboim era dawned.

Boulez made waves when he returned, just as he had elsewhere throughout his career. His two-week residency with the CSO in 1987 electrified audiences with programs featuring staples of his New York repertoire—Debussy, Schoenberg, and Stravinsky. Building on this success, Barenboim tapped Boulez to cover part of his first recording agreements with the orchestra, and the French maestro more than delivered. During Barenboim's first four seasons, Boulez led month-long residencies that introduced (or re-introduced) the city to a wide palette of modernist works ranging from Bartók and Stravinsky to Varèse and Carter. Recordings of these early performances went on to win five Grammy awards. Serving as a more visible public advocate than Barenboim, Boulez also brought his ideas to the public in lectures at the Art Institute and in open rehearsals with the Civic Orchestra, which reached new heights under his baton. The CSO named Boulez its next principal guest conductor in March 1995, capping off a large celebration of his seventieth birthday. The decision made his four-year de facto status official, and he remained in this position until Barenboim's departure in 2006.

Beyond leading and recording with the orchestra during his annual visits, Boulez collaborated with composer-in-residence Augusta Read Thomas and programming director Matías Tarnopolsky to develop a contemporary music series at Symphony Center called Music-NOW. The chamber music series complemented Boulez's focus on orchestral pieces written before 1960 by featuring newer music exclusively. MusicNOW became so popular that it enticed Barenboim himself to direct some of the programs and quickly outgrew Buntrock Hall, the orchestra's rehearsal space, as its main venue. Generous endowments from passionate donors ensured that it would remain one of the country's most vital new music incubators. Boulez's deep involvement was one of the orchestra's bright spots during the economically challenging years that closed Barenboim's tenure, and the two went on a smashingly successful international farewell tour in 2005 to celebrate Boulez's eightieth birthday.

When the orchestra made its surprise announcement that Bernard Haitink would succeed Barenboim with the title of principal conductor, it also named Boulez as its first conductor emeritus. News reports suggested that Haitink would be the orchestra's chief musical advisor while Boulez would continue to serve as the lead guest conductor, but nearly the reverse was true. CSO musician contracts stipulated that only the music director could make personnel decisions, and Haitink took no interest in this role. Boulez accepted it dutifully since his long association with the orchestra had earned him the orchestra's respect and trust. By assuming this responsibility, he offered artistic and managerial stability as the search for a new director continued. Under the full leadership of not one but two of the world's most distinguished musicians, both born before 1930, the orchestra was poised to maintain if not elevate its international stature even in the absence of a permanent director.

Age didn't shrink Boulez's innovative spirit, and he delivered for the orchestra again in his new role. Audiences in Chicago and New

York continued to marvel at his batonless approach to conducting, which enabled him to articulate form and tone color in even the thorniest contemporary scores. In response to these idiosyncratic readings, Andrew focused his reviews on phrasing, shades of color, textural balance, and other details that only Boulez could reveal. Boulez continued to support new works by commissioning composers less than half his age and took it upon himself to expand his modernist repertoire with pieces by Karol Szymanowski and others. Asked at a Chicago celebration of his eighty-fifth birthday how he stayed so mentally alert, he responded that he thought continuing to learn new scores was key.

: :

Far from an ivory tower sage who appealed only to the elite, Boulez appears under Andrew's watchful eye as classical music's equivalent of a rock star—at once rebellious, charismatic, mellow, and charming. At the same time, Andrew elicited profound insights in his interviews with Boulez. The Frenchman suffered through the turmoil of Nazi occupation and had to pick up the pieces by forging his own path as a composer and conductor primarily outside France. Discussions of these life experiences slip between deep analyses of specific works and detailed recollections of formative encounters with the leading figures of modernism, particularly Edgard Varèse. With natural charm, Andrew also uncovered Boulez's wit. Asked how he would have responded in the 1950s if someone had told him he would be conducting the Bruckner symphonies with great American orchestras, Boulez quipped without missing a beat, "I suppose I would say, maybe, who is Bruckner?" So it was: Boulez brought the city Berio— Chicago brought him Bruckner.

DOUGLAS W. SHADLE

FIGURE 2.1. CSO musicians laughing in Berlin, Germany, rehearsal during 2005
European tour. Pierre Boulez, conductor; Daniel Barenboim, piano.
Photo by Todd Rosenberg. Used with permission.

A Visitor Enchants the City

Playing Bartók, Stravinsky, Carter, Messiaen

Chicago Sun-Times, **December 12, 1993** The scene in the lobby of
Orchestra Hall last Sunday morning was only slightly tamer than at
the Aragon or the Riviera on a Saturday night. Admittedly, the Michi-
gan Avenue crowd included more grandmothers with scarves and
students in baggy sweaters than the black-jacketed mosh-pitters who
storm a North Side rock concert, but the same sense of urgency—
even panic—was evident.

"I'm going in!" snapped one young man as he slipped under the
arm of an Andy Frain usher who was blocking the lobby door.

"I am a member of the governing board of the Orchestral Association, and my husband and I have seats in there," huffed a silver-
haired matron as she pushed past another beleaguered guard.

Such is the effect of the annual visit to Chicago of French composer, conductor, and music theorist Pierre Boulez, concluding Tues-

day with a Chicago Symphony Orchestra concert featuring works of Ravel and Bartók. At a time when critics of classical music question its relevance and orchestra managers decry the decline of music education and ponder the graying of their audiences, the 68-year-old Parisian turns many of these arguments upside down during his month long residencies.

While many superstar conductors cultivate an imperial seclusion, Boulez engages in standing-room-only pre-concert conversations with ticket holders and makes himself available for one-on-one newspaper and broadcast interviews.

"Look at how an art museum presents itself," he said in an interview on local radio. "It invites the public inside its house, provides varied and stimulating means of making exhibitions, offers lectures and audiocassette tours. Increasingly, they use video and CD-ROM technology. They have days for the family and the students. This must be the model for the presentation of serious music as well."

Boulez's critique of music presentation does not stop there. "We have created an atmosphere in the music hall that is cold and too structured. Concerts are held in a certain place, with tickets at a certain price, beginning at a certain time. We live in cities that are composed of many villages and we must find ways to connect with these villages."

But enthusiasm and creative thinking alone can't explain how the somewhat-rumpled Boulez, known for years for his dismissive views of music and bureaucrats not to his liking, has become the most beloved CSO guest conductor since the golden years of Carlo Maria Giulini and Claudio Abbado. His Italian predecessors were dashing heartthrobs with passionate intensity on the podium. And although Abbado included 20th century music in his programming (his semi-staged production of Alban Berg's atonal opera *Wozzeck* was one of the orchestra's greatest triumphs), both men concentrated on music that appealed to a broader cross-section of the audience.

For his part, Boulez dispenses with tails, preferring a dinner jacket, and shuns a baton. His Chicago concerts have concentrated on music of Bela Bartók, Igor Stravinsky, Elliott Carter and Olivier

Messiaen, supplemented this year by Gustav Mahler's rarely played tragic Symphony No. 6. His podium style is crisp and clear, deceptively businesslike. In his Art Institute lecture last Sunday on the art of conducting, he had some good-natured fun with those who consistently describe his work as "studied, logical and analytical."

Commitment and concentration are not mechanical, he explained, and their product is not "cold or detached." Rather, they are necessary to developing an overall arch, "a trajectory, a balance of episodes that is the essence of interpretation." When they are achieved, a conductor paradoxically achieves a level of spontaneity that enables him to lead an orchestra and an audience as if "through a series of mirrors" of the composer's original intention and hope for his piece.

Boulez calls this paradox of "acquired spontaneity" the "core of interpretation." At a time when many orchestras are using market research and focus groups to plan their programs, Boulez demonstrates that, in the proper hands, the most serious music can reach levels of popularity that any presenting organization would envy.

And it is this paradox that, when considered along with his generous intelligence, his disciplined stance and the sincerity of his charm, explains the ever-growing love affair between Chicago and Pierre Boulez.

Revelatory Analyses from the Podium

Intricacies of Berg, Debussy, Stravinsky

Chicago Sun-Times, **May 4, 2006** The Chicago Symphony Orchestra has had only three principal guest conductors in its 109-year history. And with all due respect to his two great and much missed Italian predecessors, Carlo Maria Giulini and Claudio Abbado, neither of them had the effect on the orchestra that the current principal guest conductor, Pierre Boulez, has had.

His role as chairman of the board of 20th century music and his hand in shaping the CSO as one of modern music's greatest champions was confirmed with the invitation to Boulez and the Chicagoans to open the third Musik Triennale here last week.

The world's largest festival of 20th century music, the third installment of Cologne's six-week musical orgy features all of the American "Big Five" orchestras, as well as the top European ensembles, including those of Vienna, Berlin and Birmingham, and many of the world's major solo artists.

Boulez, who marked his 75th birthday in late March, showed the stamp he has made on the CSO not only in his concerts but in those led by music director Daniel Barenboim that followed. Boulez's ongoing legacy is threefold: precision in playing even the most difficult works, an integration of the modern repertoire into standard programming, and an openness by the orchestra to new music, played at the highest level.

Opening night brought a reprise of a highly successful CSO subscription concert—Berg's suite from his opera *Lulu*, settings of poems by Baudelaire and Villon by Debussy, and Stravinsky's complete *Firebird* ballet.

Once again, German soprano Christine Schaefer was the soloist in the Berg and Debussy works. And once again, this young and highly intelligent artist showed that while her clear tone and perfect pitch have few peers in the interpretation of modern music, her voice is simply too small to be heard over a large orchestra, even in the vibrant acoustics of Cologne's Philharmonie.

This was the only criticism that could be offered of last week's programs, however. No one captures the intricacies and rhythmic complexities of a Stravinsky ballet score like Boulez. And whether playing *Le Sacre du printemps*, *Petrouchka*, or the *Firebird*, his performances are visual treats as well, as they are delineated so clearly that you can literally see each soloist and section offer up each melody and sonority.

In Barenboim's concerts, Boulez also provided a steady presence. Not only in his *Notations* for orchestra, which under Barenboim have become a staple of the CSO's repertory and a triumph of clear communication. But even in a work that the French composer-conductor probably would not give a second notice to, Manuel de Falla's complete ballet, *The Three-Cornered Hat*.

Barenboim, of course, finds the Latin passion and color in this work, which is too easily dismissed as light music. But he and the orchestra bring an articulation and structure that elevate the work and reflect their long association with Boulez.

An all-Boulez chamber program at the Berlin Staatsoper just a few days before brought this message home, too. CSO members of the Chicago Chamber Musicians, joined by string colleagues from the orchestra, gave performances of *Derives I-II* that held their own with the playing of modern music specialists and Boulez protégés, pianists Florent Boffard and Pierre-Laurent Aimard. In the intangible art of music, the ability to focus the mind is a step in the direction of lifting the soul.

Structure of Mahler's 7th Symphony

Chicago Sun-Times, **November 27, 2006** Although Daniel Barenboim and Pierre Boulez both came late to Mahler in their careers, the two conductors have become today's alpha and omega of performing the great symphonies of this proto-modern titan. Chicagoans have been privileged to share in their deeply serious but highly contrasting explorations over the past 15 years.

For Boulez, a focus on structure—rhythmic, harmonic and sectional—has been the chief means of revealing aspects of the work some miss and others can build upon in their own performances. Some have spoken of Boulez as blowing dust off of classics or examining them with X-ray specs. Instead, it is better to think of him as having a perpendicular view of serious music. That is, he has the rare and perhaps unique ability to see and control just where music is going in time and rhythm—the horizontal movement of a score—while he also hears and carefully monitors the way each note and instrument relates to the others in each bar—the vertical shape of the music from the violins down to the percussion.

So in the hands of Boulez, the 80 minutes of Mahler's 1904–05 five-movement Symphony No. 7 are not Bernstein's voyage of emotional catharsis, Solti's sound machine or Barenboim's spontaneous leap off the diving board, but a kind of rhythmic and spatial explication that remains completely musical at the same time.

This type of a combination analysis-performance is no easy task to execute and works best when Boulez and an orchestra know each other well, as is the case in Chicago. When he first conducted the Seventh with the Vienna Philharmonic in Salzburg 10 years ago, a listener could feel the tug of war between the players and their guest conductor. Here, cooperation prevailed.

With some conductors, we feel as if Mahler is anticipating the sensorial surround of a film score. With others that we are witnessing a crack-up or hearing a story of heroic inner struggle. With Boulez, undiminished physically and mentally at 81, we are instead given the sense of being present as Mahler composed the work in his hut along an Austrian mountain lake. As with the box constructions of artist Joseph Cornell, we are invited to view an object that contains a whole world and yet is itself contained.

Ligeti, Ravel, Berio, and Berlioz

Boulez's Passion Shines

Chicago Sun-Times, **November 27, 2006** Pierre Boulez has become such a familiar part of Chicago's musical life over the past 20 years that some might have taken for granted his flying to Chicago last month from Europe to step in with the Chicago Symphony Orchestra for an ailing Riccardo Muti.

As those concerts of Mahler's Seventh Symphony — subsequently televised on PBS's Great Performances — made clear, even at 85 Boulez is never about merely filling time or adding a check mark to his conducting catalogue. And after spending several weeks here working on his own projects and attending an unusual range of CSO programs as a listener, Friday night he launched the two-week series of major concerts that he was actually scheduled to lead this season.

Boulez and his contemporary György Ligeti, a Romanian-born Hungarian Jew, led parallel lives as compositional investigators that crossed with some regularity from the early 1990s until Ligeti's death at 83 in 2006. A key work in their late-career collaboration was Ligeti's sole Violin Concerto written from 1990 to 1992, with Boulez leading his Ensemble Contemporain and its dedicatee Saschko Gawriloff in the first recording just after its première. While Ligeti had opposed the formal nature of Boulez's structural idea of composing, the two men each greatly admired the originality and integrity of the other's work. If Chicago had to wait almost two decades to hear this half-hour masterpiece, at least we are hearing it with Boulez at the helm.

And with the CSO's own concertmaster, Robert Chen, as the remarkable soloist. The five-movement work is unlike any other in the repertoire, and the solo part rises from and falls back into the chamber-sized orchestra sometimes in ways that are initially indiscernible. One could even argue that the soloist should be an ensemble's leader as his or her role is to push both audience and musicians to hear music in an entirely different way: Odd sounds from a strangely tuned violin and viola. Ocarinas and slide whistles and instruments reaching for the extremes of their range. Rhythms derived from the chants of African Pygmies and cross-ticking clocks. And a real or imagined folk melody that made its way into works throughout Ligeti's lifetime. Ligeti usually shunned electronics but was fascinated with the ways people heard things simultaneously and in layers in computer and digital eras, and the beautiful and lyrical Violin Concerto and Chen's total and never show-boating involvement brings this fascination to life.

Boulez placed the Ligeti in the midst of French works that also questioned accepted forms and ideas about sound of their time. The four haunting *Symphonic Fragments* from Debussy's 1911 music for a very strange stage spectacle, *The Martyrdom of Saint Sebastian* by the poet-provocateur Gabriele d'Annunzio, opened the concert sounding almost like a space exploration. Ravel's own 1911 *Mother Goose Suite* and Debussy's 1903–05 classic *La mer* made up the second half in performances that seemed subdued only in the sense that they were never overwrought. Boulez, a connoisseur of visual art, particularly modern prints and works on paper, guided everything with an eye for subtlety that only brought out the richness and careful assembly of these four remarkable creations. That Chen returned to his concertmaster's chair after intermission only underscored the committed playing by the orchestra. English horn Scott Hostetler was most prominent among numerous fine section leader solos.

Ravel's Colors, Ligeti's Rhythm, Bartók's Drive

Chicago Sun-Times, December 2, 2006 Conductor Emeritus Pierre Boulez is leading a program of 20th century compositions of which he is an undisputed master. From the delicate colors of Ravel's noble and sentimental waltzes through the rhythmically enthralling piano concerto of the late György Ligeti to Bartók's early masterwork *The Miraculous Mandarin*, Boulez was in full control Thursday, the orchestra was playing at its best and the audience reacted to this challenging array with the enthusiasm of blissful attendees at a rock concert.

Such marvels as principal flute Mathieu Dufour's solos in Ravel's 1914 orchestration of his *Valses nobles et sentimentales* (originally written for piano), guest soloist Pierre-Laurent Aimard's seemingly effortless navigation of Ligeti's delightfully impossible score and the amazing slides of this greatest of all trombone sections in Bartók's driving pantomime were enough to send one singing into the streets.

Chicagoans have had far too few opportunities to hear professional performances of works by Ligeti, the Hungarian exile who came to the world's attention when Stanley Kubrick appropriated some of his pieces for *2001: A Space Odyssey*. Boulez and Aimard brought this piano concerto here in 1998, and the connections between soloist, players and conductor had only grown since then. By turns aggressive, hypnotic and lyrical, it is always unpredictable and yet, with these two Frenchmen, moves like clockwork.

Festive Berio Briefs, Delicate Berlioz Songs

Chicago Sun-Times, **February 2, 2008** Just when you thought you'd run out of superlatives for Pierre Boulez, the highly respected elder statesmen turns wily magician and astonishingly pulls two more rabbits out of his hat.

In his first appearance this season with the Chicago Symphony Orchestra, he offered a new suite of four stunning brief works by his late contemporary Luciano Berio, and with the great mezzo-soprano Susan Graham, the finest performance of Berlioz's song cycle *Les nuits d'été* that this listener has ever heard.

Boulez has assembled four occasional pieces, written by Berio from 1978 to 1989, that reveal a strong resonance with Boulez's own venture into large-scale orchestration in his *Notations* series. Under the rubric *Quatre dédicaces* ("Four Dedications"), the suite contains rich and knotty piles of winds, brass and strings with unusual subdivisions between solo players and sections and within sections themselves. Festive works of about three minutes each, written for Rome, San Francisco, Dallas and Rotterdam, they are shots-in-the-arm for the repertoire, collectively and individually.

Berlioz is credited with inventing the orchestral song cycle, and his *Nuits d'été* ("Summer Nights"), Op. 7, has been a part of the standard repertoire for a century or more. What made this outing different was Boulez's focus on Berlioz's intent of delicate scoring for a reduced orchestra. From the throbbing of the winds and the quiet layering of the cellos in the opening "Villanelle" through the final measures of the closing "L'Ile inconnue" ("The Unknown Isle"), the work was revealed as both more complex and more ravishing than many might have thought. By having this carefully thought-out context around her, Graham, who can do no wrong, was able further to caress each poem and to hold notes, even the quietest, long enough to create haunting sonorities.

Tackling New Music

A Captivating New Work by Matthias Pintscher

Chicago Sun-Times, **February 23, 2008** Contemporary orchestral composers these days usually run in or near two gangs. The Complexity Gang turns out thick scores for large ensembles. But sometimes all the instrumental activity leads to a kind of brown soup without much character. The Faux Naive Gang, in contrast, follows the American mavericks of the last century: lots of melody, major keys, and open chords. Too often this crew forgets the mavericks were innovators who wrote what they liked.

Fortunately, each camp has inspired some real individuals who take the best from the gangs but dig deeper. Thursday, Chicago Symphony Orchestra audiences got their first taste of Matthias Pintscher, 37, one of Germany's most important young composers, who understands complexity but also knows how to streamline it and wed it to the theatrical and the imaginary visual.

For *Osiris*, a co-commission of the CSO, Carnegie Hall, and the London Symphony Orchestra, Pintscher begins with the scattered pieces of a 1970s artwork by postwar German bad boy Joseph Beuys and the Egyptian myth behind it of a god torn asunder by his angry brother yet brought back to physical unity by his wife's love. In the 23-minute piece, dedicated to CSO conductor emeritus Pierre Boulez, he tells the story of Osiris instrumentally but also acts it out in musical figuration. High muted trumpets and a deep contrabass clarinet offer lines like dialogue while heavily divided strings (every player has a different part) create a kind of tightly regulated set of watery tides below.

Pintscher is an astonishing colorist. He makes the players work in strange ways, but the results are both gently captivating and brilliant.

Who else but Boulez could have pulled off this world-premiere performance in the limited rehearsal time of U.S. orchestras? He approached this new work with total seriousness and utmost care. The virtuoso members of the CSO responded in kind.

From Stravinsky to Szymanowski

WFMT Broadcast, **March 2, 2009**

PATNER: You're doing a lot of Stravinsky on these programs and the marquee item is the full *Pulcinella*, including the songs. I wonder if you might say something about how you came to this project.

BOULEZ: I have conducted the full version of *Pulcinella* a couple of times already. I don't like the neoclassical style of Stravinsky, I must tell you, since I was twenty. It's sterile when you compare it to the first period of Stravinsky. I find with *Pulcinella* that it takes a kind of music which had no special value and toys with it. That's a kind of stylistic game, and it's really very witty sometimes. Especially if you don't return to the original music because this music is sufficient by itself. The parody of style is a very big success. I think a little bit like Berio did when he took the Scherzo of Mahler and then changed the text to add some bits by himself. I could not do that myself, but I appreciate when it is well done, and there is a touch of humor with it. Humor in music is not really the easiest thing to be done. Stravinsky is one of the rare musicians who can do humorous things without help of a text or an explanation.

PATNER: What difference does the work make when the songs are included?

BOULEZ: Well it is complete. When you have the instrumental version then that's shorter because you have not only cut the songs, but you have also cut some places in the ballet. He made a version which is just twenty minutes and the other version is forty minutes. You never know why exactly. For instance, in the concert version of *Firebird* you don't understand why he cut short some places which are very interesting. I don't try to understand.

PATNER: But for the same reason that you do the complete *Firebird*, it makes sense to do this complete piece of music.

BOULEZ: Yes, absolutely. Because it has a succession of moments which are very logical and very well organized.

PATNER: Should an instrumentalist or a singer in this piece be looking just at the notes on the page or thinking about the encounter between Stravinsky and Pergolesi?[1]

BOULEZ: Well nobody has heard Pergolesi, me included as a matter of fact. I don't think that's music which is terribly important in the eighteenth century, but you look at it like any other music of the time. I don't try to reach a kind of authenticity or parody of authenticity. I take the text as it is. And I'm also myself toying with it. I like for instance when Stravinsky does wrong harmonies, or harmonies which are not quite the right ones, without being totally wrong. Or when he changes the rhythms and makes uneven rhythms instead of very classical even rhythms. I enjoy that, and I hope that the audience understands all the inside jokes sometimes.

PATNER: But now many players do have experience with music from earlier centuries.

BOULEZ: Well, they don't play *Pulcinella*. They play only the authentic music, or so-called authentic music, and they don't care very much for the parody.

PATNER: So a modern orchestra player is going to understand this is coming through Stravinsky.

BOULEZ: He's maybe better related to the music by Stravinsky even if Stravinsky takes some starting point from Pergolesi. A man who plays contemporary music is more able to do that than somebody who is totally involved with music of the eighteenth century.

PATNER: In the first week's concerts, you had two works of Stravinsky at the beginning and two of [Edgard] Varèse at the end. I had an idea listening to that program that it was a chance for people perhaps to think that with Stravinsky we think we know his influence today. With Varèse we forget how his influence was so deep and is still so powerful.

BOULEZ: I don't know if Varèse had an influence, really. Yes he was influential in France. Not at all in Germany.

PATNER: But certainly in this country he was very influential.

BOULEZ: Certainly, but it took time. I remember the first visit I made to Varèse was in 1952. I was in New York and he was still quite isolated. Not at all accepted by the musical world generally. His big time was the twenties and thirties. When the neoclassical wave became so important with Aaron Copland and others and populism also, Varèse disappeared. Completely.

PATNER: Some of that was his personality, too, though, wasn't it? Didn't he sort of push back at the idea of being mainstream in any way?

BOULEZ: I think he refused that, totally. He looked very much toward the future. He wanted also electronic music. He asked for subsidies to work with the Bell Telephone Company. Nothing happened. So he was quite discouraged and did not compose for quite a long time. He began to compose again after the fifties, when people like me, for instance, recognized him. I performed him in Paris in the series of concerts I was organizing. And so he was recognized although when his work was performed for the first time it was absolutely a riot because the program was totally absurd. It was a work of Mozart—I don't remember what work of Mozart—and there was *Déserts* by Varèse with all the electronics. Then at the end was the Tchaikovsky Fifth or something like that. Which was grotesque.

PATNER: That's really bizarre. Not fair to any of the composers or the audience.

BOULEZ: It was the beginning of the revival of Baroque music, and especially Italian music—Vivaldi and so on. Some people saw Varèse in the program, they thought it was maybe a kind of Vivaldi they had not heard of. It was absurd as a combination. It was not a scandal like the *Rite of Spring*. It was a scandal because the program was totally wrong.

PATNER: What do you recall from your meetings with Varèse?

BOULEZ: He showed me in his studio the kind of sketches he had
    done. It was not very far from Washington Square. That was the
    Italian district of downtown. But he was rather secretive. After
    his death I met quite regularly his widow and she told me that
    he had great fits of depression. You know he was supposed to
    have great strength and be a model for fighting everything and
    everybody, but on the contrary he had these fits of temper and
    after he saw this kind of new classical wave and being on the
    side totally and forgotten almost, he had fits of depression and
    he had difficulties surviving.

PATNER: Somebody who if he's had fits of depression has kept them
    very much to himself and who has found a way to survive is
    of course Elliott Carter. Now one hundred years old. And com-
    posing frequently and with great success.

BOULEZ: I participated in a concert for his centenary in London.
    Pierre Aimard played the new pieces for piano which were abso-
    lutely lively and very vital. And astonishing for somebody who
    is a hundred to have this kind of vitality.

PATNER: You chose, though, to do here in Chicago one of his quite
    ancient works from his nineties, *Réflexions*.

BOULEZ: I did it this week, with two performances to come. He
    wrote *Réflexions* for me. But you can multiply the number of
    strings to have a better balance and we will do it with more
    strings than I did at the first performance.

PATNER: Originally it was just written for the personnel of your
    ensemble.

BOULEZ: Yes, and we generally had two woodwinds and two brass,
    and then we had three violins, two violas, two cellos, and one
    bass. But we can make it six cellos, six violins, and two basses,
    so the volume is bigger and much better.

PATNER: Once you have a contrabass clarinet you better have some-
    thing to balance it out, right?

BOULEZ: Well you use it very carefully. We had a piece two sea-
    sons ago by Matthias Pintscher where there was a big contra-

bass clarinet solo which was horribly difficult. But this solo
for contrabass clarinet is much nicer and easier to perform.
You know in general the toughest pieces of Elliott are between
the sixties, seventies, and eighties. After that he went milder.
I think with the number of performances he had, he noticed that
there are things which are theoretically possible—you can write
them—but they come to performance very rarely because if you
have to work half an hour on one bar, generally you don't have
the time to do that. So practically you have a kind of approximation of the things and he does not write approximation. His
recent style has used more simple elements which are easier to
get properly with accuracy.

PATNER: You're saying perhaps that that's been aided by his being
frequently performed in recent years?

BOULEZ: Certainly he has more experience. And certainly the works
now are easier to perform.

PATNER: Coming back to the second week of concerts, I would say
the first composer that comes to mind when one says Pierre
Boulez is not Szymanowski.[2]

BOULEZ: No, although I have known Szymanowski for a very
long time. There was a French violinist, Jacques Thibaud, very
famous in his time, and during the war he played a piece by Szymanowski called "La Fontaine d'Aréthuse" for violin and piano.
It was very striking to me because I had never heard this type of
vocabulary before. And I have never forgotten that.

I did not have an opportunity to perform his music. But now
that I perform the Viennese School quite a lot and Stravinsky
and Bartók and Varèse, I am interested to discover others also
in depth. When you perform you have to look at the scores very
closely. This first violin concerto of Szymanowski I have done
already, and I've done also the second one, but the first one is for
me more interesting. I did it with Christian Tetzlaff and the London Symphony both in London and on tour. It interests me to do
it with another violinist now and with another orchestra. I think
you are discovering—we are all discovering Szymanowski. I will

do the first violin concerto with Tetzlaff again in Vienna this
season, and next season I will do the Symphony no. 3, because
that's also an interesting piece.

PATNER: So you're in your Szymanowksi period.

BOULEZ: Not exclusively.

PATNER: But it's interesting because there are people who say this
conductor or that composer has no interest in anything that he
isn't already interested in. But because perhaps of that memory
of that one piece, when the time arrived you're saying, "Well, let
me investigate this a little bit more."

BOULEZ: I am curious because I don't want simply to do and redo
and redo and redo always the same pieces. And you know the
program of this week I like very much because it shows three
pieces which have absolutely no connection but were written
in a span of time very limited, maybe five years. The *Sinfonietta*
by Janáček, the violin concerto of Szymanowski, and the *Pulcinella* of Stravinsky. You cannot imagine that they were by three
people who were living exactly at the same age.

PATNER: They were but just on different planets.

BOULEZ: Stravinsky and Szymanowski were the same age, both
born in 1882. And it's difficult to imagine that Janáček was
older than Debussy. Sometimes to compare facts like that is
very instructive. The story is not one branch. History has many
branches even in the same time.

PATNER: And to be able to see those branches together, but in a way
that will probably fit better than Mozart, Varèse, and the Fifth
Symphony of Tchaikovsky. Those were different trees. Not just
different branches.

BOULEZ: You could do Anton Webern and Carl Orff, one after
another.

A Musician's Evolution

A Characteristic French Sound

Chicago Sun-Times, **January 9, 2010** From Ravel's *Le tombeau de Couperin* to Marc-André Dalbavie's Flute Concerto to Béla Bartók's expansive, spooky *Bluebeard's Castle*, every piece played by the Chicago Symphony Thursday night, under conductor emeritus Pierre Boulez, was a total whole; together, they evoked an essay in composers' use of orchestral color and how a great orchestra brings those colors to life.

Musical color, the way different combinations of instruments and harmonies can create different moods, feelings and even an aural sense of the visual, has fascinated Boulez since his own student days with Olivier Messiaen in the 1940s. The characteristic French sound, both in Ravel's own writing and the Baroque period he was reflecting on, were given perfect balances by the orchestra, and principal oboe Eugene Izotov played like a dream.

Dalbavie, a student of Boulez, wrote his Flute Concerto for Emmanuel Pahud, friend and colleague of CSO principal flute Mathieu Dufour, who was the featured soloist Thursday. Surely these two remarkable musicians are among the few capable of playing this work with such seeming effortlessness. For 16 minutes, soloist and orchestra engage in a series of swirling lines with the soloist presenting cascades of notes that must flow as smoothly as a brook. The work is unusually gentle for Dalbavie, but Dufour's virtuosic performance illuminated underlying references and tensions as well.

In the one-act opera *Bluebeard's Castle*, mezzo Michelle DeYoung displayed a risky urgency, and German bass-baritone Falk Struckmann was resigned and fierce as the serial husband who can love only through death. As strong and fine as both singers were, this was, above all, a reminder of how this work is told by its large and expressive orchestra, which controls all the moods and narrates the opening of each of the castle's seven locked doors. It made you want to hear every opera played on a stage by the Chicago Symphony. What a privilege to hear all of these great artists in such a serious and hugely satisfying program.

On First Hearing German Music and on Becoming a Conductor

WFMT *Broadcast*, January 11, 2010

PATNER: As you approach the age of 85, Maestro Boulez, do you see your own life as having so far been on any particular architectural course?

BOULEZ: I think you don't build architecture; you receive the architecture by accumulating experiences and different phases of your development. It's futile to hope to have a trajectory at the beginning of this life. You don't know what will happen and you meet circumstances which force you to go into another direction. I was interested in modernity. I was very fixed in my opinions about the composers I liked or I was not interested in. For me there are five composers who were really very important and crucial in my consciousness of music. Stravinsky was the first. Then Bartók, who I discovered immediately after the war. And the three Viennese—Schoenberg, Berg, Webern—who I discovered also immediately after the war.

One must think about the situation. When I came to Paris [from Lyon] I was eighteen and it was during the time of the German occupation. There was a lot of music which was never performed—either forbidden or just ignored. The French are responsible for that also because they were interested in what was produced in France and not interested at all in what was produced outside of France. There was a complete lack of the culture of Austrian modernity, not only in music but also in painting. For instance: Klimt[3] was totally ignored for a very long time in France. Still now when you speak about Klimt and the prices of Klimt, the French are completely surprised by the reputations these painters have.

PATNER: It's still remarkable you had not heard—you who were a curious young student and composer—you had not heard

Mahler symphonies, you hadn't heard Bruckner symphonies, you hadn't heard the Second Viennese School.

BOULEZ: Mahler was forbidden as a Jew. But Bruckner was ignored by the French because of a certain amount of nationalism. Not for good reasons. I think the complete set of symphonies of Bruckner was performed for the first time in Paris by Barenboim in the seventies. That's quite a delay.

PATNER: So it took an Argentinian-Israeli Jewish conductor to bring the Catholic Bruckner from Austria to France in the 1970s.

BOULEZ: Yes, absolutely.

PATNER: And it's not only France. You can talk to musicians from Germany and Austria who didn't have familiarity with Ravel or of Debussy.

BOULEZ: The reaction of my generation was to say we want to know what the others are doing. One speaks always about the Darmstadt School.[4] There was no school. There was a meeting point. It was people who wanted to know each other. The borders were so strong during the war. It took something like five years to have more opportunity to go out of the country. Then people met, and they were really so happy to see each other, to know what the others were doing. After that, English people came, like Birtwistle.[5] All these people came to just look for something in common. I discovered Mahler really when I was living in Germany and it was the 1960s.

PATNER: You came to Paris at eighteen in the midst of the German occupation of Paris. What was your musical exposure before then? Was it from church music? Was it from groups playing in your town? Was it from the radio? Was it from looking at scores?

BOULEZ: Orchestral scores, certainly not. Piano scores, yes. Brahms was not very well known, but Mozart, Beethoven, Haydn also. And Chopin.

PATNER: At what point did you have a sense that modernism was going to be your destiny?

BOULEZ: I suppose when I heard the first modern pieces. I was still

in Lyon before going to Paris when I was seventeen. I went to
concerts and I was interested each time there was a new piece.
The maximum of modernity was Honegger,[6] who at this time
was considered a very important composer. He was much more
important than all the other ones. And I heard, for instance,
La danse des morts. I heard other pieces by him, especially the
symphony for strings and trumpet. For me it was really something exciting, which I had never heard before.

I discovered modernity through him.

PATNER: He was not viewed so much then as being revolutionary,
but in retrospect his music was going in directions the others
certainly were not going in.

BOULEZ: Then I discovered Messiaen in Paris. He was teaching.
I was in the Conservatoire in the preparatory class. And I got to
choose a teacher for the harmony class. He had the reputation
of a kind of outsider, an interesting outsider, rejected by part of
the establishment, and not only accepted but really admired by
other people. I went to a concert where a work of his was performed, and I decided, "Yes, I must study with this man." And
that was it.

PATNER: When you would hear these pieces, first of Honegger and
then of Messiaen, was it a visceral reaction, a physical reaction,
an intellectual reaction, an emotional reaction?

BOULEZ: It was a very emotional reaction because at this time you
know I cannot analyze anything. It was a first reaction. I liked it
because it was not like the music I had heard before. As simple
as that. Primitive reaction as it can be.

PATNER: Were you setting out to compose as a means of understanding, as a means of responding to what you were being
exposed to? Or were you saying, "Okay I'm now a composer"?

BOULEZ: I was responding to what I heard. I was studying piano.
Very quickly I said, "Well, piano is not my business. I don't want
to become a virtuoso." I had not the patience. And I am too late
for that because you don't begin to study seriously piano at the
age of eighteen. I was very matter-of-fact and I said, "The piano

I learn to learn technique—how it works exactly—but I will not go further than that." And then I devoted my time entirely to composition.

PATNER: You wrote these sonatas very quickly and yet they are very complex and they are still challenging people and still interesting people.[7] There are recent recordings of them all around the world. Maybe it's the one thing you share with Brahms—you wrote some sonatas early and then you didn't write any later.

BOULEZ: That's right, because now I am not at all interested in sonatas. It was a project which was interesting but I was not right for this project. I did not want to write a sonata in four movements. That was not interesting to me. So I went more and more to discover forms by myself.

PATNER: It seems that another governing principle for you has been necessity. Things that you had to write because they were in you, learning about the different instruments, different ensemble possibilities, and then conducting out of necessity, not necessarily out of choice.

BOULEZ: Conducting out of necessity because there were not many people who wanted to devote the time to study it. I was not at ease then. I was very happy when I got to the end without any kind of small accident. Then I discovered that I had to conduct, as I was in charge of this series of concerts I established myself—

PATNER: The Domaine Musical.

BOULEZ: I was the conductor who was less expensive. I was not paid anything. I learned to conduct my music particularly from organizing concerts.

PATNER: Weren't you also a music director and a pit bandleader for a theater house?

BOULEZ: For the theater, yes, but you know that music was very simple.

PATNER: But was that good experience to be able to run through these things each night?

BOULEZ: Yes, it was a good experience. The music I played from memory immediately because it was not very difficult music. Then if you repeat that fifty times you know very well what it is. You learn the materials, and therefore I was not totally ignorant when I began to conduct. But I was not really ready for difficult things. I had to learn that on the spot. But I had engaged musicians for these concerts who were the same age as I was, who were very eager also to do something unheard, and they were very cooperative. They were ready to work with me.

PATNER: If somebody had said to you in the 1950s, perhaps after drinking absinthe or something, "You know, Boulez, in the future you're going to be conducting the Vienna Philharmonic and the Cleveland Orchestra and the Chicago Symphony Orchestra in Bruckner, and you're going to be recording Bruckner symphonies with these orchestras," would you have had a response to that?

BOULEZ: I suppose I would say, maybe, "Who is Bruckner?" No, that I would not have said.

PATNER: You might have said it for fun.

BOULEZ: Certainly I wasn't ready to conduct those kind of classical orchestras. Certainly not.

PATNER: The word in English, "fight"—one of the French words I think has been *combattre*, to fight—is a word that runs throughout your earlier writings and throughout many writings about you. I think people who have only come to know you in your recent years would say, "What is all this stuff about fighting?"

BOULEZ: When you are, as I am, very soon to be eighty-five, you cannot really behave like a man of eighteen or twenty years old. First you have a certain amount of experience and people know about this experience so they have a tendency to respect you much more than when you are younger. When you are younger they say, "He does not know anything." That was a reaction constantly when I was conducting classical music. "Well, he knows very well Stravinsky; he does not know a note of Beethoven." Which is absolutely stupid because I studied Beethoven before

Stravinsky of course. Still in my age if there is the opportunity of really saying the truth of what I think, the truth, I tell it.

When I was younger I established a series of concerts, Domaine Musical, because there were polemics without end about pieces that were not performed. How can you polemicize on a thing you've never heard? I was always ready to fight for performing things. Even things I did not like particularly, but I said, "It's important to play them because people must have their opinion." I don't want to impose my opinion on everybody. You have to be objective first, listening to something, and then subjective, to have your judgment on that.

PATNER: Another work that you're doing this season—and it will be done here in your honor as part of the commemorations of your upcoming birthday—is the Adagio, the only movement that Mahler completed for the Tenth Symphony.

BOULEZ: The Adagio is the first thing of Mahler I performed ever. It was with the London Symphony Orchestra. I had heard a very poor performance of the Adagio in Paris with not a good conductor, not a very good orchestra either, so it did not impress me very much. But after, when I looked at the score, I was really very impressed and I am still. The kind of step forward he did with this Adagio is really remarkable, because even if you compare with the Adagio of the Ninth Symphony, which is already really quite a piece, this one is really amazing—all the harmonic relationships, the kind of very audacious counterpoint. The ingredients and the tools he used are really close to Schoenberg, the closest you can imagine. Even closer than Berg. Berg is sometimes less audacious than Mahler.

PATNER: Berg sometimes, perhaps, is making a kind of bridge between Romanticism and Modernity, but with Mahler it's more jumping into something unknown.

BOULEZ: Jumping into something new. Berg is sometimes nostalgic and even in his last work—the Violin Concerto—you have all this nostalgia of G minor, B-flat major, and so on. You have all these chords which are not disturbing at all, but which are put in a kind of situation where they are more or less foreigners. In Berg, you have this kind of displacement of rhetoric which is outside the right place. In Mahler, you have complete coherence that continues constantly, but there's a kind of set of variations in between. And each time the variations are from an absolutely extraordinary harmonic language. I mean the modulation, the constant modulation—you are of course from time to time in F-sharp major—but most of the time you don't know where you are going. That's extraordinary because you don't know where you are going, but at the same time it's perfectly safe. You know that in Mahler you are with a hand that absolutely masters every moment.

PATNER: So it would have been conceivable in the sixties that your only connection with Mahler as a conductor might have been to do this Adagio.

BOULEZ: I really was not pleased at all at that time by the rhetoric of other movements which I accept now. For instance the rhetoric of the last movement of the Sixth, which I find really very intriguing, at the time I would have found that maybe bombastic. Maybe because I had heard it performed in a bombastic way. That's possible because it's so easy to exaggerate the features in Mahler.

PATNER: Barenboim would often say, "I'm a bit suspicious of Mahler," and in a way that was also saying, "I don't like this rhetoric which is sentimental or this which is bombastic." I don't think there's a right or wrong here. Very often, even among conductors, composers, a lot of this comes from the way we have heard the works or the way we have received them. If we go back to the score there's a lot to get still from Mahler.

BOULEZ: He writes expressly *nicht sentimental*, not sentimental. If you exaggerate the sentimental, the sarcasm is gone. And there's a kind of humor sometimes of the quotes—false quotes, pseudo quotes. That's really interesting for me in Mahler. That you find also in Berg, the kind of humor about his own taste. Sometime just to push a little bit to say, "Well, I am on the verge, but I will not go further."

Modernism from Mahler to Janáček

Mahler and Webern

Chicago Sun-Times, **October 16, 2010** If life gives you lemons, make a tarte au citron. That was the strategy of the Chicago Symphony Orchestra when music director Riccardo Muti fell ill two weeks ago and returned to Italy for tests. What other institution could then bring in the legendary composer-conductor Pierre Boulez to fill in for Muti, offering instead [of the original program] four performances of a major program of Mahler and Anton Webern?

There is nothing token or thrown together with Boulez, even as a substitute. "I would have done this even if I had had to rearrange my schedule," Boulez said after the concert. "For the orchestra, for the team, for Muti."

Chicagoans must find it odd that Mahler's Symphony No. 7 is seen as the ugly duckling among the composer's output. Written in 1904–05, the work had its U.S. premiere here in 1921. Even if fewer conductors program the 80-minute work, when that few include Solti, Abbado, Barenboim, and Boulez, the work is not a stranger here.

Nor should it be. Its "Night Music" sections are among Mahler's most personal creations, and the middle movement scherzo is perfect heartbreak. The range of sounds that emerges from the large orchestra—a repeated song from the unusual tenor horn, chilly timpani rolls, tuba murmurs, cowbells, and even guitar and mandolin—points to Mahler's sense of expansion and experiment. Even his approach to an optimistic finale can get under a listener's skin.

After recently hearing younger and less experienced conductors take up some of the Mahler Nine, it was beyond refreshing to hear this supposedly sprawling work guided by a master's hand. Delicacy, structure, harmonic invention are all made clear. The music is rich without exaggeration.

It was interesting to contrast the interpretations of two senior figures with Webern's 1908 *Passacaglia for Orchestra*, Op. 1. When Bernard Haitink led this 10-minute work in 2006, there was a sense of sweep, a painterly quality, as in a Monet cityscape. That depth was present with Boulez, but seemed to have been achieved out of individual points, as in a Seurat painting.

Why I Program Contrasting Works

WFMT *Broadcast*, November 11, 2010

PATNER: Maestro Boulez is in town to lead four concerts of the CSO. They were not on his schedule but he stepped up to the plate after Maestro Riccardo Muti had to step away for a few weeks to deal with medical issues. You had short notice to come in this time.

BOULEZ: Martha Gilmer [the orchestra's artistic director] called me past midnight in Paris. When I heard her voice, I say, "Oh, something is wrong." And she said, "I know that you are free." If the conversation begins like that you have very little space to say no.

PATNER: Because you have been on a sabbatical from conducting this season.

BOULEZ: I will begin the sabbatical by conducting. My sabbatical is a little bit like Swiss cheese—holes for activity. But for Chicago, I could not say no. I know when somebody like Muti is ill, he cancels because he has a serious reason. Therefore it was my duty practically to come here but it's not a heavy duty, that's a very pleasant duty on the contrary, because I love this orchestra.

PATNER: That also gives the listener a sense of your connection with this orchestra.

BOULEZ: Yes, I conducted first the orchestra in 1969. I conduct the orchestra regularly since 1986. And then I came regularly and then permanently.

PATNER: How did you decide on the Mahler Seven and why did you
pair it with the Passacaglia of Webern?

BOULEZ: The Seventh Symphony is the one I've done the least. I did
the Sixth quite a lot. I don't know why it happens like that sometimes. With a complete series of Mahler we did with Barenboim
with his orchestra in Berlin I did the Sixth and he did the Fifth
and Seventh. I was eager to do it again because I have not done
it for four years and you know that's time to reappraise, to look
at your own state of mind.

PATNER: What is the current state of mind about the piece?

BOULEZ: I always liked very much the two night musics. They are
the closest to the [Des Knaben] Wunderhorn. Also the density of
the orchestra is very thin—no, thin would be not the right word
but a transparent orchestra. I like this tendency in Mahler, when
he is not tied to a kind of bombastic experience, to bring this
refinement to the music. Especially in the second night piece the
music is transparent completely. You have nothing to do practically to make it more transparent. It is already there in the
score.

PATNER: Some people say that the guitar is not just represented in
that movement but that the orchestra becomes a kind of a sound
like a guitar.

BOULEZ: Yes, it's chamber music for more musicians. But so is the
Wunderhorn. That's a kind of chamber music written for bigger forces. I've been told that Mahler sometimes performed
the Wunderhorn with single strings, to make it really chamber
music. There are two tendencies in Mahler very clearly—the
tendency toward chamber music and the tendency toward a
big orchestra, full of brass and big sounds.

PATNER: But there's a way to do that so that it isn't only bombast.

BOULEZ: I say bombastic because that's a word for it. You might
say "rhetoric," which is more elegant. And the Webern I chose
because for two reasons. One was almost trivial. That's because
people can come late. If there is no opening piece then they are

deprived of the full first movement of the Mahler. They have to wait almost 30 minutes. That's not good. I want them to hear the full symphony. Therefore what piece can go closer to Mahler and to go further than Mahler? And then after it you go back to Mahler.

Certainly people who have never heard the Passacaglia by Webern are struck by the beginning. You cannot forget that. This very sparse beginning with just the pizzicato of the strings, spaced slowly. And the orchestration of Webern is a kind of chamber music emphasized. Webern was a great admirer of Mahler. Berg was also a great admirer. Schoenberg, on the contrary, was very reticent at the beginning. He was not at all enthusiastic. He changed after that, maybe under the influence of these disciples.

PATNER: Later Schoenberg does become really a fanatic.

BOULEZ: I think he began to understand the way of composing like Mahler later. At the beginning he was puzzled, probably. Schoenberg's *Verklärte Nacht* [*Transfigured Night*, 1899] has a kind of development, like Wagner. Not like Mahler at all.

PATNER: In the case of the Mahler Seven and in the case of the Webern, Bernard Haitink had also done them here and each of you has a very strong connection to the piece but plays it in a very different way.

BOULEZ: A piece that is valuable allows many performances—many different *types* of performances. Of course, not if it goes overboard and exaggerates everything, or on the contrary makes everything subdued. Within a range you have different types of performances and different emphasis on that character or this character.

PATNER: On your other program you have a very well-known Debussy, a much less known Debussy, and then the [György] Ligeti Violin Concerto, which is being done by the orchestra's own concertmaster, Robert Chen.

BOULEZ: I like sometimes contrast. The same composer can bring also sometimes puzzling questions. I put these two Debussy pieces together because with *La Mer* Debussy is at his maximum of possibility and with *Le Martyre de saint Sébastien*, the four sketches, he is still looking for something else, and he's on the threshold, and he did not really go much further because he was sick. I think Debussy has simplified his vocabulary, but simplified and at the same time the continuity or the discontinuity of the musical ideas is very striking. If you look at the piano *Études*, for instance, the richness of the ideas, the invention, you think, "How can he put that in the same piece?" And in the end the relationship is very deep.

I was teaching in Basel for a couple of years and I did a program for six months at the university on the Debussy *Études*. For six months we analyzed everything, and it was very interesting to see the illogical logic of Debussy. In *La Mer*, in the second movement, "Jeux de Vagues," you can find this richness of ideas. You don't know how to connect them at first, and then finally you connect them. In the *Nocturnes* you don't have that at all; you are still very classical. The second movement of *La Mer* is much more complex.

The big ballets of Stravinsky are a set of pieces. The only one which transcends that is *Les Noces*, much later. He tries to find continuity through use of the same material. Repetition, with variation, of course. But the ideas are very simple and few, and it's remarkable how can he do it with a few ideas. So that's good for Stravinsky. But Debussy went in the other direction. More complex and difficult. Therefore the late music of Debussy is not really performed very much. The chamber music—people do it. But the instrumental combinations are not usual, like the Sonata for Flute, Viola, and Harp. That's not a usual combination. He planned to do six sonatas. The next one was to be horn, oboe, and harpsichord—a very curious combination each time. He refused the normal violin and cello and piano, for instance. He wanted a resonant instrument like the harpsichord, or like the harp, but not the piano. He tried to make a combination between, for instance, the viola and the flute, which are two different families, or the oboe and the horn, which are also two different families. It's very interesting to see the direction he was going, and I give a taste of that when I do these sketches for *The Martyrdom of Saint Sébastien*.

PATNER: And the Ligeti?

BOULEZ: I chose the Ligeti because it was also a kind of demonstration not against the West, but to be independent from the West. He came to the West in '56, after the events of Hungary. He was confronted with Stockhausen in Cologne, me in Paris. He came to the West at a moment when the big revolution was already there in the West, he came late after that, and he did not want to be totally absorbed by this type of writing. He wanted to be different from what the western people were doing—big intervals, and disjunctive themes, like Schoenberg and Webern were doing. He wanted to have, on the contrary, continuity.

His demonstration was with half tones, micro tones, and polyphony, but in a very limited melodic range. The rhythmical aspect of his music was very complex from the very beginning. And sometimes he went so far in the demonstration that it was difficult for him. He wanted to have the gestures to show, "I am independent." So suddenly you find the big octaves with four pitches, then the same octave of F-sharp. But thirty years later you say, "Why this F-sharp, in octaves?" There is some part of Ligeti's demonstration that has gone nowhere because the time has changed.

PATNER: But he did have that chronology to confront those choices, because through no fault of his own he's born in one area, he lives through the Nazis and then the Communists, and then '56. He had a terrible experience.

BOULEZ: That was not easy. And that's a thing he never spoke about. Myself, I heard from that through friends of his. Because he was absolutely silent about his experience. I think his father or one of his brothers died in a camp.

PATNER: I think both.

BOULEZ: It was very difficult for him to overcome this experience.

And you know, the humor [in his music] always seemed dubious. I mean, you know, you laugh and then after you say "Why
did I laugh, really?" That was a kind of frightening life. The
humor is very sarcastic. Sometimes you are absolutely afraid of
the humor. In his opera it's the same exactly, you know, the kind
of macabre humor.

PATNER: He even puts that as the title, with his *Le Grand Macabre*.

BOULEZ: After that he abandoned all these effects. He was afraid
that it turned into a mannerism, and he didn't want to be a kind
of mannerist even in his own manner, let's say. A moment that
is very important in his output is the trio for violin, horn, and
piano—an homage to Brahms. That was important because he
tried to find some way of getting classical without all the mannerism of his previous period. The rhythm became more and
more important. And I think that was the influence on the
repetitive people in the States here.

PATNER: You mean the so-called minimalists?[8]

BOULEZ: Minimalists, yes.

PATNER: With their constant repetition.

BOULEZ: He did it in a bit more refined way because he had a science of writing which was higher and more effective [than mini-
malism]. In the Violin Concerto [1989–93], I think the movement
I like the most is where the writing itself, with pitches, is in
phase with the rhythmical writing. Sometimes, maybe as a kind
of demonstration, he used melodic lines which are more or less
half popular, half classical, and there is a discrepancy between
the rhythmic writing and the pitch writing, and that's very
strange sometimes. But that's in the Piano Concerto [1985–88]
more than in the Violin Concerto. The violin concerto is a very
good piece.

PATNER: And it's become—I don't want to say a best seller—but it's
become very popular with audiences. It's interesting, it's virtuosic.

BOULEZ: Nothing to be afraid of for the audience. You show the virtuosity of the player, and that's always very impressive. He was

very gifted for pleasing the audience. He did not want to please, maybe, but it pleased the audience. And I don't find that a sin. I find that's proof that he found an audience receptive to what he was thinking.

PATNER: There is a difference between simply having some ideas that might be very interesting ideas, but they're sort of one idea at a time, and having that ability of Ligeti to kind of take this in three dimensions and to be thinking in terms of pitch, and of rhythm, and of phase, and of effect, rather than just, "Ah, I have a beautiful melody," or "I have an idea for some clapping."

BOULEZ: Maybe that's the difference of country also. You know, Bartók is different from Schoenberg, different from Webern. Even at the very beginning. Bartók would never have written the Passacaglia by Webern, never. That's typical Austrian, Vienna. And he was proud of his specificity. I think in the same way Ligeti was proud of his specificity. That's borderline. They don't belong to the empire. They are apart. If you see the quartets by Bartók, you cannot think of them without thinking of Beethoven. But they have a rhythmical specificity that Schoenberg never had. If you look at the second quartet by Schoenberg and the second quartet by Bartók, which are approximately the same date, you cannot see the same influence there of Beethoven. They are very different. Bartók is another language.

PATNER: In December you return to a piece you've done here once before, the *Glagolitic Mass* of Janáček. You open with the *Transfigured Night* of Schoenberg. Is this again so that people don't come in and miss too much?

BOULEZ: No, because with *Transfigured Night*, they have to miss thirty minutes. That's not done to be kind to latecomers. That's done for showing this period. Janáček was born ten years before Debussy, and he died ten years after Debussy. So his career is quite vast before and after. Ravel was twenty years later, born approximately twenty years after Janáček. It's difficult to establish a chronology of Janáček according to the dates. If you compare to what was written at the time, Janáček still is in infancy when Debussy wrote *Prélude à l'après-midi d'un faune*. The *Lachian Dances* and the *Prélude à l'après-midi d'un faune*, you cannot make a comparison. That's two different people and two different moments of music. The modernity of the late Janáček is more modern still for us now than the modernity of Debussy, which has been totally absorbed, not to speak of the modernity of Ravel, which is totally absorbed.

PATNER: It's a reminder again that the time of one's life is very important, and yet also the individuality which exists outside of the time is very important, and somehow over our lives these things do or don't come together, and that is the person we create.

BOULEZ: It's like a big tree with a lot of leaves in all corners sometimes. You have very big branches, that's true. You know, the three Viennese belong to the same branch, sure. But you cannot put Bartók on this branch and you cannot put Stravinsky on the same branch. That's impossible.

PATNER: And then, even with accepted timelines, if you take, over centuries, the timeline of things happening in Japan or in China, it's like reverse sometimes. Things were invented hundreds of years before and other things not arriving for hundreds of years later.

BOULEZ: What is the saying in Shakespeare, *Hamlet*, things are more complicated than dreams of philosophy or something like that. I don't have the quotation right, but in French I can say it.[9]

A "Glagolitic Mass" for the Ages

Chicago Sun-Times, **December 4, 2010** Those who've experienced the live concerts with Pierre Boulez over the past few weeks have witnessed again the combination of this great orchestra with a composer-conductor of unique powers of inquiry and presentation.

Boulez wraps up his residency this week by revisiting a work he led for the first time just 10 years ago, Leos Janáček's 1926–27 *Glagolitic Mass*. Since his last Chicago outing with this theatrical 45-minute work, Boulez spent several years working on and conducting Janáček's last opera, *From the House of the Dead*, a contemporary of the Mass, throughout Europe. The experience has underlined the conductor's conviction that Janáček's music is not at all designed to please Western ears or to conform to European expectations.

It growls, it shouts, it talks as people talk with each other, it screams to heaven as they scream. His late works can feature fanfares for a celestial kingdom of the mind, and three sets of timpani help to make clear in the Mass that this kingdom can be terrifying as well as glorious. As Brahms did, as Verdi did, Janáček, another non-believer, makes his own text for this mass, even, to underscore the Eastern effect, setting the liturgical excerpts, sections, and scraps that he selected in a disused Old Slavonic and giving even that an extra Czech spin. The work is both thrilling and heavy. There are multiple calls for mercy, but not for peace.

Duain Wolfe's chorus (also up for a Grammy for Muti's Verdi *Requiem*) delivers, and how: barking, purring, demanding, as if the animals from Janáček's fantasy *The Cunning Little Vixen* had become overwhelmed with human passion.

Last time Boulez paired the explosive Janáček with Stravinsky's contemplative 1930 *Symphony of Psalms*, another case of East confronting West. This week he offers the 1917 string orchestra version of Schoenberg's *Verklärte Nacht* ("Transfigured Night"), Op. 4.

I don't know how it connects, if at all, with the Janáček, but I do know that in a lifetime of hearing and loving this swirling, shimmering, hypnotic work, I have never heard it played with such beauty and delicacy. It even earned a rare extra curtain call from the crowd.

III

Bernard Haitink
(2006–2010)

Whereas Daniel Barenboim had developed a strong relationship with the Chicago Symphony long before he joined as director, Bernard Haitink had maintained virtually no presence in the city save on the shelves of audiophiles. Haitink's name was synonymous with the venerable Royal Concertgebouw Orchestra of Amsterdam, which he led for a quarter century. When he debuted in Chicago in 1976 and gave the local premiere of Shostakovich's Fourth Symphony, players and audiences instantly connected with his magnetic baton. He made an acclaimed return to Chicago with the Concertgebouw in 1982, which the CSO and Solti reciprocated with a successful trip to Amsterdam's famed hall in 1985. When Haitink returned to conduct the CSO again in 1997, everyone felt as if a mystical bond between conductor and orchestra had formed over the decades, even in his absence. According to one player, "Haitink made a few adjustments, tightened the belts, and the machine was running perfectly." *Tribune* critic John von Rhein called his appearances "love feasts" on the stage. Haitink thereafter remained on Henry Fogel's "Dream Sheet" of guests—those he wanted but who always seemed too busy to snag.[1]

The 2004 announcement of Barenboim's departure came as a shock to many, leaving the city to speculate about who might replace him. When Solti had announced his retirement, it was immediately clear that either Claudio Abbado or Barenboim would follow in his footsteps. This time the field was wide open. Riccardo Chailly, Haitink's successor at the Concertgebouw, proved to be the musicians' favorite but had not directed the orchestra since the 1990s and didn't express any interest in the position. Esa-Pekka Salonen, superstar director of the Los Angeles Philharmonic and another player favorite, told the orchestra that he wanted to channel more energy toward composition rather than taking on a new leadership role.

The search committee quickly concluded that an interim director would buy them time to make the right permanent choice. Claudio Abbado, one possible option, said he loved the orchestra but lamented that his failing health would not allow him to take on the responsibility. In a happy coincidence, Haitink had long been scheduled for two weeks with the orchestra in March 2006, and the results were spectacular. Critics praised his rare ability to meld his artistic vision seamlessly with the orchestra's strengths in tremendous performances of Beethoven, Weber, Brahms, Webern, and Hindemith. The Dutch maestro had barely arrived back in his home base of London when Deborah Rutter flew there to offer him the position of principal conductor, a title granting him musical oversight of the orchestra with drastically reduced management responsibility. Since he had stated publicly that he was no longer interested in taking on significant new projects, his acceptance was a surprise. The prospect of working with an all-star team like the Chicago Symphony had changed his mind.

Just as Haitink's tenure began, the orchestra developed a new in-house record label, CSO Resound, and initiated a syndicated radio series to revive its presence on air—and especially on the internet— after years without a commercial recording contract. In the absence of a permanent music director, the orchestra musicians themselves played a distinctive shared role with management and recording staff on these projects, engendering a harmonious relationship from the outset. Local control over recording equipment and engineering further elevated the level of collaboration, and the orchestra func-

tioned well as a team on these creative endeavors. Eager to add to
his recorded catalog, Haitink welcomed the opportunity to inaugurate CSO Resound with Mahler's Third Symphony. He later earned
a Grammy for his recording of Shostakovich's Fourth—the piece he
had introduced to Chicago thirty years earlier.

: :

Andrew's portrait shows that the mild-mannered elder statesman of
the podium, who had survived the Nazi occupation of his homeland
sixty years earlier, embraced his new role with the spark of a leader
half his age. Though he was in residence only four to six weeks per
year, his repertoire with the CSO ranged from classics like Mozart and
Beethoven to living composers Peter Lieberson and Mark-Anthony
Turnage—and of course the city's beloved Bruckner, Mahler, and
Strauss. He even learned Haydn's grand *Creation* and traveled on tour
with the orchestra in China, both for the first time in his career. Haitink's profound Beethoven cycle elicited some of Andrew's most intense appreciation of orchestral music. Audiences everywhere roared
for Haitink and the orchestra, and Andrew thoroughly enjoyed going
along for a ride that no one would have imagined before it took place.
In his interviews, he even uncovered Haitink's dry wit. "It is a throat
sickness," he said, describing the Dutch language. The army of gen-
erals that Barenboim had assembled became Haitink's fountain of
youth. "I have a feeling that if I stopped conducting, life would be
difficult," he once told John von Rhein. "Music is the reason that I
go on."[2]

DOUGLAS W. SHADLE

Taking the Stage in a New Role

Anticipating His Arrival

Chicago Sun-Times, **October 15, 2006** "Don't be so humble," the line
attributed to Golda Meir goes. "You're not that great." The rare flip
side of this, of course, is that one does occasionally encounter indi-

FIGURE 3.1. Bernard Haitink on Concertgebouw steps during 2008 European tour.
Photo by Todd Rosenberg. Used with permission.

viduals of genuine accomplishment matched by equally great and genuine humility. And Chicagoans used to connecting the Chicago Symphony Orchestra with the larger-than-life figures of Fritz Reiner, Sir Georg Solti, and Daniel Barenboim will have to start adjusting their expectations when the quiet, self-deprecating Dutchman Bernard Haitink, 77, makes his first appearances at Orchestra Hall as the new principal conductor of the CSO, beginning Thursday.

Given neither to grand physical or personal gestures, Haitink, former longtime music director of Amsterdam's Royal Concertgebouw, London's Covent Garden opera house, and the London Philharmonic, among many other appointments, communicates both musically and personally with a quiet voice, unexaggerated movements, and a somewhat dry sense of humor.

"The last person to ask about me is probably me," Haitink chuckled in a recent phone conversation from his apartment-hotel in New York where he was staying while leading the London Symphony Orchestra in a well-received cycle of the Beethoven symphonies at

Lincoln Center's Avery Fisher Hall. And what about music? "Well, that is also rather hard to talk about, isn't it?" he said, again laughing.

Haitink's musical experience and interests were shaped by his wartime childhood in Amsterdam: He was 11 when Nazi Germany overran the Netherlands and was in his mid-teens when they were driven out. After the war, there were still restrictions, albeit different ones, on who could conduct and play with symphony orchestras and which composers could have their works performed. The Concertgebouw's famed music director, Willem Mengelberg, for example, was banned from work in the Netherlands in 1945 because of his co-operation with the Nazis.

"I can never forget when, just after the war, I was able to get the album of 78s of Bruno Walter and the Vienna Philharmonic with [contralto] Kerstin Thorborg and [tenor] Charles Kullmann performing Mahler's *Das Lied von der Erde* ['The Song of the Earth'] in its first-ever recording in 1936," Haitink said. "I would play these over and over again. I had never heard this music or anything like it before. I am still enthralled by that experience."

That fascination with the great composers has continued over the six decades since that discovery. Haitink went on to some fame for his performances of Mahler and a very different Austrian composer, Anton Bruckner. Despite their temperamental and biographical contrasts, these two composers both loved large forms, and Haitink will feature their works in his two weeks of CSO performances this season. This week brings a single work, Mahler's Third Symphony, and in May, Haitink will lead Bruckner's Seventh Symphony.

"With Mahler, the emotions are very much on the surface, but, and how should one say this," Haitink thought aloud. "The conductor must see beyond that surface but not presume to think that he knows more than Mahler knew."

It is just this sort of concern for musical accuracy and a disdain of overinterpretation that was a part of what won Haitink over to the CSO musicians almost immediately when he led them at Orchestra Hall last season after an absence of nine years. In March, he faced an orchestra whose members were still greatly divided over music director Daniel Barenboim's impending departure, but Haitink managed both to take their minds off these debates and provide them with needed inspiration.

According to Michael Henoch, longtime assistant principal oboe and a member of the CSO's music director search committee, "There was just a very special relationship that was evident from the moment of our first rehearsal with Maestro Haitink."

On Early Years and Lucky Breaks

WFMT *Broadcast*, October 16, 2006

PATNER: Since you are in many ways new to us here, I wonder if we could hear a little bit about your own background, perhaps about your childhood.

HAITINK: Oh my goodness. I've been conducting more than fifty years now. After Chicago I have to go to Amsterdam because there is a concert scheduled on the 7th of November where fifty years ago in 1956 I had my debut. I don't know if you know the situation in Amsterdam but in the hall there's this huge staircase where one has to go down. That concert for me came very unexpectedly. I had to conduct for Carlo Maria Giulini, who canceled. It was a short-notice engagement. And I came down that staircase and there were all the subscription ladies sitting there, and I heard a lady say, "My God, what a baby!" And the press wrote, "It will take a long time before Haitink will get a hold." Well finally, I'm there.

PATNER: I'm wondering about the period before that debut fifty years ago. Did you come from a musical family?

HAITINK: No, not at all. I had all the odds against me. I wanted to play the violin when I was eight years, and there was a family suspicion that I wanted to play the violin because I had a friend who walked always with his violin case to school. They thought I wanted to imitate him. But I got lessons. My teacher was a violinist of the Concertgebouw in Amsterdam. My parents were not musical. They went to concerts because you had to do that when you belonged to a certain social circle. Amsterdam was a very small and provincial town in many ways. My teacher said to my parents, "You must really bring that boy to concerts." He was a great admirer of Willem Mengelberg. And Mengelberg was not that young anymore; this was in 1938. He said, "Maybe it's the last time that Mengelberg will do the *Saint Matthew Passion* and that boy has to go to the *Saint Matthew Passion*." So I went.

PATNER: So here you were, a nine-year-old boy, going to see the *Saint Matthew Passion* of Bach with Willem Mengelberg at the Concertgebouw.

HAITINK: Exactly. I was sitting behind the chorus seats, because it had already sold out. And I saw a lady all of a sudden in tears. It was an aria in the *Saint Matthew Passion*, and I discovered that music could move people. It was quite a landmark thing for me.

In the meantime I practiced my violin with mixed results and then another landmark in my life, and not only in my life, the Germans marched in in 1940 and changed the whole way of life in Holland. All of a sudden we were an occupied country. Amsterdam was a very Jewish town. I had many Jewish friends and slowly but surely the Germans started to do what we all know now they did. And that was a terrible time. And I lost some very good friends. Some survived, but not too many. And as my mother had a Jewish grandmother . . . my parents, they didn't like me going to the Concertgebouw anymore because the hall was infested with German officers. But again my violin teacher said, "No, that boy, let him go. It is so important for him. Let him go." And so I went. From 1940 to 1945 I went regularly to concerts. Even in the last year, which we called the "Hunger Winter."

There was no electricity anymore, nothing. The orchestra played in a physical setup so that they could have the light from the windows on the desks on Saturday afternoon. One hour of music, that was the most they could do, and some played with little mittens. And still people came. Finally it had to stop because the Germans compelled all men between sixteen and sixty to go to Germany to work in the factories. I was just too young to fall into that bracket.

So, it stopped, all the music. But then after '45, after liberation, I picked it up again. And there came an avalanche of music which I'd never heard. Jewish composers. Mendelssohn. Mahler, which had been forbidden. Russian composers who had not been allowed. French music had not been favored. So all these things came—British music, American music. All new. And so I was totally overwhelmed again. And my country came on to its feet again.

By then I was sixteen. My school career was not a success. I never could focus. So I went to the conservatory as a violinist. I was not a great talent, but could just manage. I played in the school orchestra. I think I was principal of the second violins. And it was conducted by a very special musician whose name was Felix Hupka.[3] I went to him and said, "I want to be a conductor, and I would like to have lessons." He said, "Well, I'm terribly sorry. I don't think you have talent and that's it. Goodbye."

So, I practiced my violin, played in the orchestra, and a year later he was rehearsing the Tchaikovsky violin concerto with the concertmaster of the conservatory orchestra. And he said to me, "Hey, you wanted to be a conductor. Okay, do it. I want to listen to how it sounds in the hall." And there I was. So I conducted I think the third movement of Tchaikovsky. Afterwards he came to me and said, "It's okay, I will give you lessons." And I said, "Well, which scores should I bring?" He said, "Scores? Bring your violin. You have to learn to play a phrase properly." My violin teacher didn't like that necessarily. And so it started.

And then my studies were interrupted by my compulsory national military service, which was not a thing to write home of. I was a total waste of Dutch tax money, totally. When I came back I wanted to apply to take a conductor's course at the Dutch radio orchestra, which at that time was very good. And I applied and I got the answer, "No, because you are still a student at the conservatory." But then the director of the conservatory, who was an extremely nice man, said, "Well, he's a sort of idiot, and if we let him apply he will see that it will not happen, and he will have had the experience." I had to conduct for my entrance examination. There were two conductors as judges, who would do the course. One was a Dutch conductor. The other was a German conductor, Ferdinand Leitner, who was general music director of the Stuttgart Opera. I had to conduct the *Oberon* overture by [Carl Maria von] Weber, and the Dutch conductor said, "That's a hopeless case. He's an idiot." But the German conductor, Leitner, said, "Well maybe he's an idiot but I would like to try it out with him." There were two groups of twelve and I was number thirteen; he created an extra.

So my life was always very odd. I did that course and they said, "Okay, you should come back next year. In the meantime you have to audition for the radio philharmonic orchestra with your violin because we think it's very good for you to play a year in that orchestra." Which was very good advice. So I played in that orchestra for a year. Then I came back again for the second year and at the end I got a job as a sort of apprentice conductor at the Dutch radio orchestra. There were four concerts scheduled for me with the chamber orchestra, a sort of promenade orchestra that played lighter works. But then the conductor of the official orchestra became very ill and I had to jump in. And then Carlo Maria Giulini canceled, as I said earlier, and I had to jump in for him at the Concertgebouw. And that started it.

PATNER: You jumped in and fifty years later you're still in.

HAITINK: Yes, exactly. And one of the prominent players of the Amsterdam orchestra said, "Well, that boy, he doesn't know a thing, but he is a conductor." And I met him I think forty years later. I said, "Martin, lovely to see you again. And you know, I still don't know a thing, but I'm still a conductor."

PATNER: I want to go back, just briefly, and I know it's a very pain-
ful and difficult period, but I think it's important for younger
people, to understand how devastated the Netherlands and Belgium were [during the Nazi occupation].

HAITINK: Inundated, everything was taken away. The last year there
was no food anymore. We were very lucky. We didn't suffer. But
other people really suffered and people died. I mean, it was an
awful time.

PATNER: And from people I know of your generation and older,
I know that much time went into reconstructing culturally and
emotionally, as well as the time that had to go into reconstructing physically. Mengelberg, for example, was banned from conducting because of those concerts that he had continued to
present.

HAITINK: He was banned for life. That was changed after ten years,
but then he died just before the ban would have been lifted.
I think in a way that was a blessing because he was eighty and
he died. There would have been terrible, unpleasant situations
in the concert hall if he had come back. The anti-German, especially anti-collaborator feeling, was quite strong in Holland.

PATNER: The number of role models within the Netherlands, for a
future conductor, was small. I mean if you grew up in Vienna,
say, or in Munich, or in Berlin, maybe there was a phone direc-
tory page filled with them. But in terms of actual native Hol-
landers who were in the field—

HAITINK: Well, yes and no. Because quite quickly the Concertgebouw was allowed to play again. They were accused of collaboration and they were not allowed to play, but after six
months or so the Concertgebouw opened again and people
were hungry for music. And you know at that time, conductors
were not booked as now. This idiocy that we have to book for an
engagement in three years' time didn't exist.

I remember that Otto Klemperer was living under very dire
circumstances in a New York flat. He didn't have work anymore
because he had this terrible accident where he had this brain

problem.[4] He had friends who said to the Concertgebouw, "We would like you very much to invite that man because he's a wonderful musician. You will see." And he came. And it was an incredible success. And he did a lot of concerts with the Concertgebouw. And many conductors came. I heard so many great conductors. Erich Kleiber—there was a whole Beethoven cycle several times. Wilhelm Furtwängler was finally allowed to come back when he was still young, made a tremendous impression. And a whole list of conductors. I think I nearly slept in the concert hall.

PATNER: So in a way there was an advantage to there not being many local conductors because you had this great orchestra and the great conductors of the world came through.

HAITINK: But there was one Dutch conductor, who, before the war, when Mengelberg was there, was already much more than an assistant—he was called principal conductor—and he took over the orchestra after '45. It was a bit of a lukewarm beginning, maybe, but then he made an enormous stride and he established the orchestra again and he became quite famous. He was a wonderful musician and did the first tour to the United States where they opened at the United Nations and then did an enormous tour together with Kubelik, who was one of the loved conductors in Holland.

PATNER: I'm going to let you say his name because Dutch is the most mispronounced language.

HAITINK: It is a throat sickness. Eduard van Beinum.[5]

PATNER: And van Beinum did build and rebuild that postwar Concertgebouw.

HAITINK: He was very loved also in America. He became, later on, music director of the Los Angeles Philharmonic. He was very respected at the Philadelphia Orchestra. And once more he had his tours with the Concertgebouw that were enormously successful. But he died pretty young, when he was fifty-seven.

PATNER: Particularly young for a conductor. Conductors tend to go on for very long careers, we hope in your case as well.

HAITINK: Oh, one doesn't know. I wish I had a cat's seven lives. But
who knows?

PATNER: I want to ask you about one more thing from that postwar
period. When we spoke recently on the telephone you told me
about getting an album of 78s of Mahler's *Das Lied von der Erde*.

HAITINK: I think that was the first thing I heard because recordings were not existent. But there was a small shop with a fanatic
owner and he had the first 78 recordings. For me they were the
first. Toscanini with the New York Philharmonic. And Bruno
Walter. It was a fantastic experience. Now there's so much.
Everything's recorded a hundred times. But at that time it was
a very special thing.

PATNER: And this was music that you didn't know, you hadn't
heard? Mahler certainly wasn't allowed to be broadcast during
the war.

HAITINK: Oh, no. Not at all. And Mahler frightened me terribly.
I was too young to understand the emotions and I found it a very
frightening experience. With Bruckner I always felt at home; it
was easy to understand for me. But Mahler was a problem.

PATNER: And what about Mahler today, sixty years later?

HAITINK: Oh, I have done some symphonies in my life and—

PATNER: But what does he do for you today emotionally?

HAITINK: Enormous emotions. Very often at the surface but very
often very deep. He is a wonderful composer. My only worry is
that it is done too often, and I don't exclude myself. I remember when I started I had quite a working relationship with the
London Philharmonic. In the seventies in Amsterdam Mahler
was already very much accepted, but in London when you did
a Mahler symphony, you had half an empty hall. Now when
you want to have success, want to have a full hall, one conducts
a Mahler symphony. Mahler always said, "My time will come."
But I'm not sure if he would have been happy with this sort
of—I don't know—glut of performances. I don't know. But
once more, I'm a culprit myself.

A Mahler Third for the Ages

Chicago Sun-Times, **October 21, 2006** Bernard Haitink debuted as CSO principal conductor with a performance of Mahler's massive 100-minute Third Symphony that was one for the history books.

One of the world's great orchestras, without a music director for the first time in almost 40 years, has put great expectations on the humble but highly respected Dutch maestro. And from the moment he signaled the chorale of nine horns that opens this tremendous score, it was clear that these hopes were well placed. Authoritative without being dictatorial, sympathetic while maintaining a point of view, thoughtful without being pedantic and delicate without timidity, Haitink showed that he was here to bring out the mysteries of this magical piece, one that contains an entire world, and that he wanted to meet the CSO's players at a mountaintop of artistry that they would share with the composer.

With limited fuss but great intensity, Haitink demonstrated that even the most ethereal and seemingly chaotic moments in Mahler are fused with logic. He revealed the never-absent pulse in the final, heaven-aiming slow movement which had a way of carrying the audience even when time appeared to stand still. He can float an orchestral pianissimo to rival the greatest Verdi soprano and he can have the players give their all while keeping each voice delineated and in balance.

Haitink does this in total partnership with the players, sensing the strengths of the individuals and the ensemble that Solti and Barenboim built—Jay Friedman's singing trombone, flute Mathieu Dufour's blending with Jennifer Dunn's piccolo, Christopher Martin with third-movement-long solos for trumpet and post horn[6] of heart-rending tenderness—as if he had known them for years.

That these forces were joined by the women's voices of the Chicago Symphony Chorus and an ensemble of the Chicago Children's Choir, impeccably prepared by Duain Wolfe and Josephine Lee, and by the woman who owns the soloist's parts of this piece, American mezzo-soprano Michelle DeYoung, only meant that all of the elements of perfection were in place. This was the beginning of a beautiful friendship indeed.

Impressing with a Wide Repertoire

Lutosławski and Bruckner Go Together

Chicago Sun-Times, May 12, 2007 "So many bridges!" French composer Olivier Messiaen would tell the young Pierre Boulez and his other students when Bruckner's name would come up. And the way that different conductors traverse or respond to those extensive thrusts and hopeful connections can be fascinating.

With Bernard Haitink, one has the sense that Bruckner's bridges themselves are the subject of observation. Thursday night in the Seventh Symphony, it was as if he was taking us on a sort of refined Grand Tour of uncharted ruins. Swells of volume and shifts of tempo came with a kind of aristocratic gentleness that eliminated bombast while sounding inevitable. Shifts and transitions, even in the famous Scherzo with its alternating sound worlds, seemed effortless.

Yet this was the sort of naturalness that comes only after years of experience, not to mention an almost extra sensory connection with the orchestra. This includes an understanding of connections within the ensemble as well, with mellow Wagner tubas played by the horn section laying a foundation for delicate and overlapping wind solos.

These qualities—of both a fine touch and hand and a comprehensive and long view—were apparent in the program as a whole. The late Witold Lutosławski's *Chain 2: Dialogue for Violin and Orchestra* (1986) calls on its soloist, here the elegant and incisive CSO concertmaster Robert Chen, to engage with the orchestra in a set of determined and "ad lib" exchanges. Lutosławski[7] was a modernist who somehow found ways to assimilate experimentation without alienating his audiences. In retrospect, the programming of *Chain 2*—given its overlapping and combining of disparate materials and its complex marriage of heart and head—with the Bruckner showed a stroke of genius.

But this ability to find the unexpected in works we thought we know was also present in Beethoven's brief, eight-minute *Coriolan Overture*, which opened the concert. From its first stately measures to an almost impossibly quiet ending, Haitink showed us whole worlds we never knew were there. Haitink demands and earns our attention, measure by measure. Attentiveness is his byword.

A Transparent Mahler Sixth

Chicago Sun-Times, **October 20, 2007** What a roll the Chicago Symphony Orchestra is on! A month in Chicago and touring Europe with Riccardo Muti and now the first of three subscription concert weeks with principal conductor Bernard Haitink. Happy players, happy audiences, happy management, even happy critics. How can all of this be?

Some of it is a matter of psychology. Daniel Barenboim did some serious rebuilding of this orchestra, making dozens of outstanding hires, taking the responsibility for several much-awaited retirements and pressing members toward a greater chamber music quality and flexibility in their playing.

But his term as music director was marked by his extraordinary passion in difficult as well as inspiring ways, and some players chafed under his demands. While his abilities at harnessing divided emotions made for some great performances, the underlying morale began to fray.

Enter Haitink and Muti, with principal guest conductor Pierre Boulez offering continuity. They have reached points in their own long, illustrious careers where they are as pleased to be in Chicago as the musicians and audiences are to have them.

Look no further than this week's concerts, where Mahler's massive Symphony No. 6 is played by Haitink and the orchestra with a transparency, even a delicacy, that seems to stop time. It does so almost literally: This work of searing sadness clocks in at about 80 minutes; Haitink stretched it to just about an hour and a half.

Maybe the players felt the length, but the listeners surely never did. When have the two trios of the blazing scherzo movement sounded so gentle, like lullabies? When has the andante felt so personal? Always avoiding bombast and steering fully clear of saccharine sentimentality, Haitink led the massive outer movements as if telling a very sad story for the very first time.

The Chicago brass was lyrical, even in the work's famous climaxes, with tuba Gene Pokorny putting the "m" in mellow. The quiet interplay between concertmaster Robert Chen and principal horn Dale Clevenger took us to the essential Mahler.

Too Spare Mozart, Massive Masterful Brahms

Chicago Sun-Times, October 27, 2007   The Chicago Symphony Orchestra concerts this week can be thought of as three unique—and largely unrelated—character studies: of a conductor, a composer, and a beloved soloist.

Opening with Mozart's first major orchestral work, the Symphony No. 25, K. 183, known as "the Little G Minor" in contrast to Mozart's late, great Symphony No. 40 in the same key. Neglected until the 20th century, the work gained popularity from the film *Amadeus*.

Principal conductor Bernard Haitink has scored high marks in Chicago for lean and clear interpretations of masterworks. But his presentation of this product of the then 17-year-old boy genius was perhaps too spare and clean. The two G Minor symphonies are Mozart's only ones in a minor key and surely some "sturm und drang" was telegraphed by this choice. Playing the piece as purely logical actually can seem illogical and with a small ensemble we might have asked them to play more boldly.

The second study is that of a composer of our own time. Mark-Anthony Turnage is one of two current CSO Mead composers-in-residence, and the 47-year-old Briton has thus far offered several inoffensive works with well-orchestrated sound worlds. Using a large orchestra, Turnage's 16-minute commission *Chicago Remains* has passages of powerful chordal blocks and sonorities that never frighten but also rarely lead anywhere.

The last act of these concerts belongs to pianist Emanuel Ax. At 58, this always-delightful performer is one of the true owners of the great and ever-popular Brahms B-Flat Major Second Piano Concerto, Op. 83. Ax knows that this huge 48-minute work is a thing of beauty and he carried the orchestra through its many waves of melody and massive sound in a manner of total dialogue and unified vision.

From principal Dale Clevenger's opening horn call to principal John Sharp's playing of the haunting cello solo that opens the slow movement, everyone was on Ax's same masterful and eloquent wavelength. Ax was so excited by Sharp's playing that he rounded the podium twice to pull the shy performer over to stage right to share his bows. It was generous and classy, like everything else about this performance.

Lieberson Edges to Kitsch, Mahler One Soars

Chicago Sun-Times, **May 3, 2008** Bernard Haitink starts this week's concert with an oddity, Ravel's 1929 orchestration of his own 1895 piano piece, *Menuet antique*, a sort of French-Impressionism-meets-Kurt-Weill work. In addition to its inherent beauty, the *Menuet* also demonstrated how Haitink calibrates every section of the orchestra with both clarity and grace.

The death of mezzo-soprano Lorraine Hunt Lieberson from breast cancer just under two years ago hit the classical music world like no other blow in recent memory. The chance again to hear *Neruda Songs*, a work written for her in 2005 by her husband, Peter Lieberson, was a bittersweet occasion, especially as Lieberson himself is now battling lymphoma.

Kelley O'Connor was Lieberson's own choice as his wife's successor in the work, and she brought a careful intelligence and Iberian flavor to the five settings of the Spanish writer's love poems. The vocal lines are Lieberson's greatest accomplishment, while the orchestrations edge towards kitsch. Haitink knit them all into a moving whole, and the composer was clearly moved when he took the stage.

Haitink's Mahler is the product of decades of consideration and probing study. This week, Haitink does with the First what is often claimed but rarely true about other performances: he takes the score, often at a slow pace that requires extra attention, and makes it float and sing and move anew. Rather than playing it as a race to its final climaxes, Haitink made the brass huzzahs of a piece with all that came before. And if you have ever heard anything as beautiful as the third movement, Mahler's world within a world, I hope that you know how lucky you are.

Chicago's Greatest Ambassador

London—On the State of the Orchestra

Chicago Sun-Times, **September 14, 2008** After two sold-out concerts each in London and in Amsterdam, and critical glory in both music capitals, several things emerge about the state of the Chicago Symphony Orchestra:

First, the pairing of Dutch maestro Bernard Haitink and the Chicago Symphony is happening at exactly the right time for both sides of the coupling and is getting results that far exceed those expected from any sort of "caretaker" or interim period. Haitink, who turns 80 in the spring, is at the height of his interpretive powers, and as he revisits major works from his half-century-plus career, the Chicago Symphony is his ideal instrument. The orchestra in turn looks with great respect to a man who matches his musical skills and experience with the greatest civility.

Second, despite the emotional roller-coaster of the end of the Daniel Barenboim era and the initial aftermath, the orchestra is in excellent shape, rivaling any time in its storied history. Younger and veteran players blend their energies in a common purpose. Strings sound as they never have before, the woodwinds are virtuosos, individually and collectively, and the famous Chicago brass is undimmed if also more elegant. There are matters of individual players and tensions, as there are in any orchestra, and the temporary return of retired principal clarinet Larry Combs is a reminder of how important it is to fill his chair with another exceptional talent. But this orchestra is envied around the world with reason for its work, performance ethic, and artistic results.

And third, the Chicago Symphony remains one of Chicago's greatest ambassadors—probably its greatest one, period. Georg Solti saw this as a necessary role to add to the orchestra's professional and artistic profile, and under Solti, Barenboim, and Boulez, that reputation did not falter in the cities the orchestra visited. When, rightly or wrongly, Americans are viewed either with suspicion or stereotypes in many countries, and when Chicago and Haitink show the world what has been accomplished there, and do so with so many women musicians and diverse nationalities, it demonstrates that culture is one of our city's—and our country's—greatest offerings.

Another special partnership has begun with the return of London-based American pianist Murray Perahia to the ranks of Chicago Symphony soloists (he is performing Mozart's C Minor Concerto, No. 24, K. 491, in all three cities on this tour, including the last stop, Lucerne, Switzerland). Perahia and Haitink bring a similar perspective to Mozart—elegant, refined but not at all stuffy. But more than this, Perahia is a truly collaborative artist, and he listens to his orchestral colleagues as much as he plays with them. In the concerto's slow movement, he somehow imitates and reflects solo violins, flute and oboe.

Acclaim in Tokyo, Hong Kong, China

Chicago Sun-Times, **February 16, 2009** Some 35 years after the first major American orchestra visited the People's Republic of China, the Chicago Symphony Orchestra became the final top ensemble to make its debut here as it closed a three-week, five-city, ten-concert tour of Far East Asia with two sold-out performances at the new National Centre for the Performing Arts in the Chinese capital.

With 11 Chinese-born players and some 20 Asian members, the Chicago Symphony has the largest representation of Eastern musicians of any leading Western orchestra, and throughout this tour of Japan, Hong Kong, and mainland China the sense of homecoming and of connection between peoples was palpable.

From Yokohama to Tokyo to Hong Kong to Shanghai to Beijing, crowds greeted the orchestra with waves of applause and waited in lines at the stage door to meet performers. The reputation and teaching experience that many non-Asian players have in the Far East meant that the orchestra as a whole had the classical equivalent of rock-star groupies grabbing up available tickets even when top prices reached almost $500 (U.S.) in Tokyo and $200 and more in Hong Kong and China.

Principal conductor Bernard Haitink, who turns 80 next month, also was making his first visit to China (and Hong Kong as well, in his case), and he is revered here in a way normally reserved for legends. Banners with the Dutchman's face and showing the maestro in action on the podium hung throughout cities on the orchestra's itinerary.

Standing ovations are not a part of concert ritual in the Far East, but a happy audience can keep curtain calls going for 10 minutes and more. At Tokyo's famed Suntory Hall, audience members would not leave even after the musicians had exited the stage, demanding that Haitink come out for a solo bow. Claques of brass fans shouted bravos from student galleries and cheap seats in every city when performances of Mahler's Sixth Symphony and Bruckner's Seventh, massive works both, came to an end.

Programs also included Haydn's Symphony No. 101, "The Clock"; Mozart's No. 41, "Jupiter"; and Richard Strauss' *Ein Heldenleben* ("A Hero's Life") with Taiwan-born concertmaster Robert Chen as the brilliant soloist in the latter.

"The Chicago Symphony is characterized by its intensity, its sense of common purpose and its insistence on playing each piece at the highest level," Haitink told the *Sun-Times.* "When you add the sense of these qualities that the Asian players bring as a part of their cultural heritage and the insistence on excellence that Japanese and Chinese audiences insist on, I can say that this tour has been one of the most wonderful and moving experiences of my long career."

Bruckner Beyond Words

A Historic Performance of the Eighth Symphony

Chicago Sun-Times, **April 18, 2009** Bernard Haitink has turned his transitional role as the Chicago Symphony Orchestra's principal conductor into a historic period of collaboration and growth. Haitink, now 80, has long performed the works of Anton Bruckner. Rather than finding celebrations of sound or Romantic statements in these pieces, Haitink follows the pathbreaking efforts of Eugen Jochum, his predecessor as music director of Amsterdam's Concertgebouw Orchestra, and sees the Bruckner symphonies on Bruckner's own terms—as efforts to communicate desires and thoughts that cannot be expressed by words alone.

We are guided through a story with many digressions and unexpected recoveries. As Austrian as Bruckner was, Haitink seems to marry him with that ultimate French narrator, Marcel Proust, to produce performances that must be viewed from different angles in space and time even to begin to comprehend them.

This understanding makes Haitink an ideal guide to Bruckner's most challenging work, the C minor Eighth Symphony of 1884–92. Thursday night with the CSO, Haitink offered revelations on the level of Pierre Boulez's encounter with this work beginning 12 years ago. But where Boulez makes us take on the structure of this 80-minute work, Haitink keeps us focused on the line of the argument, however many times Bruckner makes us think the line has been interrupted.

Each movement is laid out clearly, from the big noises of the Allegro, to the jaggedness of the Scherzo, to the inner depths and prayerful heights of the Adagio. Just when we think the conductor is being too indulgent of Bruckner's longueurs in the Finale, he shows us how all the themes fit together and allows us to listen back in our minds to the unfolding we have just experienced.

Every member and section leader within the orchestra rose to this occasion. Conducting from a chair due to a pinched nerve, Haitink was even given the rare honor at a first performance of the players insisting that he take a solo bow without their standing. Right they were.

A Profound Beethoven Cycle

Nos. 5 and 8

Chicago Sun-Times, June 4, 2010 From the moment Wednesday at Symphony Center that Bernard Haitink signaled the first notes of Beethoven's *Fidelio Overture* and then those of his Eighth and Fifth Symphonies with the Chicago Symphony Orchestra, you knew you were in a special place.

Perhaps you knew it even before those rippling and rhythmic measures sounded out. The full house was unusually attentive and palpably expectant. In cities where Beethoven festivals are done frequently, either as money makers or from lack of programming vision, there's not much to such an occasion. But for one of the world's finest conductors, at 81, to lead the Chicago Symphony in a survey of the nine symphonies by this most charismatic and revolutionary of all composers is something different.

This series of nine concerts, many chamber music performances and three free symposia also marks the end of Haitink's four years as the Chicago Symphony's principal conductor.

As a longtime subscriber and I noted, that means there is a lot of love in this space. Love for Beethoven and love from the audience, love from the players for a consummately professional and richly experienced conductor who gave them leadership at a time it was almost desperately needed, and love from a conductor for an orchestra "that does something very difficult," as Haitink told me. "It allows me simply to be myself and to say musically what I might have to say."

Beethoven is about the totality of human possibility, and this is not a subject that changes—except perhaps for the worse—or loses its power as time goes by. And Haitink knows—as well as anyone active in music today—that it is we who have to open ourselves to this great musical maker and thinker.

Of course he understands the pacing and the relationship between different and changing tempi in each piece and each movement in a way that few others do. Of course he has a psychic-seeming way of carrying the sense of dotted rhythms between himself and the orchestra without beating out every count. Just those opening measures of each work contained as much unseen rippling as the flutter of a butterfly's wings.

But he also is so in the moment at each moment that we forget what is happening next in works that we might have heard dozens, even hundreds of times. Haitink draws this same watching out for the next turn from the CSO players—from Daniel Gingrich and James Smelser's ruddy horn calls and leadership, to Eugene Izotov's heart-stabbing oboe solo in the Fifth, to trombones that are just right— tuneful, buoyant, and never too much.

It's magic. But it's magic that comes from decades of work, of trial and error, of training and practice by everyone on that stage. When these master musicians turn their full attention to one another and to Beethoven in such a concentrated way, you are reminded of why you are here—here in this hall and even here on this earth.

Nos. 2 and 3

Chicago Sun-Times, June 7, 2010 Structure in music was something Beethoven both knew a great deal about and exploded for all time over the course of his prolific career. So it's also interesting to note the structure of the Chicago Symphony Orchestra's first-ever Beethoven Festival with its principal conductor Bernard Haitink. To present the nine symphonies requires choices in order and pairing, and they can be instructive.

On Wednesday, Haitink kicked off the three-week survey with an underestimated entry, the Eighth, and then the work—when not in the right hands—most overexposed, No. 5. The match was a reminder that all of these works have something to say, and we need to give each of them careful hearing.

The program Saturday also brought a giant, No. 3, "Eroica," and a lesser-heard opus, No. 2. But here we had back-to-back earlier creations, from 1802 and 1803, and playing them chronologically offered building blocks, points of expansion, and components given what might be called creative destruction in the larger, later composition.

Again, Haitink commands our listening. The meticulous Dutch conductor never makes claims to definitiveness, especially with Beethoven, whom he has revisited in full cycles three times with three different orchestras in just the last three years.

Nor does he want us to hear the symphonies piecemeal—"I think we all need to really spend time together with Beethoven to begin to get close to what he is doing," he told me in a recent interview.

Pacing is key for Haitink—to his career as well as to each piece. His intense study and re-study of Beethoven scores—particularly their tempo markings—has brought him to perhaps the most illuminating set of choices before audiences today. Fleet, without being rushed, Haitink's tempi are about the inner sense of urgency in these great works, not about whipping up sound for effect. If some mistake this for caution, that's their loss.

Possibly aided by the orchestra performing without stage risers, the strings continue to shine and sing in ways new to the orchestra's history. Daniel Gingrich and David Griffin led the superb horns, and Haitink waded into the orchestra at concert's end to shake hands with principal flute Mathieu Dufour and principal oboe Eugene Izotov.

Nos. 4 and 6

Chicago Sun-Times, **June 12, 2010** We have been fortunate in the four seasons that Bernard Haitink has graced the Chicago Symphony Orchestra as principal conductor to see and hear him in a wide range of music—large-scale symphonies from Bruckner, Mahler and Shostakovich, 20th century works from Britain, France and Poland, new work, Classical period work, choral and instrumental pieces, and those featuring both piano and vocal soloists.

But we've missed out on a big part of his long career by never hearing him in opera, even in concert form. Time, money, and other legitimate priorities all played their parts. But this week's installment in the Chicago Symphony's ongoing Beethoven Festival, heard Thursday, gives more than a small taste of what Haitink brings to the world of opera and song, and not only because it opened with a commanding performance of the often raucous and lesser-played "Leonore" Overture No. 2, written in 1805 for Beethoven's sole opera, *Fidelio*. In fact, the thought really wouldn't leave my head during the quicksilver playing of the Fourth Symphony, a work that is too often seen as merely occupying the space between the composer's signature "Eroica" and Fifth Symphonies.

In Haitink's experienced hands, we hear Mozart echoing through the half-hour-plus 1806 work—but fortified and expanded upon. Beethoven scaled back his instrumentation to a Mozart/Haydn ensemble and length after the mighty Third Symphony. But he didn't limit his curiosity. In many ways, he successfully spins out and develops more moods and story lines in this work than he does in the one he actually wrote for the theater. With great economy (and Haitink is made for economy), Beethoven gives us the equivalents of arias, ensembles and accompanied recitatives (by instruments taking solos). And as he did in the overture, where a listener always wonders if the players will accidentally make a move from the more frequently played "Leonore" No. 3, Haitink made sure that the Beethoven's thrill in the unexpected underscored the pulse of the final movement.

It's the Sixth Symphony, the 1807–08 "Pastoral," that we're accustomed to thinking of as storytelling, what with Beethoven's own descriptive movement names—"Merry Gathering of Country Folk," "Thunderstorm," and so forth. But Haitink knows that how the tale is told musically is what matters here, not a lot of acting out or trying to create a film score before its time. It was as if we were hearing a fine opera company in the gardens of a country house, except our singers were flute Mathieu Dufour, oboe Eugene Izotov, bassoon David McGill, and guest clarinet Patrick Messina of the Orchestre National de France—blending with his colleagues as if he lived here—with horns Daniel Gingrich and James Smelser supplying brilliant atmospherics. Haitink gave us a "slow" movement taken at an almost brisk pace that worked sublimely.

Nos. 1 and 7

Chicago Sun-Times, June 17, 2010 One of the many things that makes Beethoven unique among composers is that he and his music have maintained their intense popularity for two centuries. That popularity has not varied much in kind, either. Audiences then and now find the same power, humane insight, and sense of inspiration and hope in his works.

These factors might seem to make putting on a survey of all of Beethoven's symphonies an easy task: Everyone's going to like them anyway, right? In fact, it makes the challenge for conductor and orchestra even greater. Falling into habit or rote can dull any work, no matter how great.

Wednesday night at Orchestra Hall with the Chicago Symphony Orchestra, principal conductor Bernard Haitink demonstrated that there has been no danger of this in the Chicago Symphony's three-week Beethoven Festival. After a lifetime spent with these pieces, as both player and conductor, Haitink's current perspective is capping a set of three recent cycles intentionally given with three different orchestras. Haitink also has looked deeply into his own musical experience to emerge with a perspective that allows listeners and players to hear each symphony anew and in the context of all nine entries.

So this week's concerts, the festival's penultimate program, came off less as a marathon of three distinct works that took us from 1799 to 1812 than a climb up a mountain of Beethoven's design and accomplishment. The First Symphony, the calling card of a 29-year-old genius, filled with subtle and not-so-subtle transformations of

Mozart and Haydn's earlier creations, was followed by that opera in an overture, the 1804–05 "Leonore" No. 3. The program's second half held the nonpareil Seventh from 1811–12 with its outbursts of joy, its solemn meditations and its lessons in harmony that could sweep up any listener.

Haitink's understanding of Beethoven's sense of structure was underlined by bringing three works with slow, deceptive introductions together on the program. His insight that the coda of "Leonore" No. 3 relates to and ties together all parts of the piece showed that it is much more than a thrill ride. His reassembling the elements of the famed second movement of the Seventh resulted in a performance of the Allegretto like none I've ever heard and, I'm prepared to say, surpassing any others played here.

No. 9

Chicago Sun-Times, June 20, 2010 Haitink brings his astonishingly clear and subtle survey of the full series of Beethoven's symphonies with the Chicago Symphony Orchestra to a dramatic close this weekend at Orchestra Hall with the last of them, the great and still revolutionary Ninth, the so-called "Choral" Symphony. And while he will continue to visit Chicago — he is slated to conclude the CSO's next season with two weeks of concerts — these performances also bring to an end his four seasons as principal conductor here. And just as Friday night's concert helped us to see the symphonic Beethoven whole, so this summing up allows us to observe a period in the orchestra's history that can now deservedly be called the Haitink Years.

Concert and tenure alike are and have been marked by inquiry and an almost quiet upsetting of expectations. There is the 81-year-old maestro's combination of gentle politeness with steely determination. His dry and wry Dutch wit. His small but highly individual catalog of physical gestures. All of these, along with his characteristic 8:04 p.m. concert start time, will be sorely missed.

But the gift of his time here will resonate beyond yearning. While we may have heard more emotional performances of the Ninth, none was as revealing as this one. None made you think more than this one.

This became fully apparent with the slow, third movement where Haitink showed the webs that Beethoven is weaving—and, we now understood, was always weaving—in this work and came to full flower in the finale where every part of the orchestra, the massed and expert Chicago Symphony Chorus and the four American soloists—soprano Jessica Rivera, mezzo Kelley O'Connor, tenor Clifton Forbis, and bass-baritone Eric Owens, the latter particularly fine—were heard as a part of a complex whole, not merely more rocks in a sonic avalanche.

As with the brief, beautiful and almost never performed choral song setting of Goethe verses, "A Becalmed Sea and A Prosperous Voyage," that opened the evening, Haitink gave us a Beethoven full of surprises. It's clear he's still curious about every measure of these works. How privileged we have been that he has shared his own voyage and spirit with us.

Mahler by a Master Interpreter

A Ninth Symphony That Flows to the Last Notes

Chicago Sun-Times, June 4, 2011 The Chicago Symphony Orchestra has played Mahler's Ninth Symphony for just over 60 years, starting when George Szell in 1950 led a performance here of a work then considered an oddity and a jumble. It later became the province of Chicago's greatest leaders: Solti, Giulini, Levine, Boulez, and Barenboim.

There are artists whose biography lifts the estimation of their creative output. And then there are those, perhaps no more so than Gustav Mahler, whose masterpieces actually get bogged down by constant "identification" of personal details and alleged intentions in the score. Few conductors have played so important a role in the biography of Mahler's music while leaving the composer's real or imagined biography to others than Bernard Haitink, whose career began and developed in Amsterdam, the city most receptive to Mahler's music.

Even before the concert Thursday began, there was a sense of occasion: this great Mahler champion, now 82, leading this great Mahler orchestra, which has such affection and respect for Haitink, in the Ninth for the first time.

These expectations were met and then some. Haitink's signatures were all there—an innate sense that music flows, a control of dynamics that is total but never mechanical, an understanding of both individual lines and the way they exist when woven together (see the fierce end of the rondo-burleske), a pacing that starts before the downbeat and remains at work until after the last notes have died away.

There was more. It almost sounds silly to say this, but Haitink tamed the sold-out audience. You could hear the quiet. You could feel the attention. Even between movements, coughing and rustling was at a minimum. This actually relates not only to the conductor's prestige, but to his understanding of the work itself. The breathing of the strings in the opening *andante comodo* refers to every part of the piece to come. The four movements are finely defined and constructed, but are always a part of the whole symphony (here 82 minutes of music).

The rich, 21st-century sound of the CSO strings and their concertmaster Robert Chen, bequeathed to us all by Barenboim, was rarely harnessed as fully as it was Thursday. Leading the violas, assistant principal Li-Kuo Chang, with Chen, brought a tenderness and elegance to his solos that was brilliantly matched by such principals as flute Mathieu Dufour, oboe Eugene Izotov, cello John Sharp, bassoon David McGill, clarinet John Bruce Yeh, bass clarinet J. Lawrie Bloom, and piccolo Jennifer Gunn.

Is the piece "about" death? Life? Struggle? Acceptance? Rebirth? Haitink knows that it is—like any truly great work of art—about all of these. His Ninth, with its unusually spacious scherzo/ländler and animated final adagio movement, reminds us that the piece is about us.

A Fourth Symphony of Depth and Lightness

Chicago Sun-Times, October 22, 2011 In his recent years with the Chicago Symphony Bernard Haitink has shared a lifetime of experience with Mahler that began as a student listener at Amsterdam's Concertgebouw and included his 28 years leading that orchestra. Haitink's presentations are not of the urgent, emotions-on-the sleeve school that became too accepted in the States after the Mahler revival of the 1960s. Rather, they have an almost Shakespearean knowingness, one that allows for both depth and lightness to unfold naturally in performance.

Haitink has waited until now to bring us one of his favorites, the initially simple-seeming but highly personal and structured Fourth Symphony. Haitink reveals the piece as yet another that benefits from hindsight, and a hindsight free of the nostalgia often ascribed to the score.

Petals unfold but remain nested in one another. The four distinct and varied movements flow logically, even warmly. Haitink stretches the work slightly to almost an hour—still Mahler's shortest entry—but this, too seems right on.

The only shame of the week is that the illness of German violinist Frank Peter Zimmermann removed Berg's great 1935 concerto from the program and the substituted Schubert Symphony No. 5 shifted the time references of the pairing. Working with an appropriately reduced ensemble, Haitink gave the earlier piece just the right mix of elegance and youthful spirit.

A New "Creation"

On Learning a New Work at Age 85

> *WFMT Broadcast*, October 24, 2011
> PATNER: If you think of a camera lens and if you take the camera
>   and you look at Mahler Four and then to its right the Berg Violin
>   Concerto from 1935, you get kind of one feeling. If you move

the camera lens left and you have Schubert on the left, and then Mahler Four on the right, you get a different feeling. Yes?

HAITINK: It's a totally different inroad, yes. But both are possible.

PATNER: Isn't that interesting that both of them are possible—you have played both combinations. That says something good for Mahler. He doesn't need anything more good said, but it says something additional about him.

HAITINK: I have to confess that his Fourth Symphony I like the most of all his symphonies. It has this wonderful chamber music quality. There are not too many bells, and resurrection and so on. It's just pure music. And it's a wonderful, intimate piece. I'm a bit worried about it because I think in a way that I would like that to be the last piece I ever conduct, so that's dangerous.

PATNER: I don't know if it was the first, but it is certainly a Mahler work you have played for a long period of your career.

HAITINK: It always came back. But I try not to play these pieces too often because when you do it too often, it loses something of its magic. It should be for a special occasion where you feel fresh and then the orchestra doesn't play it too much. And the Schubert Fifth Symphony. The orchestra had not played that for a while.

PATNER: It is a magical piece, isn't it?

HAITINK: Oh, it's wonderful. It's wonderful. Schubert, a boy of sixteen, who composed this. I mean, how can one imagine that?

PATNER: Somebody said all Schubert is early Schubert because he didn't live very long. People sometimes associate lightness or joy with youth, but that kind of lightness and joy is something that would normally come with life and age and experience, and yet, as you say, he had it at sixteen.

HAITINK: It is such a sunny piece. It's wonderful.

PATNER: So we went from a sunny piece to perhaps, in some ways, one of the sunniest Mahler pieces, but still with a sense that was looking, perhaps, to the future.

You are shortly going to be conducting a new work. It's not unusual for people to add a work to their repertoire, but you are adding a very major work, and not a brief work, and you're adding it not at the very beginning of your career. Haydn, *The Creation*, the great oratorio written at the end of the eighteenth century and late in Haydn's own composing.

HAITINK: At the end of his life. He was not a young man anymore.

PATNER: How does this come about?

HAITINK: How do these things happen? Maybe it came up in a meeting. Maybe it was suggested to me. We decided to do it, and then there was a problem that when it was composed by Haydn, the libretto was in two languages, German and English. And normally it is done in German. But being here, in an English-speaking, American-speaking country, I said, "We have to do it in English," so there we are. Maybe the English is a little bit old fashioned, but the German is also terribly old fashioned.

PATNER: And it's quite possible that the German that he used and the English that he used were kind of back and forth, right? Wasn't he living in England and then he went back to Europe and was using texts that were pulled together for him probably from different translations?

HAITINK: The man who wrote the text was Baron van Swieten, an Austrian who was partly Dutch, and he had a great influence on Haydn. He made a text for him and even had musical suggestions. But it was, as far we know, composed in Esterházy, in Europe. It was composed, I think, because his friend Salomon, the London agent, could promise him performances. Haydn's hero was Handel, and he wanted to write an oratorio as successful as one of the Handel's oratorios. I think he had the *Messiah* in mind. So we are nowadays very conscious of historical performances, God help us. But he wrote it for 200 musicians. He had an enormous chorus, you know, and orchestra. I try to be more ... not too much, but maybe a bit more vegetarian in that respect. But I have twelve first violins. So going down in the strings it's ten, eight, six, four, and then a chorus of eighty. And I must say, I have a chorus where I am able to make quite a good noise.

PATNER: I guess the question is not so much how did it come up now, but given that you have done Haydn throughout your career, why had you never turned to it before? Was there not an opportunity or it was not something that grabbed you, as they say?

HAITINK: I have strange things in my character. I'm not a schemer. I take things how they come. And sometimes I suggest things, of course. But an important example in my life, the whole Mahler thing. When I started doing Mahler, it was a totally closed book for me. My predecessor, Eduard van Beinum, died far too young, and I became linked to the Concertgebouw. They had a huge contract. You know how it is. Business has to go on. I think they took terrible risks with me because I was very young. But Phillips, who had an exclusive contract with the orchestra at that time, insisted that they will do a Mahler cycle. And I said, "Well, I can't do it in one or two years. I need ten years, every year a symphony, and let's see how it works."

PATNER: So as a young man you were able to recognize, both artistically and personally, that "yes, okay, we'll do it, but I can't do this as a smorgasbord in two years."

HAITINK: They wanted to bring it out. But then they had to agree because of the situation. At that time there was not so much competition. Nowadays it would be totally different. There are some very talented younger conductors who would jump at it. But at that time, in my country, I was the only white hope.

And coming back to Haydn, you know, it's very funny with Haydn, very strange. Every orchestra musician, wherever you go and you do a Haydn symphony, they will say "Oh, what wonderful music, we should play that much more," and it never happens. I don't exclude myself. I haven't done enough Haydn. I have done it, but not in the amount which I should have, because he's a wonderful composer. He has wit. He has an incredible fantasy. He surprises you all the time. It's never stale. And he admired Mozart so much. So what more do you want?

PATNER: Somebody who both admired Mozart and had known him, and must have always, in his head, tried to turn over how, how, how.

HAITINK: What a culture, no?

PATNER: So given all of that, why not *The Creation* earlier?

HAITINK: Good question, and I can't answer it. Just that it happened. These things are logistical sometimes. Can I get the right chorus? That's always a problem in Amsterdam. But in London they had their own chorus, but I never touched it. I don't know why. And I have to be honest, I'm not young anymore, and it's nice to have a new challenge.

PATNER: Obviously you could go about this, given your history, your abilities, in any number of ways. If you wanted to, you could work strictly from the score. If you wanted to, you could sample concerts or performances. You could read, you could not read. How did you begin the preparation for this once it was decided?

HAITINK: Reading the score. Reading again, again, again and trying to hear it because sometimes there are very amazing harmonies, all of a sudden, changes of key, and it takes time. You have to read the text and what the music says about the text, and what it doesn't say. And it took me a long time.

PATNER: I know from having been privileged to visit you there that you have a wonderful study on top of your house in Lucerne, and a nice desk, and you said to me, "That's the most important thing in my house, because it's big enough I can spread out the score."

HAITINK: And then if I get not so much bored, but have a moment of staleness, then I look out to the Rigi, the mountain, and well, I think, "It's not that bad."

PATNER: Do you mark in that initial score? Do you make notes on a pad of paper next to it? Do you keep it in your head?

HAITINK: I have different scores. The score we have now here lying on the table is for me the definitive one. But before that I looked at a smaller orchestra score. I made notes with pencil. And now what I call the official one has blue pencil. Red sometimes, and even black.

PATNER: Do they mean something different, the blue, the red, and the black?

HAITINK: For me.

PATNER: For you, okay. This is a work that very much has sections. It has three large parts and then it has numbers, as we say. Does that become a part of your work after you have gone through the whole score, to think about the way it breaks down, or is that a part of the way you put it together from the beginning?

HAITINK: That happens because of practical reasons. First I had the piano rehearsal with the chorus, so I did the chorus bits. And then I started the orchestra alone rehearsals, which is important because the orchestra parts are very detailed, very important. There Haydn uses his wit and his surprises that are in the orchestra. I have my rehearsals with the soloists. And then we have to put the thing together.

PATNER: How do you see Haydn having put it together? Do you think there is a special plan? Do you think there is a through story that he's attempting to retell?

HAITINK: It's the story of the creation. And whatever you think about that, that is a personal thing, it is there. I'm sometimes a little bit surprised when you hear "... and God said it was good." Nowadays one has to ask, is it really good? But there's a certain naïveté there, and one has to respect that.

PATNER: I'm thinking back, I'm sure it's true for many people, some version of it, when I was a child in the 1960s it was still very popular in the liberal Jewish education to perform cantatas. And we did a creation cantata, and we would sing, little children, "And God said it was good, ki tov," which is the Hebrew— "and God said it was good." And to this day, when I see that, I think, "Well, that's a pretty naïve sounding thing. What does that really mean, and would he still say that, if there is a he?"

HAITINK: Exactly. But one has to face that it was composed at that time. I don't know what Haydn really believed in. Was it tradition or was it his personal belief? He is quite funny at the end in the recitative, Adam and Eve, and it's on a personal level because his marriage was not great. At the end of one of the recitatives Adam says, "You have to be obedient." He doesn't say it once, but continues three times repeated, bom, bom, "You have to be." I don't know if the audience will get it, but that's tongue in cheek.

PATNER: When you look at the two big oratorios, *The Seasons* and *The Creation*, one of them obviously starts and ends on Earth, the other one starts in the heavens and ends on the Earth. But for Haydn it's very important that the Earth part of both stories, the human part of both stories, is what we are left with, isn't it?

HAITINK: That's the greatness of Haydn, that he's so human. And when you talk about the introduction, that is an amazing piece of music, five minutes. There's no tonality. There is just, yes, chaos, but wonderful chaos.

PATNER: The only other times I can think you have that is in some of the French Baroque composers. There's a couple of pieces by Rameau where they just kind of—*rrrr-rrrr-rrrr*—to give you a sense of the Earth opening, the Earth being created.

HAITINK: Bach, the *St. Matthew Passion*.

PATNER: Of course.

HAITINK: There are wonderful places in the accompaniments of the recitatives also when the orchestra is playing about the worm who creeps out of the Earth, the whales, the big whales, and so on. It's very familiar. It's like a picture book.

PATNER: Again I think of the way in *The Seasons* the farmer's life is hard, but it's also humorous. And if we don't both look at our lives, but also look with some winking, then it's not good. I think that's part of the Haydn thing. You have exceptionally intelligent soloists and it is very important that a singer understands the text, right?

HAITINK: It's very important because they have to do so many subtle things by themselves in the recitatives. I can't do everything myself. I have to trust them and to leave it to them and to the possibilities.

A Very Happy Occasion

Chicago Sun-Times, **October 29, 2011** Former principal conductor of the Chicago Symphony Orchestra, Haitink is guided almost exclusively by the twin stars of musical integrity and personal humility. When you add his decades of experience to the time that he puts into study and contemplation of scores, you wish that he could take up any and all masterworks he has yet to perform.

Though he has had the lifelong acquaintance with Haydn that is a part of a classical musician's life and has shown a special affinity for his symphonies, Haitink had never led the late, summing-up oratorio *The Creation* (1796–98) before this week's concerts. Thursday at Orchestra Hall, you could hear not only the results of the conductor's study and insights, but also a lifetime of reflection on the meaning (and limitations?) of religion, of poetry, of tradition and of that great framing era that Haydn helped to close out and that Haitink's native Netherlands played such a key role in establishing: the Enlightenment.

Inspired by the massive oratorios of English tradition, especially those of another native German speaker, Handel, *The Creation* is very much a work of texts, for both soloists and chorus. The words, whether performed in German or, as here, in English (Haydn made dual versions) inspire the music, even when the instrumental parts of the score preview the vocal lines. What is this Biblical creation story really about, both Haydn and Haitink seem to be asking. Would the Creator still pronounce His work as "good" today? Can we know any more in the end than that innocent-then-fallen couple Adam and Eve?

It is hard to imagine this 110-minute (with Haitink's sometimes stately tempos) musical narration having a better instrumental or choral presentation than it had here. Suspicious of piety and allergic to pomposity, Haitink found the work's simplicity and unfolded the intricacies that two centuries of listeners and players have called Bach-like. Without breaking flow, he inspired passages on the bringing forth of animals and the other creeping, crawling and swimming things that were, as they should be, laugh out loud funny.

Reduced strings, wind sections and soloists were all a part of a single team, curious and eager. Duain Wolfe's CSO Chorus, almost always a marvel, showed a coiled strength and a contrast between near silence and C Major celebrations rare even in its own illustrious history.

As the tale-telling archangel Uriel, English tenor Ian Bostridge was all that this part can and should be: knowing, confident, confiding, hypnotic. He also had the distinct advantage of total command of the English tongue, something that often defied Swedish soprano Klara Ek and German bass-baritone Hanno Mueller-Brachmann, also attractive, younger singers more believable as the Edenic couple of the work's third and final part than they were as Uriel's companions Gabriel and Raphael. British fortepianist James Johnstone and CSO principal cellist John Sharp were the ever-attentive and supportive continuo players.

Filled with infectious energy in this residency, Haitink looked very, very happy as the seventh day received its last "Amen."

Beethoven's Greatest Mass

Beethoven's "Missa Solemnis"

Chicago Sun-Times, October 27, 2012 It's the most extraordinary work by a great composer you've never—or very rarely—heard performed live. It's a setting of the solemn Roman Catholic Mass by a man whose own religious beliefs had little to do with Catholicism or liturgy of any kind. It's 80 minutes of power, delicacy, surprise and wonder. It strains the range of its singers and vocal soloists, particularly the sopranos, and it is so quiet at times, it barely can be heard. It's led by one of the most important living conductors, one of a handful of artists with the necessary insight and long personal and professional history who can pull off the work and command total focus from performers and audience.

It's Beethoven's *Missa Solemnis*, heard Thursday at Symphony Center, and its performances this weekend by the Chicago Symphony Orchestra and Chorus under the leadership, at once authoritative and wholly sympathetic, of former principal conductor Bernard Haitink, 83, are not to be missed.

For *Missa Solemnis*, Beethoven took the standard mass text and more confronted it than set it to give voice to his own independent religious impulses. "From the heart—may it go—to the heart!" Beethoven famously inscribed on a work others might have thought should be addressed to God Himself. Racing through most of the text of the Credo—the basic expression of Christian belief—he peppers the concluding Agnus Dei section with abstract martial sounds, "war episodes," while writing in the score that he urges man to hold on to Beethoven's own ideas of "inner and outward peace."

In the Credo, Beethoven writes eerie, floating wind sounds around "Et incarnatus est," one of several passages unlike anything else in Beethoven, or in other music of this time, for that matter. The work follows with an almost welcoming, natural set of sounds around "Et homo factus"—"and became man." Haitink takes all of this and makes it of a piece. He shows how parts that seem disparate actually cohere, such as how the sudden instrumental opening and the choral and solo responses of the Kyrie, God and man—and woman—each stating his or her case, fit with the quiet, almost accidental-sounding end of the Agnus Dei and the work as a whole.

A reduced orchestra, and a chorus of 83, play and sing as a unity and as if they had been working with Haitink on this for two months instead of just two or three days. Duain Wolfe expertly prepared the chorus in Beethoven's odd dynamic markings and Germanized Latin ("Dona nobis PATZ-em").

Soprano Erin Wall, belated CSO debutante mezzo Bernarda Fink, tenor Anthony Dean Griffey in his first subscription concerts, and Haitink favorite, German bass-baritone Hanno Mueller-Brachman, were what Beethoven wanted as a solo quartet—well-matched but highly individual voices. Concertmaster Robert Chen and other instrumental leaders, especially winds and Daniel Gingrich's superb horn section, were breathing with Haitink, and the composer.

Every visit to Chicago from the Lucerne-based Haitink is a gift, especially one such as this. It is often said that there can be no perfect performance of the *Missa*. I'm not sure what kept this one from disproving that observation.

IV

Riccardo Muti

(2010–)

Riccardo Muti made his debut with the Chicago Symphony at Ravinia Park in 1973. Like Daniel Barenboim before him, he had not yet served as music director of a major orchestra, though the city's most cosmopolitan listeners might have heard him conduct operas at the Maggio Musicale Fiorentino in Italy. Noting that the tip of Fritz Reiner's famous baton had moved only in the space of a postage stamp, *Tribune* critic Tom Willis felt Muti brought something altogether different: "Visually, his music making starts in his back and proceeds thru a martinet's arms. Some of his gestures are so angular as to approach comic opera stereotypes. Everything is larger than life. Soft is softest; loud, loudest. [. . .] Above all, his music is perfectly clear." Love or hate the style—he certainly made an impression. When Muti returned to conduct a subscription series two years later, Willis assured readers that his movements "should not blind the listener to the superior musical quality of all that he did." Chicagoans would have to wait thirty-two more years to see this special conductor with their orchestra again.[1]

Muti reached international superstardom soon after his appearances in Chicago. By 1980, he had already earned the virtuoso conductor "quadfecta": a US orchestra (Philadelphia), a European orchestra (London's Philharmonia), an opera post (the Maggio Musicale), and a generous recording contract. Critics hearing Muti's Philadelphia Orchestra noticed sudden changes in the ensemble's famed "Ormandy sound," with one listener describing the new timbre as "more versatile and a shade or two more lithe in its phrasing if perhaps a bit less lush in its tone." Muti explained his approach to Bernard Holland of the *New York Times*: "I want this wonderful orchestra to be able to play with a cleaner, more direct style—with less perfume. On the other hand, I want to keep always the possibility of bringing back this perfume when it is needed." Muti's profile soared even higher when he became director of La Scala, the most famous opera house in the world, in 1986. Over time, however, the demands of juggling multiple positions began to wear on him, and he decided not to renew his contract with Philadelphia in 1990. "I need time to be not only a musician but a man of culture," he told *Times* reporter Allan Kozinn. "As I said to the orchestra, I want to find myself."[2]

Muti's introspection led him to champion the lofty idea that music can unite us. With only three years under his belt as director of the Philadelphia Orchestra, he led eighty-seven players in a free "concert for humanity" protesting nuclear proliferation. According to concertmaster Norman Caro, the maestro boldly agreed to lead the orchestra without fearing negative responses from the board or the public. Over time, Muti's political engagement transformed into a broader humanitarian enterprise. Beginning in 1997, he led concerts with the Ravenna Festival orchestra in cities torn by violence and discord, including Sarajevo, Beirut, Yerevan, Jerusalem, Moscow, Istanbul, and even New York City in the wake of the September 11 attacks. These concerts, known as "Le Vie dell'Amicizia" ("The Roads to Friendship"), were meant to promote mutual understanding and to demonstrate that classical music is the common inheritance of us all.

Looking beyond politics, Muti also cultivated a scholarly side. Just months after the anti-nuclear concert in Philadelphia, he collaborated on a concert version of Verdi's *Macbeth* with the prolific opera critic Andrew Porter, who routinely called for presenting musical texts as accurately as possible. The two engaged in a lively discussion before the show to demonstrate how a new critical edition of the score reflected Verdi's wishes while cutting away generations of performance traditions that had nothing to do with the composer. Muti later collaborated with the distinguished musicologist and University of Chicago professor Philip Gossett on performances of other Italian operas. Daniel Barenboim, meanwhile, had openly rejected Gossett's work during his tenure in Chicago, calling his new critical edition of Verdi's *Requiem* "absolute nonsense." Gossett resigned his position as an orchestra trustee in response but later welcomed a collaboration with Muti and the orchestra on performances of the *Requiem* that ultimately dazzled the city.

As Andrew's first reviews indicate, Muti immediately charmed the city and became the focus of a courtship dance with Chicago Symphony president Deborah Rutter when he returned to the orchestra after an absence of over three decades. And Rutter knew that the dance had no guarantee of a marriage. Muti had danced with the New York Philharmonic after his 1999 debut, not long after Kurt Masur announced his resignation. His concerts there led composer Greg Sandow to call him "the Michael Jordan of conductors" as speculation about his imminent acceptance of an offer simmered to a boil.[3] But, to everyone's amazement but his own, Muti called off the engagement at the eleventh hour, citing his responsibilities at La Scala. The Big Apple fluttered again when Lorin Maazel, the Philharmonic's eventual choice, decided that he would leave the post in 2009. Muti, who had since given up his post in Milan, returned with sizzling guest appearances just before management announced that Alan Gilbert would be Maazel's successor and that Muti would serve as principal guest. New Yorkers sulked as they watched Rutter and the Chicago Symphony take the dance floor with Muti and end the night with a kiss. Muti's about-face after making repeated claims that he would never take over an American orchestra left one jilted Philharmonic player, a violist, to wonder, "I don't know what Chicago has that we don't have."[4]

Muti instantly won over the city with his charm in front of the public, especially by promising to continue his humanitarian mission of bringing classical music to ordinary people—"in schools, hospitals, even prisons," he told reporters. Several writers took jabs at Barenboim for not living up to similar ideals and hoped that Muti meant what he said. Following through on his word, the orchestra's Citizen Musician initiative and the formation of the Negaunee Music Institute made these ideals come to life on his watch. Under the auspices of these programs, orchestra musicians have continued to perform in local churches and detention centers. Muti also faced the inevitable challenges of a permanent director. Key principal players, including bassoon, clarinet, double bass, and horn, left or retired not long after his tenure began, but he rapidly appointed exceptional successors to the first three positions while the orchestra's second horn rose to the challenge as an outstanding acting principal.

Beyond the local community, Muti has continued focus on maintaining the orchestra's international preeminence by taking it on tour and supporting innovative digital projects. All the while, he has developed an eclectic but vibrant repertoire, expanding the orchestra's palette to include major works by Italians like Verdi and forgotten gems by a surprising cast of characters like Scriabin, Berlioz, Cherubini, and Shostakovich. Critics routinely praise his concert performances of Verdi's music as setting a new standard of musical and dramatic precision, elegance, and power.

: :

Andrew's portrait of Muti is by far the most personal, and it is therefore the richest of the four in this book. Andrew began covering Muti as the orchestra tried to woo him as its next director, and the two developed a deep friendship that leaps off the page in their interviews. The two bonded over a shared appreciation of the arts as Andrew followed Muti and the orchestra during its courtship dance. Over time, Muti shared his innermost thoughts about his childhood, his encounters with the Chicago community (including throwing out the first pitch at a Chicago Cubs baseball game!), the potential of music to bring about positive changes in society, and ultimately the profound meanings of specific musical works. Feeling comfortable with

FIGURE 4.1. Riccardo Muti leading the orchestra in Verona, Italy, on 2007 European tour. Photo by Todd Rosenberg. Used with permission.

Andrew, Muti puts his profound musical insight, sharp wit, passion for music, and embraceable humanity on full display in the interviews. And it becomes clear over the course of Muti's tenure that Andrew believed he could hear all these qualities in the orchestra's performances on stage.

DOUGLAS W. SHADLE

A Musical Romance

Anticipating His Return

Chicago Sun-Times, **September 9, 2007** On the eve of a full month of season-launching concerts at Orchestra Hall and then on tour across Europe with the Chicago Symphony Orchestra, at 66 Riccardo Muti appears relaxed and happy as he spends the first period of his adult life without a position as music director of a major international orchestra or opera house.

Having previously led the Maggio Musicale in Florence, the London Philharmonia, the Philadelphia Orchestra, and, for 19 years, Milan's La Scala, he is now, "How do you say? A free sword. A free lance. What can I tell you?" he says with a laugh.[5] "I am a Southern Italian man, which means that by nature I am lazy. So I am enjoying my freedom."

Muti knows that American orchestras would love to establish a relationship with one of the few conductors whose name and image still cause excitement in the larger world, to say nothing of his decades of experience. But the combination of his character, he says, and his intense loyalty to any orchestra he does lead, have caused him to turn down offers, twice, to head the New York Philharmonic and not to do much guest conducting beyond those ensembles with whom he already has long-standing relationships. This explains his absence from the CSO podium for an astonishing 32 years.

"I have nothing against America," Muti says, sipping a freshly brewed Italian espresso in his living room. "My years in Philadelphia were very happy. But I also know the Vienna Philharmonic first and best. And I have my new Luigi Cherubini orchestra in Ravenna for young Italian musicians. And now I make a relationship with Salzburg for their spring [Pentecost] festival where we explore the forgotten world of Napoli in opera and concert. It is a matter of time and emphasis."

So why come to Chicago now when the CSO is in the midst of a highly-publicized search for a music director? And why spend so much time with the orchestra? "First of all, please write it down that I am not a candidate for anything. I am not on any list. Not to be a music director, a president, or a pope! But Deborah Card—she is very persuasive. She courted me. And this orchestra is one of the great orchestras of the world—one with the highest standards—so it is also an honor. And an honor to take them on some Italian debuts [in Verona, Turin, and Rome]. But it is not a competition. I should have come last year, to wet the feet, but I could not. So this year we wet the feet and the whole body all at once and we do so in five nations!"

And if there is a good chemistry after "getting wet" together for a month? Could there be some sort of relationship? "Non posso vedere nel futuro! (I cannot see into the future.) But I hope we will at least like each other!"

First Chicago Concert after 32 Years

***Chicago Sun-Times*, September 14, 2007** The curiosity and excitement that was building for Friday night's opening of the Chicago Symphony Orchestra's 117th subscription season was far more than the usual anticipation of the new cultural year. Riccardo Muti was returning to Chicago for the first time in, astonishingly, 32 years.

The Italian maestro did not disappoint Friday, even if he offered up an odd program long on atmospherics and short on major compositions. Perhaps the highly independent musician wanted to show that he could find the musicality in any work and create a sense of suspense and artistic merit even in a series of pieces usually known more for being sonic showcases.

Certainly Prokofiev's 1928 Third Symphony in C minor, Op. 44, cobbled together from his then-unproduced opera, *The Fiery Angel*, is not much of a piece and its absence from the CSO's repertoire is wholly understandable. Yet Muti took this Soviet-era psychodrama and treated it with all of the respect and reverence that he might bring to a sacred "Stabat Mater." Each movement was given its own character with a remarkably enviable clarity. In the kitschy scherzo, Muti brought out an amazing transparency in the violins that made sure that enough was never too much.

This unusual delicacy, this sense of care, this ability to bring out the subtlest and quietest playing from the virtuoso principals of the orchestra's wind and brass sections wholly characterized the program's second half of Spanish and pseudo-Spanish music of de Falla and Ravel. Even Ravel's overprogrammed *Bolero* seemed to have been broken down to its basic structure and then ingeniously rebuilt anew.

This is a very special guest indeed.

Getting Better Acquainted

Chicago Sun-Times, **September 15, 2007** As in any relationship, the second date can be as or more revealing than the first in the world of the symphony orchestra. Riccardo Muti made his first appearance in 32 years with the Chicago Symphony Orchestra on Friday night and his second less than 24 hours later for Saturday's "opening night" gala concert at Symphony Center. By the second date, the Italian maestro almost seemed like an old friend.

There were distinct differences between the two concerts, even in the large portion of Iberian-themed works by de Falla and Ravel given both nights. Muti's four decades on the world's top podiums have been marked not only by his musical insights and skills but also by his cleverness and charm.

Friday night, the CSO's first "normal" subscription program, was essentially all business, with Muti shunning most solo bows and other divo trappings. He kept his stage movements to a minimum, although Chicagoans did get their first taste of the "Muti jump" a couple of times: Sometimes at a large crescendo the conductor propels himself straight up in the air like a child skipping rope.

Saturday night, before the many formally attired benefit patrons, we got Muti the showman. Opening the evening, the "Star-Spangled Banner" was played with the force and speed of the Italian national anthem at a World Cup match. In de Falla's second suite from his *Three-Cornered Hat*, Muti physically enacted much of the dance in his direction of the orchestra. And there were even solo bows with nods of the charismatic Neapolitan's famous center-parted long black hair.

But there were also interesting musical and stylistic points being made. In the repeated portions as well as the program's operatic excerpts from Verdi, Puccini, and Francesco Cilea, it was as if Muti was offering a musical argument, an Italianate alternative to the clear influence of Austro-German traditions under former music director Daniel Barenboim.

The overture to Verdi's *La forza del destino* told us the story of the opera, emotional as well as melodic. In three vocal excerpts, Muti showed that his European reputation as a superb orchestral accompanist and environment builder is well deserved.

On His Early Musical Experience

WFMT *Broadcast*, September 19, 2007

PATNER: I can't think of any other way to start than just to say thank you, Maestro, for coming back to Chicago and spending so much time with our orchestra.

MUTI: It's astonishing that I have not come here for thirty-two years. Actually it's very strange to see the same hall that you remember when you were young, and to see the hall rejuvenated, but I'm not rejuvenated at all.

PATNER: You're still juvent! You weren't missing from Chicago because you had done something bad or because someone didn't like you, but you have always in your career been very devoted to the orchestra or opera company that you are with at any particular time.

MUTI: When I came to Chicago in 1972, I started also with the Philadelphia Orchestra. Already in 1975 Ormandy spoke to me about the possibility of becoming principal guest conductor, the first time that somebody was appointed principal guest conductor during the long Ormandy era. And in 1979 I was appointed music director and kept that position until 1992. Already when I was principal guest conductor it was clear that I gave Philadelphia a sort of exclusivity. It was not a choice between the two orchestras, but one orchestra was giving me the possibility to become music director. I was young, and it was very exciting to be music director in one of the great orchestras in the world.

Also, when I was appointed music director in Philadelphia, I still was music director in Florence at the Maggio Musicale Fiorentino and music director in London with the Philharmonia Orchestra, so I had *three* positions. That is absolutely insane. Or, if we want to say, immoral, because a music director should only and exclusively take care of his orchestra. His own orchestra.

I left the Maggio Musicale Fiorentino first, and then I left the Philharmonia to devote myself to the Philadelphia Orchestra. Then, in 1986, came La Scala, and I was able to keep both positions in La Scala and in Philadelphia until 1992. I didn't want to leave the Philadelphia Orchestra because it was a love affair from the beginning to the end of my tenure there. But I realized that La Scala really needed a commitment from me. When I decided to leave the Philadelphia Orchestra, I remember that for weeks I was thinking about the moment I had to give the bad news to the orchestra. I will never forget when I said to the orchestra after rehearsal, "I have something to tell you." I will never forget the eyes of the musicians after I gave that announcement. But life forces you to make choices.

PATNER: There's a short novel by the writer Isaac Bashevis Singer called *Enemies: A Love Story* [Farrar, Straus, and Giroux, 1966]. It's about a man who without planning it winds up in three marriages at once. Perhaps you were extricating yourself also from this and didn't want to let go of the favorite wife before you took another favorite wife.

MUTI: I loved Philadelphia and I loved La Scala. Of course, La Scala gave me opportunities to do opera, which is one of my passions.

PATNER: When you have worked to go back to the intention of the composer, you have used the phrase, in both Italian and in English, that you are "driven" to this—driven to research. Where does that drive come from?

MUTI: I never, when I do an opera, or a symphony, just study the score. But I try to learn as much I can about the history of the composition and all the other elements. For example, one of the composers that I conduct and who is not very popular today is Luigi Cherubini. And you can't conduct Cherubini if you don't understand the entire Neoclassic world in art. There is a style in Cherubini that has nothing to do with Haydn, nothing to do with Gluck, nothing to do with Beethoven, but has Haydn, Beethoven, and Gluck and the Neapolitan school combined.

That I do also for Mozart. In Salzburg, Karajan invited me to do *Così fan tutte* in 1982. I was very scared, because to do *Così fan tutte*—an Italian conductor in Salzburg after nine years of the *Così fan tutte* of Karl Böhm—was like suicide. To be killed. But my approach came not from the music to the words but from the words to the music—so from Da Ponte to Mozart. I worked, I worked, and then I met an old musicologist in Vienna. As you know, *Così fan tutte* takes place in Napoli, my city. And I said, "You know, it's very strange why Mozart and Da Ponte put this story in Napoli. Napoli is mentioned only one time in the opera and there is nothing in the music, no element of the Neapolitan songs or Neapolitan atmosphere." And this old musicologist said to me, "You know, the story of *Così fan tutte* really took place in Vienna. And Mozart and Da Ponte wanted to tell the actual story between the two men and the two girls that exchange— you know, sort of a *ménage a quatre*. That happened in a village that now is part of Vienna, but at the time was a little bit outside Vienna. Neustadt." "Neustadt" means "Neapolis."

PATNER: Aha, of course.

MUTI: The origin of the name Napoli comes from Greek, "Neapolis." "Neapolis" in German is "neue Stadt." So they were telling the story that happened in Neustadt, saying it was Napoli.

PATNER: They played a little game, and they both loved games.

MUTI: This is not essential for the interpretation of the opera but it's an answer to why the opera takes place in Napoli.

PATNER: I'm still curious—there are conductors, some of them of great accomplishment, who spend more intuitive time and much less time on the research. Was this interest in research something that grew over time or was it something from your family or your childhood?

MUTI: It comes from my teachers, from my family. This was always part of my education.

PATNER: Your father was a medical doctor and interested in music. I think he sang.

MUTI: He sang very well. He lived in Molfetta, on the Adriatic, twenty-five kilometers north of Bari. So, we are talking about

the south part of the Adriatic coast. These towns of the south
of Italy were all very musical because Italy was united a little bit
more than 100 years ago, but before that those regions made
up the Kingdom of the Two Sicilies, and the capitol was Napoli,
where there was an important musical college and the conservatory. One of the most important in the world. So all the poor
families sent boys and girls to the conservatory—mainly boys—
to study music, hoping that they could become important musicians or become important singers, become rich, and help the
family. The region has a great musical tradition. My father sang
when he was twenty-one years old with a local orchestra that
was made of professional people and nonprofessional people.
He even sang the Verdi *Requiem* and Rossini *Stabat Mater*. When
I was thirteen or fourteen years old and was starting to play the
piano, I accompanied my father in the *Stabat Mater* of Rossini
and the Verdi *Requiem* at home. So this music is part of my soul,
of my body.

My father thought that it was important to learn music but
never thought that I would have the qualities to become a very
well-known musician. That came little by little. When I was
fifteen years old I decided to go to Bari, to the conservatory
and do the examinations for the fifth year of the course. The
piano course in Italy takes ten years, so you must do the examinations in the fifth year, then after the eighth year, and then
the diploma. Even though I didn't study at the conservatory,
I wanted to take the examinations to have a degree one day,
just for my pleasure.

At that time the director of the conservatory in Bari was
Nino Rota.[6] Everyone knows about Rota's music for [Federico]
Fellini's *La Strada*, and others. Rota was really a wonderful musician. He was not generally at that time there for the examinations because he was busy with Fellini writing the music for
one of his films. But that day—destiny—he was there. We were
many boys and girls waiting to do this examination and at 2:00

afternoon, so very hot, in Bari, south of Italy, the end of July, very hot, 40 degrees or something.

PATNER: In the 90s in Fahrenheit. Or a hundred degrees.

MUTI: He opened the door and said, "How many are left?" And we were three boys, and I didn't want to do the examination that day because I felt very nervous, so I said, "We are only three but can we come tomorrow?" He looked at me, he said, "Who are you?" and I said, "My name is Muti. I come from Molfetta." And he looked deeply in my eyes and then he said, "Come with me." And then he brought me into another room where there was a piano, and said, "Play something." The official committee was continuing with the examination of the other students, but I played the Polonaise of Chopin in G-sharp minor. And he said, "No, you will do the exam today." So then I did the examination and at the end of the performance he said, "We have given you the maximum of the votes. The highest vote. Not for how you have played today but for the way you will play or can play tomorrow."

PATNER: It's like an experience of poetry.

MUTI: I went home and gave the news to my father. My father couldn't believe it. In September my father went to Bari because he had to make some visits to patients. I went with him and the driver. And because one of the visits was very long, I said to the driver, "Why don't we go to the conservatory because I want to see all the votes?" Dieci. Ten, you know, to see this—

PATNER: Your great moment.

MUTI: I knew that those were the votes, but I wanted to see them. So I was there and that same day Rota came back to the conservatory. He had been absent from the conservatory since the day I did the examination and he came back that day and I was looking at these votes, and he passed and then he stopped and said, "But are you Muti?" He said, "What are you doing here?" I said, "I just came." And then he called me into his office and he said, "You know, I think that you should be part of this conservatory, because then you meet other students and you will hear the way they play."

So we had a family council. We are talking about the mentality of old Italian families. Even from Molfetta to Bari, where the conservatory is only twenty-five kilometers away, to go alone was something extremely dangerous to think about. I remember it was my mother, my father, my grandfather, and they thought about it and they decided, yes, I could go to Bari. So in the morning I started in the classical liceo, where I studied eight years of Latin and five years of Greek, too.[7] At that time the schools were very tough. And three times a week in the afternoon I went to Bari.

And then my family moved back to Napoli, which was the victory of my mother. My mother was Neapolitan and couldn't wait for the moment when she could force my father to move to Napoli. And so the entire family moved to Napoli and what about me? Should I stay in Bari or should I go to Napoli? So we went to speak to Nino Rota, and he again proved to be a great man. He said, "In one year this boy has learned so much that now the conservatory of Bari is too small for him. Napoli is a very important conservatory, and I will write a letter to the director of conservatory in Napoli to recommend him."

PATNER: Rota's music for Fellini is like a commentary on what is going on in the film, a kind of underscoring that tells you about characters. Obviously, he was someone who could look into somebody.

MUTI: When you hear the music of Rota, immediately you think about Fellini. And when you see the movies of Fellini, you hear the music of Rota. Even if the volume is very low. That was a collaboration that was very similar to that of Prokofiev and Eisenstein. Many times Prokofiev wrote the music first, and Eisenstein created the image on the music written before. And sometimes this was the case also between Fellini and Rota.

I loved him. He was an incredible musician. And very

refined. Even when you conduct the music of the Fellini movies, you have to know that he was an extremely fine musician. He played *Wozzeck* by memory. I saw him. When we hear [*sings*], the theme of *La Strada*, we think that maybe he was a very light musician. It's not true. He knew the entire repertoire, and he was a wonderful pianist also. And he could play *Wozzeck* by memory.

Touring Together in Europe

Chicago Sun-Times, October 14, 2007 "Amour, toujours l'amour." So the French have said since they invented love. The Chicago Symphony Orchestra, under the podium leadership for the past month of Riccardo Muti, might make the same observations of its just-completed swing through Europe, which began with a three-city Italian campaign, swept through Germany, nested for several days in Paris and tunneled under the English Channel by "Chunnel" train to wrap up its embrace in London.

Audiences and critics were enraptured, and in London at tour's end Muti and orchestra leaders from both management and the players' elected representatives fell over each other publicly praising the connection established between the now free-lance Italian maestro and the American orchestra searching for a new music director.

"Never in my 40-year career have I ended such a month wishing it would not end and feeling both refreshed and challenged," Muti told players, patrons and guests at a reception atop the recently refurbished Royal Festival Hall, where the CSO had just played two sold-out concerts. "I know that I want to have a strong and close relationship with you in the future."

Presenting in his unusual repertoire of Tchaikovsky, Hindemith, Scriabin, Prokofiev, de Falla, Ravel and Schubert a sort of summary of the contributions of the CSO's modern leaders, he displayed the ensemble's embodiment of Fritz Reiner's standards, Jean Martinon's eclectic programming, Solti's electricity and muscularity, Daniel Barenboim's rare flexibility, and Carlo Maria Giulini's refined elegance.

In the words of principal clarinet Larry Combs, retiring at the end of this season after 34 years with the CSO and on his last tour outside of the United States, "Muti has a way of being highly respectful and deferring to us as players and soloists while at the same time getting us to give our best and give him the results that he wants. There is something that is very mutually gratifying about that and helps to account for the success he is achieving."

"At this point in my life," Muti told me over lunch in London, "I am sure that nothing happens without a reason. There must be a reason that this great orchestra and I have come together at this moment in our histories. And I am really thinking hard about what this should mean."

Announced as New Music Director

Chicago Sun-Times, **May 6, 2008** Confirming what had been an open secret, the Chicago Symphony Orchestra has appointed the charismatic and renowned Italian conductor Riccardo Muti as its music director, beginning with the 2010–2011 season.

"Something excites me very much about this orchestra, these players, this dynamic city of Chicago, the leadership of this organization," said Muti, who has been a much-sought-after free-lance conductor since leaving La Scala in 2005 after a 19-year run. "It was not what I was expecting, but it is what I am excited about."

Known for his youthful appearance and a wide repertoire ranging from the Baroque to the contemporary, Muti will be the oldest incoming music director in the CSO's history. The legendary Fritz Reiner was 64 at his CSO appointment in 1953.

"At this point in my life, I don't have to prove [anything] to anyone," said Muti, "but I want both to devote myself to making music with the Chicago Symphony and to bringing music to the many communities of Chicago and to new generations. This is our future."

Triumph in the Verdi *Requiem*

What Kind of Work Is It?

> ***WFMT Broadcast**, January 14, 2009*
>
> PATNER: The Verdi *Requiem*—a requiem, a concert work, an opera?
>
> MUTI: Verdi's *Requiem* certainly is not an opera, but it is a great work of a great opera composer. Verdi in the *Requiem* uses the same language that he used in his operas. His operas are full of human feelings. And the same thing is true of the *Requiem*. The text that is one of the most terrifying texts of Christianity, in the language of Verdi, becomes not a work of Christians praying their God, but a work that underlines the pains and the worry and the fear of all of us, considering what our future will be.
>
> This work represents exactly the way the Italians, the Latins in general, but the Italians in particular, create a relationship with God. In the Lutheran or German or other religions, the relationship between man and God is of great respect or great faith in what will be the future—or even if you don't believe in God, there is a certain atmosphere of friendship between man and God, of trust. In Verdi it's exactly the contrary. There is a war between man and God, practically from the first note of the chorus, "Requiem." It's not a statement. The chorus asks for peace. And this is very important for the way the chorus should sing the first word. It's not a passive way of saying "requiem" but you are asking for *requiem*. That means, "You, God, you have created me. I exist because it's your responsibility, so you must take care of me and of my salvation."
>
> PATNER: It's a demand.
>
> MUTI: It's "we demand." And this is the general attitude that still exists in some cities or churches or religious communities in Italy, especially in the south. For example, in Napoli, where the patron is San Gennaro, this saint is very famous.[8] Not only because he's the patron of Napoli, but because his blood is in the church of Napoli. And this blood is supposed to liquefy two

or three times a year. When the blood is to liquefy, the church
is full of people that are waiting for this event. And when the
blood doesn't liquefy, that will bring bad luck, bad things like
wars or earthquake. The people start to scream against the saint,
to say bad words, calling him by bad names.

PATNER: So rather than the people saying, "Oh," beating themselves,
"we didn't do enough, we need to throw ourselves down," they
start to scream at the saint and say, "You are not fulfilling your
side of the deal."

MUTI: "You must take your responsibility. You want to judge my
sins. You want to judge my faults, but you must do something
for me, and I demand that you make me free for eternal life." So
this conflict is one of the most dramatic aspects of the *Requiem*.
In Bruckner, in Brahms, the attitude is completely different.
There is a tenderness. There is a melancholy. There is a kindness
that in Verdi doesn't exist.

The "Dies irae" ["Day of wrath"] of the *Requiem* is a moment
of terror, and when the soprano in the end of the piece the
soprano says, "tremens," "I am trembling," "et temeo," "I am
afraid," then there is a long silence and that silence is really terrifying because the soprano that represents the entire world of
men and women, she waits for the answer. And Verdi writes
"lunga pausa," long silence. That silence is incredibly dramatic
because we are waiting for the answer of God to our prayer. And
after a long silence the answer is the coming back of the "Dies
irae," even stronger and more aggressive and more tragic. In fact
the finale of the *Requiem* when the soprano says the last phrase,
"Libera me, Domine, de morte æterna," and the *Requiem* answers
with the chord of C major, with the tonality that generally is
the tonality of serenity, of delight, of tranquility, in the *Requiem*
this chord takes a color that is very disturbing because it doesn't
give us a feeling of quietness, but becomes a sort of big question
mark. It's not "I am sure that you are going to make me free."
There is a question mark. "Libera me, Domine," but is it going
to happen? Nobody knows.

For that reason, the entire question about whether Verdi was somebody who believed or was he agnostic, somebody that didn't believe? This is a nonquestion. A composer that wrote such a music certainly had fear for the future. He had fear for the presence of this lady dressed in black that is waiting for all of us.

It's not an operatic piece, but the writing and the orchestration, the way he uses the voice, certainly comes from a composer that was familiar with operas. The score is full of pianissimo. Generally, the Verdi *Requiem* is played like a showpiece with effects. But studying the score, we see that it is a score with more piano and pianissimo than fortissimo. And it's interesting that Verdi wanted for the *Requiem* special voices. In fact he insisted that for the tenor he wanted the voice of a priest. It's difficult to define what is the voice of a priest. Certainly he didn't want a tenor that started like he's singing *Aida*. Because the words that the tenor is singing at the beginning, "Kyrie eleison," mean, "Lord, God, have mercy." Many times singers sing the *Requiem* like an opera, but they should sing it like a religious piece of music with a text that is extremely important for understanding the music itself.

PATNER: I felt a sense of the conversational in the rehearsal. These people speaking as human voices and as characters in Verdi's drama, it's another way he seems to bridge these different musical worlds of opera, drama, concert, and religious text.

MUTI: In fact, the tempi that I take during the several numbers are never the same because there is a flexibility as you just said that is not written in the score but comes from the understanding of the words. The words guide the music; the music does not absorb the words. So it's a conversation. This should also be true in the instruments. I said to the violins in the beginning, when they play [*sings phrase*] before the chorus comes in, they should play [*sings phrase again*] thinking that this is "Requiem" [*sings phrase again*].

PATNER: They're singing the text.

MUTI: It's not just that you play *espressivo*. You must play knowing exactly that those notes are notes that indicate the word
"Requiem." Even if nobody's singing in that moment.

PATNER: How has your relationship with the piece changed in the
years that you have performed it?

MUTI: You know I come from the school of Antonino Votto, and
Antonino Votto was the assistant of Toscanini. He learned the
Requiem from Toscanini. And so it's a direct line from Toscanini. But in the years, even if the roots are the same, the piece
has changed because I have changed. When I started to conduct the *Requiem*, I was around thirty years old. I have more
than doubled my age, and so many things have happened in my
life. And I think that for a piece like the *Requiem*, full of human
feelings, everything you have experienced in your life—good
experiences, bad experiences, happiness, sadness—these are all
elements that you bring to the score. And of course when I did
the first *Requiem*, there was great excitement to approach such
a masterpiece. But I had my life in front of me. Now most of my
life is behind me so when I conduct the *Requiem* in many places,
it's like the contact, the physical contact with the—I don't want
to sound rhetorical, but—the end of life. The colors of the first
Requiem that I conducted were still colors of the springtime.
Now they are the colors of autumn.

PATNER: One thing that is new for you quite recently is that a
few months ago you for the first time conducted the *German
Requiem* of Brahms. I'm curious, now, with them kind of back-
to-back, if you see any illumination of one by the other.

MUTI: The two pieces are completely different. And they represent
two different cultures. And definitely two different approaches
to death.

PATNER: One is the pastor, the shepherd welcoming the sheep back
and the other—

MUTI: Is a fight.

PATNER: It's a fight!

MUTI: As I said to the orchestra, to the chorus, to understand the

Verdi *Requiem*, you have to visit the cemeteries of the big Italian
cities. The cemetery of Napoli, cemetery of Rome. The big one.
The old ones. They are so scary that even the dead people want
to get out. They don't want to stay there. And they are terrifying cities. They are *città della morte*, cities of the dead. It's not
this is a garden where there are the stones and you bring the
flowers and you bring your dog, or you can sit and have a picnic.
You really enter—it's like Dante in the *Divina Commedia*, when
he started saying, "Per me si va nella città dolente, per me si va
ne l'etterno dolore, per me si va tra la perduta gente." This is the
beginning of the "Inferno" of Dante. Through me, through this
door, "Per me si va nella città dolente." In the city full of pains.
"Per me si va ne l'etterno dolore"—Through me you go in the
eternal *dolore*. It's pain.

PATNER: Sadness. Sorrow.

MUTI: Sorrow. "Per me si va tra la perduta gente." Through me you
go among the lost people. This is the "Inferno" of Dante. And the
Verdi *Requiem* is the fear of the inferno. The color is extremely
dark. But Verdi, he's searching for light. In fact at the beginning,
just F-sharp in a chord creates the illumination of the entire
atmosphere. Verdi could create an entire dramatic situation
with one chord. The orchestra was laughing because I said "one
goes from a B-flat chord," the beginning of "lux aeterna" there is
a B-flat chord, and then suddenly the next bar, a D major chord,
without any modulation. And that D major chord with this
F-sharp comes when the mezzo-soprano says, "Lux æterna," the
eternal light. So I said, "With one change of harmony, Verdi creates an entire different world." And to make them laugh I said,
"Wagner needs three hours." With all the love and respect for
Wagner of course.

Showing What Makes a Great Conductor

Chicago Sun-Times, **January 17, 2009** By programming Verdi's great
Requiem for his first concerts as the official music director-designate

of the Chicago Symphony, Riccardo Muti offered his soon to be orchestral home base a work he has been identified with for more than 30 years; it's also a work that makes some of the greatest demands on an orchestra, chorus and a quartet of vocalists.

From the moment Thursday that he walked out onto Orchestra Hall's stage till the last notes 90 minutes later, Muti showed us the summary of nearly every possible positive quality of a great conductor.

Muti sees the 1874 masterwork as a distillation of everything Verdi knew about the Italian character and spirit as much as what he had gained as the reinventor of Italian opera. The *Requiem*, for Muti, as for Verdi, is not simply an opera in the guise of a sacred work. Rather, it is a marriage of everything from Etruscan paganism to Neapolitan superstition to human psychology with the ancient rites of the Latin Church.

So, yes, the "Dies irae" thrills and envelops us with its massive force. But it is ever of a part with the singing of the strings, the eerie quiet of the opening passages, the lyricism of the tenor's "Ingemisco," the poignancy of the soprano-mezzo duets of the "Recordare" and the "Agnus Dei."

The CSO played on the edge of its collective seat throughout. Concertmaster Robert Chen led the violins from tender melodies through impossible tremolos. Winds all shined and the brass played not only with its customary power but with a full range of volume and emotion. Percussionist Cynthia Yeh and her bass drums and timpanist Vadim Karpinos offered visual as well as musical excitement.

Some 170 voices sang as one, powered from the bottom ranges, standing and delivering on cue with equal parts passion and precision. Each vocal soloist, from the formidable mezzo Olga Borodina to rising tenor Mario Zeffiri and bass Ildar Abdrazakov to Muti favorite soprano Barbara Frittoli, was there only for the music; solos were for Verdi, not the rafters, and I have never heard such a meditative and balanced quartet.

Austria v. Germany

On How Austrians and Germans Differ

WFMT Broadcast, October 19, 2009

PATNER: Your career spans a period when Bruckner was in some
ways reintroduced into the standard repertoire.

MUTI: In my years as a conductor I have conducted Bruckner mainly
with two orchestras, the Berlin Philharmonic and the Vienna
Philharmonic. With the Berlin Philharmonic I recorded two of
Bruckner's symphonies, the Fourth and the Sixth. The other
symphonies I have done with the Vienna Philharmonic. So I've
learned this music, this style, from the Vienna Philharmonic.
Next year will be forty years that I've conducted regularly every
year with the Vienna Philharmonic. When I started with them in
1971, I used to call them professors. Now I am the oldest practi
cally because they retire at the age of sixty-five!

So this repertoire I've learned from them and it has been
always a great joy for me to work with them, with a sort of combination of the Italian culture, the Italian temperament, and the
Austrian-Germanic culture and tradition. They seem to love the
way I do Bruckner, and especially the Second Symphony that in
a way is the most Italian of the Bruckner symphonies because
it's a symphony where everything sings from the first theme
to the end. The last movement is a sort of improvisation like
Bruckner is sitting on the organ and he's improvising. But everything sings from the first note to the end. And I personally don't
like Bruckner as very Germanic, but more as Austrian.

PATNER: There is a distinction.

MUTI: Big distinction, as the Austrians like to underline. Bruckner
is the extension of the world of Schubert. And in fact Bruckner
reflects in his music the sense of nature. You must be familiar
not only with the philosophical or religious culture of Austria,
but also with this feeling for nature that is very much present
in the music of Bruckner. In Mahler you have the same element,

but in Mahler everything is much more dramatic and pessimistic. In Bruckner you have always this attitude of the composer thanking God and in a way God is not the Catholic God, even if he was the organist St. Florian, God is nature itself. You feel the fact that Bruckner, when he was a boy, to go to school from Linz had to go from his house through trees and mountains, and this sense of nature, of this wonderful country you can feel in his music. Of course, there are different ways of approaching this composer. Some are very much on the basis of the religious element, but I think that every music when it's not connected with one specific reason, that is social or ethical, or religious, becomes more universal. So you can convey your feelings through the music.

PATNER: I was amazed on the tour that the CSO just made that in the notes, when they were performing the Bruckner Seventh with Maestro Haitink in Paris, the annotator from the orchestra there stated, "This is a piece about the crucifixion, and the four movements represent the four corners of the cross."

MUTI: To say that the four movements are different moments of a crucifixion means to change the Bruckner symphony into program music. I think that the writer of this program went a little bit too far. Because then you have to try to underline wood, hammers, and all these things.

PATNER: Look for things that might not be there.

MUTI: Even in the most prosaic program music like Respighi and the famous fountains or pines, in the moment of the performance you don't think about the specific views of the Appia Antica or the fountains of this square or the other square. Music at a certain point is music and has the great advantage to be an art that doesn't exist in a concrete way. A painting, you see . . . or a sculpture. Music, if the musicians don't produce a sound, doesn't exist. And when the music stops there is no music anymore.

Music is an expression of feelings and it's important to say to the public that music doesn't describe anything. It's only an evo-cation of feelings.

But Bruckner was a composer whose music was very much used and abused in certain horrible periods of our history. And to make Bruckner like a sort of gigantic expression of superman, of super power, a little bit connected to the music of Wagner—this huge crescendo of Wagner that reaches climaxes where the orchestra produces enormous sound—always we should play this considering that he was an organist and of course the organ in the church can create enormous quantity of sounds—but still not the sound of sound *effects*. Sometimes in Mahler there are elements that can be effects of speaking about nature or about this or that instrument, but in Bruckner there are no ornaments in his music. Everything is substance; at least he tries to be this way.

PATNER: We spoke last time about the Verdi *Requiem* and also about your first experiences with the Brahms *Requiem* that you did with the Vienna Philharmonic and soloists. You're going to be playing it for the first time in Chicago. Now that you've been living with the piece for a couple of years, I'm wondering what some of your recent reflections on the Brahms have been.

MUTI: There is a text, but I would not say that it is a programma-tic music. The text is beautiful words that he selected for the requiem. And this requiem is completely the opposite of the Verdi *Requiem*. The Verdi *Requiem* is battle, is a fight, between man and God. In Brahms everything is much more gentle. His approach is optimistic. Just the first words, "We will be ... blessed." We will be blessed, we will be glorified—his approach is like the mother. There is an element of *caritas*.

PATNER: *Caritas*, charity.

MUTI: Charity. It's like a caress. Even if in a certain moment it's very, very, very dramatic—but never—almost never dark.

PATNER: Seeing your gestures, which the radio audience is missing, we might say perhaps that in the Verdi there is a hand raised up,

not as a fighting fist, but as a shaking questioning one, and in
the Brahms there is a hand held out and another hand perhaps
giving a caress.

Bruckner Second Symphony

Chicago Sun-Times, **October 15, 2009** Mozart's D Major Haffner Symphony No. 35, K. 385, is a brief, high-spirited, and festive work and
a Muti favorite. It's also a piece about new beginnings as Mozart
wrote its first version as a serenade in 1782 while still in Salzburg
and reworked it the next year when he had escaped to his own life in
Vienna. Muti used it as his own seasonal calling card, demonstrating
his strong belief that delineating formal structure is a key to understanding a work of music and bringing it to life.

In a program that balances his interest in popular works and the
margins of the repertoire, as well as precision and lyricism, refinement and passion, Muti lit an electrical charge with his first step onto
the Armour Stage that did not end until his now-customary "bye-
bye" wave almost two hours and two symphonies later.

That insight serves him especially well in the program's large
work, Bruckner's C minor Second Symphony in the Nowak edition
of its 1877 version. This is early Bruckner, though first written when
the hesitant composer was almost 50. It is in some ways a primer, a
brief, for ideas and concepts that Bruckner would develop and perfect further in his later great works in the genre. Muti sees the piece
as not so much a break with the past as a continuation of Schubert's
symphonic efforts, and, no great surprise here, as the most Italianate
of Bruckner's works.

He finds courtly dances in the opening moderato movement and
has at the service of his interest in detail the Barenboim-recharged
string sections, which he treats as separate choirs, as the score requires but rarely receives.

In a piece with even more stops and starts than the better-known
Bruckner behemoths, Muti paces to perfection with the composer's
silences as clear and as moving as his many notes. His tempos are

brisk, shaving about five minutes off of more standard timings, but are never hurried, and, as always with Muti, he never overexplains in his interpretations. Bruckner, even early on, has plenty to say, and Muti lets him say it, in his own quizzical yet strangely hypnotic voice.

This work is a concert rarity, not even played by the Bruckner-besotted CSO since it recorded it with Sir Georg Solti in 1991 during his farewell season. This also means that at least a third of the orchestra has never played the piece before. They dug in with glee, demonstrating their strengths at every turn and with especially beautiful playing by the wind and horn principals.

Brahms "German Requiem"

Chicago Sun-Times, October 22, 2009   Last week's elegant and lyrical performances of Bruckner's Second Symphony showed that Muti could play a too-neglected work of this Austrian master without seeming just to bring coals to the CSO's Bruckner-rich Newcastle.

Thursday night was another example of the unexpected with the much-loved Brahms *A German Requiem*, Op. 45 (1865–1868), a work that the Italian conductor had added to his repertoire only last year, at the age of 67, for concerts with the Vienna Philharmonic at the Salzburg Festival.

Muti not only loves music, he loves studying it and it was remarkable to hear what a conductor with more than 40 years of experience with both symphonic and operatic works brought to a concert-hall staple. Here was the same level of razor-sharp analysis of every measure and phrase, the attention to balance and interplay of sections, and the support for and implicit understanding of choral singing that marked his offerings last season of his countryman Verdi's own *Requiem*, a work Muti could probably conduct in his sleep.

Under the late Sir Georg Solti, the Brahms could be a set of sonic explosions, for James Levine at Ravinia a display of polished beauty, and for Daniel Barenboim a roller coaster of psychic peaks and valleys. Muti for his part starts and stays with the score. The young Brahms chose the scriptural passages he did, those from both the

Hebrew Bible and the New Testament dealing with consolation and peace for the most part, to make a very humane response to death, not one that followed any traditional religious ritual or tradition. Every musical passage, in Muti's view, is tied into and relates and responds to these texts.

So brasses were muted but not silenced. Strings were foremost, always meditative. And wind lines ran through each section like threads of gold. Urgency was applied where the score demanded it and the timpani rolls of assistant principal Vadim Karpinos and the choruses that do deal with fear or dread appeared in proper measure making the whole work cohere as a philosophical statement.

The Chicago Symphony Chorus, prepared by Duain Wolfe and Muti himself, sounded as it hasn't since last year's Verdi, gentle and commanding in equal measure and in appropriate turn. Canadian baritone Russell Braun and Swedish soprano Elin Rombo seemed still to be settling in on Thursday but their contributions remained of a piece with a performance that was all about not only the audience listening to Brahms but every member of the orchestra and chorus listening to each other. As the baritone soloist sings, "Behold, I tell you a mystery."

And a wholly beautiful and moving one at that.

Celebrating His Arrival

Outdoors at Millennium Park

Chicago Sun-Times, **September 20, 2010** It was Riccardo Muti's desire to make his first appearance as the Chicago Symphony's 10th music director by offering what he has termed "a gift to the people of a great city." He delivered Sunday evening with a "Free Concert for Chicago" before a Millennium Park crowd estimated at some 25,000 people. Perhaps in recognition of the feast day of San Gennaro, patron saint of Muti's native Naples, predictions of rain or high winds came to nothing. And the orchestra itself played its collective heart as well as its legendary technical command to its outer limits.

This is Muti, after all, the southern Italian and the seemingly in-congruous combination of scholar and showman. And so this was repertoire that's not exactly been at the heart of the orchestra's Germanic and Central European tradition. But why not, especially in this unique outdoor setting, on a beautiful evening on one of the last nights of summer, before an audience with at least as many new-comers as veteran orchestra buffs, offer a program of a Verdi opera overture and a Liszt tone poem, Tchaikovsky's *Romeo and Juliet* and Respighi's *The Pines of Rome*?

If you want to know why Verdi's operas remain both popular and daunting to perform, listen to the care Muti brings to the overture to *La forza del destino*. A story is told, characters are introduced, themes are laid out, resolutions are achieved, all in the course of eight or nine minutes. And if a conductor can find delicacy in Liszt's *Les préludes*, there's a lot he can mine from Berlioz and Strauss and Schumann and Brahms in the months ahead.

When Tchaikovsky's *Romeo and Juliet* "Fantasy-Overture" is played from the score, as it was here, it's a much more fascinating work than the great cauldron of soup that is stirred up by too many other hands. I never thought I'd hear the so-oft-played love theme in a way that connoted young love and not old kitsch, but there it was, and not just at the first appearance either.

Italian pride was in full throttle with Respighi's *Pines*, a work introduced to the United States by the composer himself with the CSO in 1926. Muti showed that it can be played with head as well as heart on sleeve.

Verdi's *Otello*

On Verdi Opera

WFMT Broadcast, March 31, 2011
MUTI: *Otello* is the last opera, Verdi said, that he wrote for the pub-lic. Because *Falstaff* he wrote for himself.

I think that Verdi always puts himself, almost in an autobiographic way, in his operas. For example, the feeling of love in the Verdi operas changes all the time. In *Otello* of course we have Shakespeare there, but the jealousy, this feeling of jealousy, so strong in *Otello*, and the sense of mature love, is what belongs really to the soul of Verdi. Verdi at the time of *Ballo in maschera* would not write a love duetto like the finale of the first act with the cellos. That is where Otello and Desdemona exchange feelings and memories.

PATNER: It's a retrospective. It's something that would come from someone who has lived life.

MUTI: As Massimo Mila, one of the greatest musicologists we had in Italy, wrote, this is a love of a man of seventy years old. It's very mature. It's not the beast full of passion that, in *Ballo in Maschera*'s Riccardo, is different. And in Falstaff is completely different again. It's a sort of virginal love again, no? Love of youth. And so *Otello* is a very autobiographic opera. We must not forget that in that time Verdi also had a big passion for Teresa Stoltz. She was the great friend of Angelo Mariani, the great Verdi conductor born in Ravenna. He's buried in Genoa. But he's from Ravenna and he was a great Verdi conductor and he had a discreet passion for Teresa Stoltz. And they became enemies, Verdi and Mariani. Then Mariani brought Wagner to Italy. The arrival of Wagner in Italy happened for many reasons.[9]

PATNER: Yes, it was provoked.

MUTI: In every opera Verdi approaches all the feelings of friendship of jealousy, of his vision of paradise or inferno in a way that really exactly corresponds to the same period of his life. I am convinced that in every opera, in every protagonist of the opera, the real protagonist is Verdi himself.

PATNER: *Otello* works in a concert hall in a way that some operas don't.

MUTI: I believe that most of the operas work very well in concert.

PATNER: Most of the Verdi operas or most of any operas?

MUTI: Most of Verdi operas [but also Wagner's]. I remember when I did the *Ring* in La Scala, *Rheingold* was for several reasons done in concert form. That was the only one that was done in concert form, and was the one that had the biggest success because the people were concentrated on the music and on the words. I'm not against the productions even though I have had problems with the directors.

PATNER: Particular ones?

MUTI: I had many problems with some even famous directors when it was clear to me that they didn't know anything about music. Just created something. So the creation on stage fights against the music. Especially in Verdi, every chord is not there just to make a sound. There is always a dramatic meaning. Verdi, in this way, comes directly from Mozart. So unless you have a great director that helps you to understand, it's better that you concentrate on the text of *Otello* that is so beautiful that if it's translated well, people really can follow every word that corresponds directly to that note.

Verdi is different from Wagner. In Wagner you have one phrase that is in ten minutes of music. No? In Verdi every word is connected with that specific note. And so the production can be destroyed if the director is not clever enough or musical enough to understand this. This is a true story that Antonino Votto told me. He was conducting in La Scala. He was a very famous conductor from South America. And he conducted a lot in La Scala in the twenties. And he was conducting *Tristan*. Toscanini was a great Wagner conductor. He loved Wagner very much, so he brought a friend to La Scala to hear *Tristan*. And so, you know, there's beautiful music going on and going on and going on. Toscanini said to the friend, "Now you can see the difference between Verdi and Wagner. Here you see that there are ten minutes the characters are saying, 'My name is this, your name is that, how do you do, how do you do.' Verdi at this point—he would've already made three children." So this a story from Arturo Toscanini.

Otello in Concert

Chicago Sun-Times, April 9, 2011 This is what it's all been about. Why journalists worldwide have been following Italian conductor Riccardo Muti's recent health problems, his actions and statements to defend the cultural life of his homeland and his plans as music director of the Chicago Symphony Orchestra as if he were on the level of a major sports star.

I'd seen two of his staged performances of Verdi's *Otello* in Salzburg in 2008, so I knew the excitement that he generates with this score, which he knows with a scholar's care and a lover's eyes. But to have this work performed here on Thursday night before a packed Orchestra Hall audience, and to see and hear the Chicago Symphony Orchestra and Chorus wanting to give everything with this work, was enough to supply goosebumps even to the most seasoned concertgoers. The roar of the crowd when Muti took the stage after the vocal soloists were in their places was out of another time.

Verdi's operatic setting, with librettist Arrigo Boito, of the Shakespeare tragedy opens with its own roar with its famous orchestral and choral storm scene, still one of the most thrilling moments in music. No one, not even Georg Solti, whose last Chicago concerts were of this same work, gets the "charge" of this scene better than Muti. But even more important, Muti keeps the tension of that charge—and its appropriate changes and alterations—for the 2½ hours of nearly continuous music. Muti offers not a moment of manipulation or added effect. Story and music are wed, the opera is in the drama.

The chorus, prepared by Duain Wolfe and Muti, offered oceans of sound, with superb supplemental work from the Chicago Children's Choir.

But the orchestra told the story. For decades, Muti and University of Chicago musicologist Philip Gossett have argued Verdi is a composer at the level of any other in the concert-hall tradition. From the strings, cello ensembles, viola choir, brass attacks, bassoon and harp lines becoming individual characters, the case was made. Home run. Grand slam. Touchdown. Viva Muti. Viva Verdi.

A Celebratory Welcome at Carnegie Hall

Chicago Sun-Times, April 18, 2011 The first Carnegie Hall concerts of
the Chicago Symphony Orchestra with its music director Riccardo
Muti showed both of the happy sides of this newly minted cultural
coin.

Carnegie Hall is ... well, Carnegie Hall, an international pinnacle,
an American showcase, an acoustical temple. To it come the boldface
names, especially when another boldface name is also on the podium.
There in the first tier Friday night for a concert performance of Verdi's
Otello was Francis Ford Coppola with Cristina Muti, the conductor's
wife and herself an opera stage director. A few boxes away: legendary mezzo Marilyn Horne. Pianist Emanuel Ax. Ravinia's James Con-
lon. Down the aisle from us on the main floor parquet: bass-baritone
superstar Bryn Terfel. Music biographer and Muti confidant Harvey
Sachs. And critics ... in numbers you wouldn't believe.

But to it also come the true connoisseurs, the music teachers and
students, the European and Asian immigrants and refugees, "the
children of the paradise" who fill the back of the upper balcony. And
when the program at this showcase for symphony orchestras and solo
recitals holds an opera—and a Verdi opera led by the greatest Verdi
conductor active today at that—you can add the vocal coaches and
singers, the opera fanatics and the kind of people who shout "Viva
Muti!" as if they were at La Scala in Milan or the Rome Opera. New
Yorkers are a bit starved for Muti in opera: He has conducted only
once at the Metropolitan here, a year ago. But even with a rare and
much lesser Verdi work, *Attila*, audiences and critics alike thought he
raised the bar there by a league. When he headed up the Philadelphia
Orchestra he brought a series of Verdi operas in concert to Carnegie in the 1980s. People today get teary-eyed telling you about them.
Muti + CSO + Carnegie + Verdi = You are at an "event."

Muti, who has at least two sides himself, is happy to have the
musical and other celebrities there. But it's the latter group he plays
to: the people who carry scores or mouth the lyrics along with the
soloists, or the children, lucky enough to be brought by their parents

or by Grandma, hearing their first concert, their first opera, their first "event."

A man who, other than the time spent with his family and working in rehearsal, is happiest, literally, alone on an island somewhere, studying scores, Muti is going for the closest a human being can get to perfection and driving his orchestral and vocal colleagues along with him.

Chicagoans heard over the last two weeks at Orchestra Hall how exciting, how dramatic, how personal, how musical Muti's *Otello* is. How the orchestra itself tells the story. They heard a vocal ensemble largely made up of debuting and younger singers from Latvia, Bulgaria, Argentina and the United States come together for a final hour that sent chills up the spine. They heard the CSO Chorus, already the standard setter, set a new standard for depth and breadth. And New Yorkers on Friday heard the additional payoff of forces who'd given three performances already and had another rehearsal on the stage here at Muti's insistence as well as that little fire that says "Carnegie Hall."

Tenor Aleksandrs Antonenko was announced as suffering a stomach ailment and being on medication before launching into the title role. As Abraham Lincoln might have said, find out what medication and send a case to all tenors. It was his finest performance in the role to date and the first that made you think this is a fellow who really could be going places. Soprano Krassimira Stoyanova proved again that she is today's Desdemona. And Italian veteran baritone Carlo Guelfi, though still limited vocally, has the theatrical side of the villain Iago down cold, ice cold.

Vocal and instrumental soloists got lots of love from all tiers of the audience. The orchestra and chorus received roars. Terfel appeared almost hypnotized by the 30-member contingent of the Chicago Children's Choir and gave them a one-man (but what a one man) standing ovation at the end of Act 2. Muti, chorus director Duain Wolfe and CCC director Josephine Lee probably had to ask the house manager to stop the 10-minute ovation.

Open Hands, Open Heart

At an African American Church

Chicago Sun-Times, **September 24, 2011** Muti opened the season this
year not with a gala, a subscription concert or even at Millennium
Park, scene of last year's free concert welcoming the Italian conductor. Rather, the full orchestra rode down to the South Side, where it
took to specially constructed risers at the Apostolic Church of God.
More than 5,000 snapped up the free seats and filled the main wor-
ship space and a spillover chapel that accommodated some 1,500
who watched via the church's own closed-circuit television system.

The program was vintage Muti in its unusual array of European
works close to his heart and a concerto with one of the orchestra's
main principals as soloist. In introductory remarks to the members
of the historic African-American congregation, Muti said that he and
his colleagues had "come to share their feelings, their love and their
friendship." The heart, he concluded, to shouts of "Yes!" and "Amen!,"
"has only one color. And that is the color of the soul."

The overture to Verdi's 1845 operatic setting of the story of Joan of
Arc is no repertoire staple. But it already contains the elements that
would propel the composer's later great overtures to classic status,
and no one plays Verdi like Muti does.

Mathieu Dufour in Jacques Ibert's 1932–33 flute concerto was another case of a performer at the top of the world pack-lifting a lesser
work to its greatest possible heights. No technical, musical or interpretive task is beyond Dufour's ability, and he gave a breathtaking
and very personal performance.

Muti's Tchaikovsky also has a very direct personal communication. It would be much easier to play the Fifth Symphony, as audiences are used to hearing it, and just let the big themes carry the
piece while perhaps throwing in some tempo manipulations for
effect. But Muti studies Tchaikovsky and takes him seriously; the results are revelatory. Demonstrating the complexity in Tchaikovsky
makes his works more beautiful, not less.

On Performing at a Women's Jail

WFMT Broadcast, October 3, 2011

PATNER: In addition to the downtown concerts, you launched the season on the South Side of Chicago at the Apostolic Church of God.[10] I found from sitting in the audience a more attentive audience than often is found in very famous concert halls.

MUTI: I was very, very moved by this experience. Years ago I announced that I wanted to bring music to areas where people were far away from the concert hall. Now the reasons people are away from the Symphony Hall in Chicago, far away from La Scala, far away from the Musikverein, are very complicated. But certainly the fault is not of the people that are away. I don't believe that there are people that naturally are born into impossibility to get close to classical music. People that have different education, that didn't have the money to study music or to go to certain schools, they grow far away from this world. And so they see this world like a world that is foreign, strange, sometime as an enemy. In the schools these boys and girls should be able to be educated, not to learn an instrument—it's not important to play well a piano or a violin or a cello—but to be educated to move your steps in this magic forest of sounds. This is what makes your soul better. Your mind more refined. And makes people more inclined to embrace other people in the concept of harmony. That is the basic element of music. I have never met a person that, after a good experience of contact with the world of classical music, rejects this world.

When I was at the Apostolic Church of God, I was impressed by the kind of silence, the participation. I felt that the people were not there just in a passive way. I could feel that was a silence of great participation. They had their eyes wide open and ears wide open to this new world of music.

PATNER: You also paid a visit, one you have paid before, to a group of young people who at least currently cannot come to visit

Orchestra Hall, because they are incarcerated at the Illinois
Youth Center in Warrenville.

MUTI: I went back because the experience the other time was very
positive. I wanted to repeat because I think it's good that you go
back—only one time doesn't create anything, one time and then
you disappear. Going back, you demonstrate that you really care
about what you want to do with them and for them. The group
that I met this time was even better, more open, less suspicious.
It's not easy for a group of young girls that have had difficult
experiences in life to see suddenly a man from the south of Italy
that comes in—why? He wants to play, wants to speak about
music.

This time I brought a program that was a little bit different.
One aria of *Così fan tutte* of Mozart and one of *Romeo and Juliet*
of Bellini. So I could speak about composers that were geniuses
but also people that didn't have a happy life—or in any case had
a short life. I explained that Mozart died very young, and he
spent years going around Europe to find a job and everybody
preferred always an inferior person to him. He ended in Paris,
where his mother died, and at that time to have your mother
dead in Paris and have to go back to Salzburg must have been
extremely difficult. And Bellini died so young. But the theme
that I brought was love—so *Così fan tutte*, *Romeo and Juliet*. Then
I played some songs of Francesco Paolo Tosti, a contemporary of
Verdi. He was a very cultivated composer. But instead of composing operas he wrote songs that were very, very famous. All
the great tenors, great sopranos—from [Enrico] Caruso to [Tito]
Schipa—they sang these. He became extremely popular in London, where he had honors. But then he went back to Italy. His
songs are extremely popular in Italy, and extremely beautiful.

There is a girl that works there at the center, a mezzo-
soprano, and she helps the girls there to learn music, to exercise
with music. She sang these arias. And then I played a beautiful piece of Verdi, a notturno. This notturno is one of the early

works of Verdi, written for pianoforte. I played the piano and we had the flutist from the Chicago Symphony, and three singers, mezzo-soprano, tenore, and basso that came from the Chicago Symphony Chorus.

The girls were very happy about the performances and they asked many questions about how it's possible to reach excellence, that level, and they asked questions about me, the performers, and the flutist.

PATNER: According to one report you said something to these young girls about finding something that would give them a focus.

MUTI: I told them that we have to have a direction in our life. A goal. I brought up the example of Mozart. I said he was maybe the most important, greatest composer. But he was treated badly many times. In different cities in Europe, aristocrats or powerful people always chose somebody else that was much inferior to Mozart. I said, "Society many times is unfair. People are unfair. But this is not a reason that we should be discouraged and give up. We have to keep insisting and going on."

New Music in Chicago and California

By Phone from the Ski Slopes of Cortina d'Ampezzo, Italy

WFMT Broadcast, January 9, 2012

PATNER: Are you studying scores on the slopes? You have four or five premieres in Chicago just in the next few weeks.

MUTI: I'm studying many scores. I even don't see my children because they've grown up, and so they disappear on the mountains here and there. I'm working on two scores that have been written for the Chicago Symphony Orchestra and for me by the two composers-in-residence. And I must say that the scores are very complex, very complicated, but also very intense and very meaningful, very deep. I am glad of my choice in selecting these two young musicians—Anna Clyne and Mason Bates. Studying these scores I have the demonstration from the work of these composers that my choice was right. I'm studying very carefully because I give to contemporary music the same attention that I would give to a Bruckner, Beethoven, or Mozart symphony.

The two works are very different, because Mason Bates writes with electronic sounds also and is very much also in the American culture through rhythmical elements and timbres that really belong to American culture. Anna Clyne is more in the direction of interior drama in a sort of spiritual thunderstorm. These two pieces will require from me a lot of work with the orchestra if we want to do a good performance. Because the two scores are very intelligent, very astute, and need a lot of care.

I'm starting two other scores. *Space Odyssey* from a Russian composer, [Dmitri] Smirnov, is a piece that we will perform in the next tour in the spring in Moscow and in St. Petersburg. This is sort of a small short symphonic poem, not based on tonic music but full of dissonance.

And then for the first time I'm doing this piece of Honegger that I knew but I'm studying now to conduct. This is the *Pacific 231*.

PATNER: Which is a name for a steam locomotive, right?

MUTI: It's very interesting that Honegger was moved by the noise of the locomotive. You know, you can be moved by nature, by flowers, by trees. This is also a very demanding piece for the orchestra. It's a very virtuoso piece and very impressive.

Honegger's Locomotive and Mason Bates' "Energy"

Chicago Sun-Times, **February 4, 2012** A music director's selection of an orchestra's composers-in-residence reveals much about the conductor's interest in contemporary music and how it relates to the general repertoire and to the public. The Chicago Symphony Orchestra played a role in establishing what is now an accepted tradition when John Corigliano was selected in 1987 to work alongside music director Georg Solti as the CSO's first composer-in-residence. Corigliano's technical virtuosity and populist sympathies matched Solti's own tastes, which also had brought major new works from Michael Tippett and David Del Tredici.

Daniel Barenboim appointed two women composers; first, fellow Israeli Shulamit Ran and then the American Augusta Read Thomas. Both were American-trained extenders of European Modernist traditions, but they also continued Corigliano's worthy cheerleading for an eclectic range of mostly younger colleagues. An interregnum followed when the CSO, without a music director, had two non-resident composers, Osvaldo Golijov and Mark-Anthony Turnage.

Riccardo Muti shook things up when he picked two young artists with keen interests in electro-acoustic music and multimedia to share the composer-in-residence post: American-born Mason Bates and British transplant Anna Clyne.

Loyalty and devotion—whether to teachers, composers, institutions or pieces of music—is a key part of Muti's makeup. His commitment to showcase the works of Bates and Clyne even before they had written any pieces specifically for him and the CSO is strong; he has studied their scores with the intensity others might reserve for Wagner or Schoenberg. With the world premiere of Bates' *Alternative Energy* Thursday night at Symphony Center, Muti showed his commitment worthwhile.

Bates, 35, whose roots are in American composition, liberal arts, and nightclub DJ work, has produced his most convincing, integrated, and appealing large-scale work to date with electronics—which he ran himself from an onstage laptop—strategically placed within the score and in their sounding on speakers across the hall. The four movement, 24-minute work *Alternative Energy* surveys modern man's use and abuse of energy—from tinkering with Tevatrons to nuclear dependence and meltdown to a distant future's return to nature and fire while exploring different propulsions of musical energy and even toe-tapping rhythms.

Principal percussionist Cynthia Yeh was almost a compositional collaborator in helping select, test and create instruments from auto junkyard scraps. Concertmaster Robert Chen showed himself wholly at home in American and Chinese fiddling. Bates kept himself and his techno contributions in the background, letting the listener focus on his careful structuring and tight scoring across the orchestra.

Some might regard the effects as reminiscent of next-generation film scoring or computer gaming, but I found any such parallels a legitimate evocation of the zeitgeist. Muti was alert to each measure and idea, at times appearing to physically revel in discovering a new world. A happy audience and orchestra welcomed Bates back onstage for three curtain calls.

Arthur Honegger's 1923 *Pacific 231*, "Symphonic Movement No. 1," not heard downtown since the CSO's greatest new-music advocate of all time, Frederick Stock, led it in 1930, is itself an exercise in musical representation of propulsive energy. Its six-minute length made it a perfect prelude to the Bates work.

"Night Ferry" by Anna Clyne

Chicago Sun-Times, **February 11, 2012** If Chicago Symphony Orchestra audiences have not figured it out yet, music director Riccardo Muti loves beautiful sound. Of course he can bring out splendid sonority from central repertoire composers such as Brahms and Schubert, whose contributions go well beyond sonic polish and pull.

In contemporary music, at least since his arrival here, Muti's goal has been to find new voices who might use rich sound to connect to new, younger audiences and reignite interest in others disaffected by the complexities of late modernism or bored by the repetitions of minimalism.

This week's subscription program, heard Thursday night at Symphony Center, finds Muti wading at least hip-deep into luscious scores from Schubert and *Night Ferry*, a world premiere from Mead composer-in-residence Anna Clyne.

For her first major commission for Muti and the CSO, Clyne chose to write a 20-minute, single-movement work for large orchestra, gaining any additional effects from the instruments at the high and low ends of the standard spectrum and its rich, tapestry-like scoring.

Night Ferry has a long and interesting story; the process behind it involved research into the life of Schubert and his severe mood swings, poems by Samuel Taylor Coleridge and Seamus Heaney dealing with obsession, a passage on real and metaphorical seas and a painting/timeline that Clyne created in her Fine Arts Building studio.

But as with a sculptor or painter, take the tools and studio away, and it's the work that remains, in this case, a swirling evocation of dark physical and mental seas and a voyage on a courier vessel that's more important than any landing or destination. Starting with a loud and low storm in the opening measures, it evokes the launch of Verdi's *Otello*, with a series of repeated and altered falling themes in wind solos ride atop the churning strings.

Some of it seems obsessive and unchanging, but it certainly matches what a tormented but forward-moving mind can experience. It has a quality of film music, but one wonders if, as with Mozart's Turkish marches, Mahler's town bands and Ives' cacophonies, composers who have grown up amid constant soundtracks aren't just incorporating the beckoning sounds around them.

Muti clearly has devoted himself to studying and communicating this score with the greatest seriousness; the CSO delivered a performance that a composer can only dream of, filled always with beautiful playing. The piece often sounds like a concerto for CSO principal piccolo Jennifer Gunn; her tiny instrument was like a light atop the dark and eerie ferry. Bass drum, clarinet and bassoon seemed to come from the deepest waters.

Schubert's 1823 Third Entr'acte from *Rosamunde* hadn't been heard here in almost 15 years. Muti spun it like a wistful dance at a long-ago ball. Bernard Haitink played the composer's "Great" C Major Ninth Symphony here just three years ago as an almost autobiographical work about the passage of time. Muti's take was much more in the present, emphasizing Schubert's constant creative urge and technical mastery. Newly tenured principal clarinet Stephen Williamson was essential to Muti's achieving his glowing vision in these two bracketing works.

A Forgotten Classical Master

Why Cherubini Is Not Popular

WFMT Broadcast, **March 12, 2012**

PATNER: You are doing a program that has works from very different eras and completely different styles: Cherubini, Brahms, and
Arnold Schoenberg.

MUTI: It's a program where, in a way, the chorus is the star—is the
soloist. In fact there are no soloists. And it's a program that contains three different works from three completely different composers.

The *Schicksalslied* of Brahms is a masterpiece. Very close
to my heart. I've done it on many occasions, especially during
several concerts for friendship that I've given around the world.
I remember the first time was in Sarajevo. Immediately after the
war, with houses broken, people killed, not even a theater. We
performed in a stadium for 9,000 people. The first piece was the
Brahms *Schicksalslied*—song of destiny. It is one of the greatest choral works by Brahms and is music of consolation, like
his *Deutsches Requiem*, consolation for the living. The text from
Hölderlin is very profound. It doesn't require that people in the
audience believe in this God or that God. It's about our destiny,
why we have to suffer so much during our life. The introduction
and the ending of the piece is of such beauty that it really gives
you a feeling of deep peace.

Then is this piece of Schoenberg, *Kol Nidre*. One of the most
famous Jewish texts, "Kol Nidre," is just before Yom Kippur. Jews
have to repent and eliminate or cancel all the vows, oaths, and
commitments that they've made during the year just to go pure
into Yom Kippur. It's a very complicated attitude. In fact, when
he wrote the piece, Schoenberg questioned the text itself, saying, "Why should we repent about something that we avoid—
we have to avoid?" So there is a sort of contradiction. But

Schoenberg himself says, maybe the text had a different meaning or different sense for the people when the text was written.

PATNER: Written in a time when Jews were very frequently under
persecution and duress, forced to say things. Tortured, even,
to say things.

MUTI: And the piece is conceived in a very special way, with a very
small group of strings—percussion, not loud, very delicate,
here and there—and many woodwinds and brass instruments.
So practically it's conceived as chamber music. And even the
chorus should be limited in number. We will use a larger number, but the idea of Schoenberg is to have a limited number of
singers. It should be very intimate, the performance, even if it
reaches sonorities that sometimes are very aggressive and very
loud. It's written also for a speaker, that is the rabbi, that has
to read—not sing—read the text. Using the voice in different
ways, with different tones, with different timbres, with different
accents, with different loudness. But never sung.

Then in the second part of the program I will do the Cherubini *Requiem in C Minor*, with mixed chorus. I say it's a mixed
chorus because then he wrote a D minor *Requiem* for male
chorus. Apparently the reason he wrote the other requiem, for
his own funeral, with only male voices—so the atmosphere
is quite dark in sound—is because he was criticized on using
female voices in the first requiem [in C minor].

PATNER: Criticized for his understanding of how to compose for
the female voice, or for having female voices?

MUTI: They criticized the fact that he used female voices. For a
requiem the conservatives wanted to have boys—boys instead
of mezzo-sopranos—but Cherubini uses really sopranos and
mezzo-sopranos—female voices. This requiem was written for
the transfer of the bodies of Louis XVI and Marie Antoinette.
Louis XVII was the brother of Louis XVI and when he became
king he wanted to have the bodies of his brother and Marie
Antoinette buried properly. And in fact they are buried in the
church, the Basilica of Saint Denis outside Paris, where I con-

ducted several times. The last time I conducted the Cherubini *Requiem* in Paris was in Saint Denis, exactly where Cherubini himself conducted it.

PATNER: The tombs of all of these kings and others there, not only those two.

MUTI: With head, without heads. The Basilica is extremely impressive, one of the greatest churches in France. It was very emotional for me to conduct the requiem exactly where Cherubini himself conducted the piece. Apparently the entire church was covered with black curtains—must not have been a very happy atmosphere.

The *Requiem in C Minor* was very much praised by all the great composers of the time, including Beethoven. Beethoven wrote to Cherubini, "I consider you the greatest composer of our time." He said that if one day he had to write a requiem, he would have the C minor Requiem of Cherubini in front of him as an example. Like when he wrote *Fidelio*, he had the *Lodoïska*, the opera of Cherubini, as an example to follow.

We know that Brahms had a great admiration for Cherubini. In fact in his office Brahms had only three images of great composers: Bach, Beethoven, and Cherubini.

Many people ask me, "So why is Cherubini not popular?" And there are many answers. The easiest one is the fact that Cherubini is a composer that wrote music for the musicians, for the music. Like the logo of the Metro-Goldwin-Mayer, under the lion, it's written, "Ars gratia artis." That means art for the sake of art. Cherubini never tried to write music to please the public or to impress the public. *Medea* is his masterpiece. And it's a very difficult and hard opera to perform and to sing. His music also has a style that is very difficult to identify. He's no Mozart. He's not Rossini. Doesn't belong to the German tradition or the Austrian tradition. Not even to the French tradition, although he was director of the conservatory in Paris, where he had Berlioz as a pupil. He had fights with Berlioz all the time. They represented two completely different worlds. His style is neoclassic, but what is neoclassic? How to define neoclassic in music? Certainly the lines must be very pure. The musical lines. Not Romantic. So we cannot exaggerate in sentimentality or sentiment. It's not absolutely classic in the sense of Mozart or before Mozart. We consider Cherubini the [Antonio] Canova in music— Canova, the great Italian sculptor of the same period. So we have to discover the fire in the marble. This is the best definition that's been made of Cherubini. There is a fire.

PATNER: But we see the marble.

MUTI: Outside is a sort of marble. In a way the two neoclassic composers are Cherubini and Spontini. But Spontini goes even more in the direction of Romanticism. Cherubini remains neoclassic. And Cherubini impresses us today, not so much for the beauty of his melodies, but for the structure, the architecture of his works, of his operas and his symphony. That's a reason why Beethoven, who was also an architect in music, admired Cherubini so much.

PATNER: What does Cherubini do with text? How does he choose his text for this Requiem?

MUTI: It's the usual text.

PATNER: So he's not upsetting the cart the way Brahms does with the *German Requiem*?

MUTI: No. So the program will be for people that don't believe in this or that God, for the Jews that believe in their God and in their religion, and for the Christians. I hope that everybody will be happy in the end.

PATNER: I don't want to ask you to be overly personal, but did religion play a role in your life, in your development, in your family life when you were a child and a young man?

MUTI: Not directly. But indirectly, yes. Religious music was part of our education because the four big musical schools in Napoli were very much connected with the tradition of the young students singing in the church. So they wrote a lot of religious music. And the church had a great influence on the composers, commissioning a lot of religious music. In fact without the church, the history of music in Italy would have been extremely different. This is something that the actual church has forgotten.

PATNER: We see the same thing of course in art. Whatever the individual views of Michelangelo, Leonardo, Raffaello, even Tiziano, Tintoretto—the language they worked in, and the commissioners of so much of their work, was going to be the church. It doesn't mean they are pious or impious, but that they are working in a language and they're using that to develop the progression of art itself.

MUTI: Also we must not forget that until the middle of the nineteenth century the pope was a king. He was the king of a state. And in fact in the region where I live, in Romagna, where Ravenna is, that region was under the pope for centuries. That's the reason why the priests many times are not very popular now.

Without the insistence of certain popes on Rafael or Michelangelo especially, we would not have all the works of art that we have today. Palestrina, Marenzio, Orlando di Lasso, without the influence and the insistence of certain popes, they would not have written what they wrote.

PATNER: But something then happens in the twentieth century—not only after the Second Vatican Council, but in general—this idea that the Church should connect to people but that it won't connect to people if it uses the great music of the past. Why, when you walk into a church, do you hear somebody playing guitar?

MUTI: I've been very critical in my country about this. The fact is not only that they play with the guitar—it's not the instrument—but the way they use it: a very amateur, dilettante way. The text also that they sing sometimes is so stupid. It's so superficial. We don't have to sing Dante in the church. But the Ave verum of Mozart would be wonderful for any religion.

Cherubini's *Requiem*

Chicago Sun-Times, March 17, 2012 Riccardo Muti's devotion to the lesser-known composer Luigi Cherubini is so great, he named one of his children for this figure who straddled the Classical and Romantic periods of the 18th–19th centuries. Not one of his three biological children, but his Italian youth orchestra, founded in 2004, that seems almost as close to his heart as his family.

It's clear why Cherubini (1760–1842) speaks to Muti. Like the Chicago Symphony Orchestra music director, the composer believed in classical structure, formal shaping and marble-like finish. A man of the theater, he wrote 30 or so operas, only one of which, *Médée*, remains in the repertoire. Muti shares this love of drama set within certain strictures.

Much has been made of the praise Cherubini received from no less than Beethoven and Brahms and later, Berlioz. But tastes change and influences and role models do not always match the accomplishments of their devotees.

So it is with the 1816 *Requiem in C Minor*, perhaps Cherubini's most celebrated concert work and one that has been championed by a small but select group. The 45-minute work is absolutely fascinating; Muti led it Thursday, with 145 members of the Chicago Symphony Chorus, with total commitment and a sculptor's hand. But its fascination lies more in how it paved the way for the great 19th-century works in the same genre by Brahms, Verdi, and even Fauré. Without soloists, flutes or in several sections, even violins, it is an explanation of darkness and form, which Muti understands deeply and makes sing at every moment. Particularly engaging are the moments of ambiguity, including the end, where the "Agnus Dei" has the listener poised in the Catholic dilemma of finding a way through God's wrath into his perpetual light.

An Emotional Return to Italy with "His Orchestra"

Concert and Celebration in Naples

Chicago Sun-Times, **April 27, 2012** "I am so glad that I was born in this city," said Riccardo Muti in his Orchestra Hall music director's suite before he and the Chicago Symphony Orchestra left for a six-city tour of Russia and Italy. "Naples is such a special place and it shaped me so much."

For Muti, bringing the orchestra which he has led now for 17 months to Naples has been more important than world tours, Carnegie Hall triumphs, a historic return by the orchestra to Moscow and St. Petersburg last week. Even more so than the opera in Rome, Italy's capital, in the presence of president Giorgio Napolitano, Muti's fellow Neapolitan (regarded as the savior of Italy for his appointment of a new, clean government after the corrupt Berlusconi years).

"Rome is now the capital city, but it was always the city of the popes, not the nation," Muti said. "Naples was the capital of a kingdom, a coming together of peoples over the centuries to create a rich and unique civilization, sometimes wild, sometimes crazy, but always alive and compelling."

Monday in Rome, Muti was received as a celebrity—he is honorary music director for life there—complete with paparazzi and impromptu TV and radio news conferences at his dressing room door, something reserved in the States for Hollywood stars. When he spoke at the end, there was an air of occasion as he underscored the connection between the cause of Italian unity advocated by composer Giuseppe Verdi (whose overture to *La forza del destino* was the subsequent encore) and the "universal unity of music."

In Naples on Wednesday night, with the same program of Nino Rota (Muti's mentor), Richard Strauss and Shostakovich, there was a much greater sense of homecoming and a much more casual give and take.

"Remember," Muti said. "In Napoli, people feel they may shout directly to the priest, the politician, the bishop—even to God himself! So why not to a conductor?"

And so it was at the Teatro San Carlo, Italy's oldest and most beautiful opera house, and the theater of Muti's youth. As he acknowledged the sustained applause for the Chicago Symphony, there was a lighter sound of the south in his voice; shouts started coming from everywhere in the house. "Maybe I shouldn't say too much," he said, laughing. "I can say something I shouldn't."

"Say what you like," one woman shouted in Italian. "You are divine here!"

When he mentioned that Naples was his home, a woman shouted, "But I know that, like me, you are from Puglia!"—the southern region on the opposite side of "the boot" from Naples.

"Yes," he said, to cheers. "I am split in half. But I was born in this great city, and all of me is from the south!"

At a post-concert supper, Muti was emotional. "I must say I was very anxious about this concert. I wanted [the orchestra] to like being here, to like playing in this theater of Donizetti and Rossini. To appreciate this town and its mix of cultures on your day off tomorrow. I wanted the people in this theater and in this city to appreciate your great musical ability and to understand why to be your music director in this, the last period of my life, is one of the greatest gifts of my life."

"After this tremendous performance, I can relax," he said. "We have brought together Chicago and Naples at last." Pointing toward tables laden with local specialties, with a firm wave of his arms, Muti gave his last instruction for the night: "Tutti a mangiare!"

Embracing Eclecticism

On Baseball and Programming

WFMT Broadcast, June 18, 2012

PATNER: This time we get to welcome a star of a sport that I didn't know was even known in Italy and that is baseball.[11] Do you know the word southpaw?

MUTI: No.

PATNER: That's baseball talk for a left-handed pitcher.

MUTI: How do you spell?

PATNER: S-O-U-T-H-P-A-W. So they have posted "Muti—throws L, throws left, conducts R, conducts right."

MUTI: I conduct also with the left.

PATNER: Do you use both?

MUTI: I think that many people were surprised to see that I throw the ball with the left hand. But I am, as we say in Italy, ambidextrous. Certain things I do with the left hand because, for example, if I have to throw a stone with the right hand, I cannot.

Considering that the only thing that I know how to do in my profession, in my life, is to move my arms in the air, I think the fact that it is very easy for me to move the left hand helps very much in conducting, because then you can underline, indicate the expression of the music without having the problem of a left hand that doesn't know what to do.

The baseball game was my first experience. My sons are here and they like baseball, all the American sports, so they decided to go to see the Cubs against the Detroit Tigers. And I said, "Okay, I have a free afternoon so I will join you." So when they heard that I was going, they offered me the first pitch. I was very nervous because of course if you make a disaster, even if then people say, "Oh, you know, this is not your profession," it's still something that hurts. And as the music director of the Chicago Symphony, to throw on the ground and to make a disaster . . . So I practiced here [at Symphony Center] in the corridor two or three times, but with a shorter distance. So when I saw the distance, I was a bit worried. But when I saw this player waiting with his glove, I said, "I have to find the strength." And then I thought if I do a downbeat very strong, a strong downbeat has a lot of power, it can help. And then, it went right there.

PATNER: Absolutely.

MUTI: It was a perfect pitch.

PATNER: Well, let's shift from one kind of athleticism to perhaps another. Bruckner's Sixth and the first violin concerto of Niccolò Paganini, how do they fit together, or do they?

MUTI: They don't fit at all together. The Bruckner Sixth is one of my favorite Bruckner symphonies. I am a Bruckner fan. This symphony has one of the most beautiful adagios that Bruckner ever wrote. Little by little I want to do all the symphonies of Bruckner.

So what to do in the first part. Generally, with Bruckner, you do something of Schubert since Bruckner is the continuation of the Austrian tradition. Or Haydn or Mozart. But I wanted to do something with our wonderful concertmaster, Robert Chen, and I asked him what he wanted to play. The Paganini concerto is for me to be at home because all the concertos of Paganini are practically operatic works. He uses the violin not only technically and in a virtuosic way, but he puts in the instrument all the style and the tradition of singers of his time. When the violin is not involved in acrobatic technical passages, he goes immediately to languid and romantic melodies where you could put words, like an opera of Donizetti or Rossini, or Bellini.

So there is no connection. Two completely different parts. But why not? It is not necessary I think that the program must have a program.

PATNER: You are doing a work that has never been done before by the Chicago Symphony Orchestra. In fact, it's been done in this country by few orchestras, even though it is by Shostakovich, and America has been almost Shostakovich crazy for decades. It is his last major orchestral work, and one of his very last works, the suite of verses of Michelangelo Buonarroti, Opus 145a.

MUTI: I came to this piece when I read somewhere that Shostakovich had put in music some of the poems of Michelangelo. My first reaction was how is it possible to put in music these verses that are so beautiful, but so difficult even for a cultivated Italian to understand the real meaning. I was very curious how this would work in Russian language. Of course the Italian text, even if you don't understand the words, it's so beautiful. For example, in one of the poems [Giovanni Carlo di Strozzi's epigram for Michelangelo's sculpture entitled "La notte"], we read, "La Notte, che tu vedi in sì dolci atti dormir, fu da un Angelo scolpita in questo sasso, e perché dorme ha vita: Destala se nol credi, e parleratti."[12] And Michelangelo answers, "Caro m'è il sonno, e più l'esser di sasso, mentre che 'l danno e la vergogna dura; non veder, non sentir m'è gran ventura; però non mi destar, deh, parla basso."[13] Now, even if you don't understand, it's so beautiful and so musical, that you can create the music.

PATNER: Italian, as a language, fits so naturally with lyricism and singing.

MUTI: So like a river. But the choral atmosphere that Shostakovich uses with the orchestra and with the voice, especially in the low register and the high register using the entire range of the bass baritone voice, is so Michelangelo, and this dark, menacing atmosphere, I really think it is one of the greatest masterpieces of Shostakovich, with a great orchestration, and with this use of the cellos, basses, and contrabassoons. And then suddenly in the end, the celesta.

Yesterday I was very impressed and touched by the fact that Maestro Pierre Boulez was at the concert and came to see me. I consider Boulez the most important musician living today, and I have for him the greatest and deepest respect. When he came in, because he's not only a great man and a great musician, but a humble person, he said, "I thank you for introducing me to this piece; I was not at all familiar with this music. I didn't know it." He made some enthusiastic comments about the score, and he found it one of the greatest works of Shostakovich. The fact that it is not performed very often depends on the fact that you need a cultivated audience, a patient audience—

PATNER: The work is about forty-five minutes.

MUTI: And the moments of great excitement are very few. Generally it's very pensive, very thoughtful. The other thing is that you need a great singer. This piece has been translated also into German and has been sung by German singers, but the German language doesn't work because it doesn't fit with this music.

PATNER: Several of the musicians told me, in the last days, that when you are conducting—this is something the audience wouldn't have a way of knowing—when you are conducting a work with text, you want the instrumental musicians to have the text.

MUTI: Always I've done this in my career. Even when I do operas I ask the library of the theater to prepare the libretto and to put it on every desk of the musicians so the musicians can read it, can follow it when they are not playing. Especially in a piece like this, if you don't know what he's saying, he can speak about tomatoes or vampires, you don't know.

PATNER: You stole my story about Maestro Boulez because I was speaking with Boulez at the interval and it is not a secret that overall Boulez is not a fan of Shostakovich's music. When I did an interview with him after he had been settled in for a few years in Chicago, I said, "Maestro, you are at home here now, you're staying here, and you don't need to give Americans only one side, you can say some of the things you might say at home, so let's go through some of the people you don't conduct." And I would mention Brahms and he would say "too perfect," or Beethoven, "I love Beethoven." I said Shostakovich and he said, "Nothing, nothing." I said, "Well, but what about the quartets?" "No". "What about the piano music?" "Nothing—he's the Meyerbeer of the twentieth century." So when I saw Maestro Boulez last night, I said to him, "Is this now your favorite Shostakovich?" He laughed and paused and he said, "Actually this piece is a revelation, and this performance is a revelation." So you have made an historic contribution here.

MUTI: He is not only a great musician, but he is open-minded. I'm sure that tomorrow he will come back to hear again this piece.

PATNER: Well, that I think I can guarantee that this will be the first

time Pierre Boulez has voluntarily heard a Shostakovich work
twice.

MUTI: Or maybe three, I will see.

PATNER: If someone were to hear a performance by you in the early
1970s of the Fifth Symphony of Beethoven, and they were to
hear the performances you are giving now this week in Chicago,
what do you think they would find different about them?

MUTI: I think that the greatest influence in my conducting as a
musician and as a conductor has come from the Vienna Philharmonic. I have conducted this music a lot with the Vienna Philharmonic, and the Berlin Philharmonic, and that gives you a
certain solidity and confidence.

One thing has not changed in the years and that is the
tempi—quite bright, not slow. For example, I strongly believe
that the first movement of the symphony is allegro con brio.
This ta-ta-ta-ta, ta-ta-ta-ta rhythm element gives life to the
entire first movement. I disagree with the so-called tradition
where before the fermata there is this big ritardando. In a period
of our history, Beethoven has become sort of a messiah of a certain ideology, Beethoven and Bruckner. So there was a bigger
emphasis on certain things to make them even more powerful
and majestic. There is enough drama and tragedy in this music,
and to keep the music tight is much more Beethoven's style than
to make it over romantic. The second movement is andante con
moto. Andante comes from the Italian language andare. Andare
means "to go." Andare. Many times andante is taken like adagio, slow. But andante means andiamo. Andiamo means "let's go."
And andante con moto—con moto is not with a motorcycle but
means "with movement." So even more. Con moto. Don't slow
down, go.

PATNER: You're saying let's read what he wrote. He made choices for
every note, for every tempo marking, when he used German,
when he used Italian—that's very specific.

MUTI: The metronome markings of Beethoven are so fast that some
people believe that he had the wrong metronome.

PATNER: The second cycle that Solti did he tried to do these
extremely fast metronome markings.

MUTI: But then you are concerned about the speed, not about interpretation. Nino Rota, who was a very important musician, and
who put metronome markings on his scores, always said to me
that the metronome speed that you put on your score in the evening is wrong the next morning. It's true, because you are tired
and you are happy, you are drunk, you have a bad stomach problem, a headache, and you feel that that is the metronome of that
moment. In the morning you are another person. We know that
Brahms when he conducted his symphonies in Vienna in the
Musikverein, and he conducted two, three, four times, changed
the tempi, the mood, the atmosphere sometimes dramatically
from one evening to another evening. He was not in contradiction with himself, but the mood was different. So I don't believe
there exists a right tempo and a wrong tempo. There can be if we
go to extremes. But if you are convinced of what you are doing,
then it makes sense.

For example, one of the greatest and incredible experiences
I had was in the late seventies, I did the Schumann Piano Concerto in Salzburg with the Vienna Philharmonic and Sviatoslav
Richter, and in the second movement the cellos always, in every
orchestra, when this phrase is coming [hums], you can see in
their faces they are very happy that their moment is coming,
the great phrase of the celli. And when we arrive there, the cellos, the Viennese, they were ready with their instruments. And
they started. [hums] And Richter said, "Oh no-no-no, no." He
was very kind. This should be like chamber music. [hums] And
I remember because I was on the podium that the eyes of the
Viennese cellists, they looked at him like, "What is he saying?"
But then after two, three, four times, and at the moment of the
concert, everybody was convinced that that was the right way
to do it. Then one month later I was in Edinburgh with the Philharmonia, and I did the Schumann piano concerto with Gilels.
So I thought that the way that Richter indicated was the Russian

way, and I was prepared to [*hums*]. And Gilels says, "Oh, no-no-no, no." He says, "Langsam." [*Hums, much slower*] I felt that, you know, I had to be ready for all kind of desires.

PATNER: That reminds me also of a pianist whom you still work with who is a very special artist, and that's Radu Lupu. One evening he was performing on tour with the Chicago Symphony and it was Brahms's second piano concerto, and there was a moment in that grand opening movement where everybody in the audience, the orchestra, the conductor and Lupu, they're all looking at each other because things started to go in a different than expected direction, but in a beautiful direction. In fact it even felt like a plane lifting off. And the next year I asked him about this and I said, "When do you know?" And he said, "I know when it starts to happen, when I'm playing."[14]

MUTI: There are some miracles that happen, fortunately very seldom, because if not it would not be exceptional or a miracle. Something like this happened to me when I was conducting one evening with the Vienna Philharmonic the Bruckner Seventh Symphony. In the adagio, I don't know how and why, suddenly I felt that the entire sound of the orchestra was changing and the entire atmosphere was becoming higher than I was producing, something that was out of my control, was too beautiful to be conducted by Muti. It was so fantastic. That went on for three, four minutes, because in the moment then, when you fully realize that this miracle is happening, then it disappears.

PATNER: It dissipates.

MUTI: It becomes good, but the magic goes.

PATNER: Some kind of Santo Spirito was there, but once it was recognized, then it went back.

MUTI: It vanished.

Virtuoso Paganini and Rare Bruckner

Chicago Sun-Times, June 24, 2012 As Friday night's concert showed again, all parties are beneficiaries here of a wise joining of a highly experienced conductor entering the autumn of his career—Muti turns 71 next month—with a historically leading orchestra made newly flexible in recent years by a set of uniquely brilliant helmsmen in a city that knows how to make an important figure feel welcome if that figure wants to be made welcome.

Muti's repertoire and programming can be almost maddeningly eclectic. When I asked him last week on WFMT how Bruckner's too-neglected, astonishingly deep hour-long Sixth Symphony fit with the virtuosic demonstrations of Paganini's First Violin Concerto, he responded emphatically, "Absolutely nothing!"

The Paganini arose to fill out a program with the Bruckner, always a tricky proposition, and also to give a showcase with the orchestra's refined concertmaster, Robert Chen. With Chen you get elegance, and once you got past the idea that Paganini means all of the showmanship of Kreisler or the magic of Heifetz, you appreciate his approach. Chen understands what Muti brings out in the orchestral accompaniment of this early nineteenth-century music: Paganini was a peer of Rossini, Donizetti and Bellini, the masters of Neapolitan opera. There are things to think about in this music as well as to be amused or amazed by. And this was what Chen spun out for us, complete with Carl Flesch's cadenza, so sympathetic to this approach.

And then the Bruckner. If Muti had us leaning in to the Paganini he knew he could capture the full house completely with these four movements of spiritual meditation, exploration and celebration. This was one of those total experiences where the attachment between score, conductor, orchestra and audience became a unity. The four principal winds, horns led by associate principal Daniel Gingrich, the reborn bass section with its new, young principal Alexander Hanna all came together with the properly directed—read never too loud—brass and the now silky strings to make you want to come back and hear it all again Sunday afternoon, the last downtown concert until late September.

Muti still has work ahead of him if he wants to keep this level of mission up. There have been timpani auditions this week, and a legendary principal and some key wind players past their prime have to be brought to understand that the movement of this great ship requires new hands on deck. But this season has shown that Chicago has the right captain. The partnership could become historic.

Novel Prokofiev and Shostakovich

Chicago Sun-Times, June 16, 2012 Riccardo Muti's concert selections can evoke a late-night grocery run: items he loves or is intrigued by go into the cart whether or not they will make a structured meal. This week's menu moves from a trivial, if biographically interesting, Prokofiev salute to one of Stalin's massive construction projects, to the belated Chicago Symphony premiere of one of Shostakovich's last major works (and a chilling one at that) and then to everybody's favorite: Beethoven's Fifth.

Muti has many oddities in his longstanding repertoire. Prokofiev's 16-minute *The Meeting of the Volga and the Don*, Op. 130, is a "festive poem" from 1951 that the cellist Msistlav Rostropovich later claimed he suggested to the composer as a means of getting some money from the Soviet state when Prokofiev was literally starving before his death at 61. If Muti had not decided to make some post-performance remarks about the sarcasm of such moments as the work's string of comical false-endings, it would have been almost impossible to justify this paean to the achievement of slave labor. Perhaps 200,000 Gulag inmates were worked to the bone and worse to build a canal (and a 33-ton copper stature of Stalin) between these two great rivers. Principal trumpet Christopher Martin and colleague John Hagstrom provided stirring double fanfares. Otherwise this was "Thomas the Tank Engine" stuff.

In sharp contrast, Shostakovich's 1974 *Suite on Verses of Michelangelo Buonarroti*, Op. 145a, is very serious stuff, indeed. The emotionally tortured composer's last orchestral work was written as Shostakovich was dying of heart disease and lung cancer. In a cool, 45-minute survey, its chilling verses from the great Italian Renais-

sance artist, in Russian-language renderings, set against spare scoring for a large orchestra, create fascinating moments of musical
space and emptiness that underline the despair of many of the poems'
on death, Dante's exile, and personal integrity.

As for Beethoven, Muti offered a driven performance that stirred
the sold-out crowd to four curtain calls. More interesting were the
quiet touches of oft-overlooked detail, particularly in the andante
movement, a veritable percolator of surprise. In contrast to former
principal conductor Bernard Haitink's almost mystical performance
in 2010, this was a young man's Beethoven with much red meat.
But given conductors' longevity and that he came of age after World
War II, Muti, with all of his experience and accomplishment, still has
much to contribute.

The Challenge of a "Universal" Mass Setting

On the Right Style for Bach

> *WFMT Broadcast*, April 8, 2013
>
> PATNER: Some would say it's really not until the beginning of the
>   last century when Albert Schweitzer said Bach is not only about
>   patterns, and look at how interestingly these notes go up and
>   down, he is about culture, he is about representing musically for
>   us what is the soul, what is life. One of the main works that dis-
>   cussion led to is the Mass in B Minor.
>
> MUTI: Thousands of people have been discussing this mass, how
>   large the ensemble should be, which style should be followed.
>   In the first part of my musical life I devoted a lot of attention
>   to Baroque music so I studied all the problems of how to per-
>   form Baroque music today. I don't reject the so-called histori-
>   cally informed practice. I don't reject the Romantic approach.
>   In both cases we have great conductors that believe in one or
>   the other. Many times we have Baroque performers that believe
>   that this is the way, the other is wrong. But when I think histori-

cally informed, my question is: informed by whom? We know
that Bach never heard the entire mass when he was alive. After
his death, through his son, the mass had a certain circulation in
Vienna, in London, then disappeared completely. And so we had
to wait until Mendelssohn to give it life again, but with a huge
gap. When we play Bruckner today, or Mahler, or even Brahms,
we know that is a tradition that has gone through generations.
In Bach, especially with this work, we don't know anything.
Also, according to many musicologists, two-thirds of the mass
is made by pieces that existed before.

PATNER: They may have gone back as much as thirty or thirty-five
years, and it's a compendium.

MUTI: The beginning of the mass, the Kyrie and the Gloria, were
dedicated to the emperor and meant to be a sort of homage. Of
course the emperor was Catholic, and so the mass sounds like a
Catholic homage. But the Kyrie and Gloria work very well also
for a Lutheran service. So the mass, at a certain point, became
complicated piece by piece with different styles. We know when
Bach moved from Leipzig to Dresden, he was in contact with
[Hasse, Caldara, Lotti], and he studied Pergolesi and Palestrina.
The Italian influence on a German construction makes this
piece extremely intriguing. In the same mass you have the style
of the Renaissance period and then up to the preclassical period,
different styles from Palestrina, from Caldara, from Alessandro
Scarlatti. And all the German unknown composers at that time
that sometimes had more resonance and were more famous
than Johann Sebastian Bach.

We know that when Spontini conducted the mass, he used
ninety-six choral people. We have eighty now in the big hall at
Symphony Center. He used sixty-eight musicians. So already he,
at that time, used a number much larger than the first performances of the part of the mass at the time of Bach. Then at the
end of the nineteenth century and the beginning of the twentieth century we have performances by Hermann Scherchen,[15]

for example, that used a gigantic number of performers because the mass, little by little, lost its purpose as a liturgical piece and became a piece for concert, so *la grandiosità*.

PATNER: This was the time of *grandiosità*, the time of oratorios and large choral singing all around Europe and the US.

MUTI: And we have the great performances of Solti, Giulini, Karajan, and still today we have conductors that believe in this kind of approach. My approach is in between. I don't believe in performances with mosquitos, you know, because in the end Bach was a very passionate man. Not from the number of the children that he had. He was a man of great vitality. And I'm sure that if he had discovered the possibilities of the organ that we use today, he would have preferred it.

PATNER: One of the reasons the transcriptions sound so right is because he's anticipating it mentally.

MUTI: If we become so radical, then why not turn off all the electric lights in the hall also and make people sit on wooden seats?

It reminds me a story that really happened. When in Napoli, at the beginning of the twentieth century, they had musical circles and they had all the great pianists, Schnabel, Fischer, they all played there. One day arrived Wanda Landowska who played a concerto with the harpsichord. There was a teacher, a lady with a big hat, one of the typical representative Neapolitan ladies, teacher of piano in the Conservatorio St. Pietro, and going out after the concert, she shouted in full voice, "We tried so hard to have a Bechstein here and now we have to hear this broken iron!"

PATNER: Then, of course, among the quote, unquote, "purists," they thought Landowska was playing not a harpsichord, but playing some kind of a piano, fortepiano.

MUTI: There is another issue about what kind of singers to use. We have the names of the singers who sang the numbers of the mass for the first time. The soprano was the very famous Faustina Bordoni. The tenor was a castrato, Giovanni Bindi. And then the basso and contralto, the names are Cosìmo Ermini and

Margherita Ermini. So four Italian singers. What is incredible is that most of them used to sing in the "intermezzi buffi," so in the comic operas. That destroys completely what has become the tradition of a certain way of singing without vibrato, with a voice that sometimes reminds me of the trains that go from Vienna to Berlin, this kind of *eeeee*.

Bach wrote his music paying great attention to the meaning of the words. I remember the first time I did this mass in Vienna with the Vienna Philharmonic and a chamber choir that is one of the most famous specialists in this repertoire. They are intonation perfect. It's incredible. But when they started to sing "Kyrie elei ..." I collapsed. In the Musikverein for me it was the first experience to hear sounds like knives.

PATNER: Or like a drill.

MUTI: I said, "Do you realize that you are saying, 'Lord have mercy'? If you say, 'Lord have mercy' in this way you go to the inferno immediately with the direct train."

That doesn't mean that I have in my pocket the truth, because I know that I don't know. But I have studied a lot about how to perform Baroque music. Even Harnoncourt, who was the one that started all this, has said don't believe that going through these formulas how to do the trills, the vibrato, non-vibrato, the old instruments, that we recreate what Bach wanted. It's just a modern way to approach ancient music. Nobody will ever know how it sounded.

PATNER: You did it in Philadelphia in the '85–'86 season. If somebody had dropped in to the Academy of Music almost thirty years ago and then they dropped in to Orchestra Hall this time, would they detect something that had changed?

MUTI: I'm aware that I've changed dramatically as a person. You know, life brings good things, bad things, tragedies also. You learn more music and so all this makes you a more complex, not necessarily better, but more complex person and conductor. My experiences in Baroque music started with the Virtuosi di Roma of Vivaldi that was played in a fantastic way that today would be

old-fashioned but you felt really the gondolas and Venice. That
was the spirit of that city.

PATNER: I should say that Maestro Muti's face is especially animated
as he talked about Venice there.

MUTI: What I was taught was the expression. With all the chorus
masters I've been working with for fifty years now in Italy and
outside Italy, the expression of the words is fundamental. When
Bach writes "Crucifixus" and you have this—[hums] bum-bum—
it's clear that he's thinking of the crucifixion, the driving of the
nails in the crucifixion. Bum-bum. When he speaks about the
ground, and then we have the shaking of the ground, the earthquake. Or when speaks about Christ, he gives an aria with a
solo horn, a sort of heroism. It's not a Flemish composer that
is involved in just pure technique.

PATNER: At the same time I'm guessing that this need for expression and clarity is also a reason not to go too far in the other
direction, with too large of a chorus or too large of an orchestra
because then you wouldn't get this communication.

MUTI: The first thing is the purity of the counterpoint. That's the
reason why, for example, if you do the chorus with two voices
of soprano, two second sopranos, two contraltos, et cetera, you
lose the *grandiosità* that is needed in certain places, but you have
clarity. The counterpoint needs clarity and expression. One of
the most important rules of Baroque is not to be over-Romantic
because you become ridiculous then—like until thirty years ago,
many orchestras used to play Mozart like Bruckner.

These movements have been important to clarify certain
things. But when they become radical and say, "This is the way,
all the others are wrong," that's a mistake. It's the style that is
important, not the number. We know that when Salieri conducted Haydn's *Creation* in Vienna, he used 1,000 performers. It
is not a legend because in Vienna there is a document with all
the fees that were paid to the chorus and the musicians. Now if
you play a Mozart symphony with seven contrabasses, immediately the critics would say, "Oh, it's wrong because it's too big."

But Mozart likes big sonorities. The point is not how many players, but which style you follow.

At the time of Solti, the recent studies on the Baroque performance were not existing. The more we go on, the danger is that if we study too much the theory, the practice becomes a disaster. Little by little we are going in a direction where the extremists, radicals, start to say that, for example, the Vienna Philharmonic is too old fashioned for Mozart. So little by little we destroy the possibility that a modern symphony orchestra can play a large repertoire.

PATNER: But at the same time, if we can learn something, we should learn.

MUTI: I'm not rejecting them. It's like in religion, when the Catholics are too extreme, or the Muslims, or the Jews, or whatever ... it's only one God. You can use the systems if you are able to know the systems of the eighteenth-century early music. But who those people were, the heart is the same—same color, the same way of beating time.

Too Solemn and Sober

Chicago Sun-Times, **April 13, 2013** Few works are more esteemed as grand contributions to Western civilization than Johann Sebastian Bach's Mass in B Minor. Neither Protestant nor Catholic, the work is universal, though the Latin language and some structure comes from the latter tradition. (Bach, however, was a devoted Lutheran.) Written in parts over 35 years with no plan that it would be performed in Bach's lifetime, it was directed to a posterity of unknown distance. (It sat in drawers for more than a century after Bach's 1750 death before receiving its first full performance.)

It sums up and weaves together the styles, scoring and experiments of Bach's full career with lessons from his keyboard, chamber, orchestral, choral and vocal music integrating harmony, counterpoint and invention.

But is grand enough when reviving this work? For Riccardo Muti grandeur seemed to be the chief goal Thursday at Symphony Center, but solemnity and anonymity reigned for much of the time. And a long time it was, too, two hours and five minutes, plus a full intermission.

Muti has spoken, insightfully and humorously, about the need to navigate between doctrinaire ideas of "historic performance" of earlier music and grandiose cathedral performances with hundreds of choristers and players. But the issue here was not the types of strings or bowing or the size or restriction of the sound of each instrument—areas where Muti's call for a middle ground, embodied here by 85 singers and an orchestra of 55, makes great sense. But the so sober, museum-like presentation too often lacked the very liveliness and personal connection that the long-experienced conductor contends "period performances" miss.

Bach front loads the five-part work with a lengthy Kyrie, compact in text, but thick with choral and orchestral writing. Here, this set a weighty tone that dominated the first half, including the second-part Gloria. After the break, Muti's ideas and practice came together much more fully on the nine sections of the Credo. The CSO Chorus, prepared by its director Duain Wolfe, had often been uncharacteristically muddy up to that point. It now came fully alive, and Muti delivered the central "Et incarnatus est," "Crucifixus," and "Et resurrexit"—the core of the Christian creed—in all three dimensions with incarnation, the nail hammers of crucifixion and the glory and splendor of resurrection essentially enacted. That same spirit and execution was present in the well-known concluding "Dona nobis pacem." One wished that this feeling could be projected back through the full two hours-plus. Perhaps it will be during the work's remaining performances.

Orchestral clarity and articulation were there at all times. And solo parts were enviable and more both on their own and while interweaving with the four vocal soloists. Principal flute Mathieu Dufour is always worth the price of admission alone, and oboe d'amore players Eugene Izotov and Scott Hostetler and bassoonists David McGill and Dennis Michel matched him in insight and tenderness. Horn Daniel

Gingrich and concertmaster Robert Chen offered elegance and a certain stateliness. The continuo accompaniment of cellist John Sharp, bass Alexander Hanna, organist David Schrader, and harpsichordist Mark Shuldiner also embodied Muti's ideas with supportive style.

Vocal soloists reflected Muti's preference for lesser-known young European singers, in this case, mezzo Anna Malavasi and soprano Eleonora Buratto (both Italians), and Albanian tenor Saimir Pirgu and Czech bass-baritone Adam Plachetk. One can understand why "stars" as used by Carlo Maria Giulini, say, in his well-known recording, do not appeal to Muti for a devotional and ensemble work such as this. But the general lack of distinction and the failure of the two women singers to demonstrate any personal connection with the essential poetry they were singing (Pirgu and Plachetk fared better) also kept this major performance achievement from reaching heavenly heights.

Finding the Sacred in Verdi, Vivaldi, and Mozart

Why Italians Are Different

WFMT Broadcast, June 16, 2013

PATNER: Perhaps you can reflect a little bit on the end of your third season as music director.

MUTI: I feel that when I come here the sound comes back to what is my ideal of sound that is a mixture, not scientifically studied, but naturally conceived, a mixture of the concept of sound that is the Vienna Philharmonic that has been the orchestra that I have conducted most in my life, together with the strength, the power, the energy, physical energy of the Chicago Symphony. The two things together make this orchestra unique today.

PATNER: An example from my listening that's happening this week is a performance of the Bruckner First Symphony. Your understanding of the piece and your affection for the piece and the ability both to be gentle and to give energy were married absolutely.

MUTI: There is always a sort of mental attitude that the Italians
are good at Italian music. But this is absolutely wrong because
we have in Italy a long and important Wagner tradition, for
example. Before Toscanini and in the time of Verdi, Angelo
Mariani from Ravenna introduced Wagner in Italy with *Lohen-
grin* in Bologna. Verdi and Boito went there to hear. And then
the great tradition of Toscanini at La Scala, Furtwängler at La
Scala. We know that Wagner liked and admired the Italian way
of approaching his music because it has a *cantabilità*. Many
times in the German performances it's very heavy and not clear
what happens in the counterpoint in the different lines. We have
an approach that is much more cantabile. We sing every part.

That was the way Toscanini did it. The *Tristan* of [Victor] de
Sabata is still considered the greatest performance of *Tristan*
in the history of Bayreuth. The same happened with Bruckner.
In this country it is said, "This is a Bruckner orchestra, this is a
Mahler orchestra." An orchestra, even a mediocre orchestra, in
the hands of a great conductor that understands the music of
Bruckner or Mahler, can sound like a Mahler orchestra, a Bruck-
ner orchestra.

PATNER: But there are orchestras with better resources, aren't there?

MUTI: The resources, yes. But then you have to have the conductor that knows how to use them. Toscanini always said, "Non
esistono cattivo orchestra, esistono solo cattivo direttore." Bad
orchestras don't exist, only bad conductors exist.

There are some stereotypes. There are some traditions
of German music being too heavy. When you take [Hans]
Knappertsbusch you hear what is very heavy, and not very clear
in the middle, but then you take Erich Kleiber and everything is
much lighter. And [Herbert von] Karajan also. I think that certain German music became more heavy during the Nazi period
to underline the power. Many of the so-called traditions became
an exaggeration or a caricature, like the ritardandi in the opening of the Beethoven Fifth Symphony. There is no reason to
arrive at the climax making ritardando, exaggerating. The stylis-

tically more reasonable approach that came about in the seventies has been extremely important.

PATNER: Anything that provokes the artists to go back to the score and try to erase, temporarily, in their mind, recordings, other traditions, and to see what they find there, is going to be a good thing.

MUTI: But we have to be careful when we say to go back. For example, in one place in Europe recently *Norma* has been done with all the old instruments and with a voice that has nothing to do with *Norma*. These things can be done in places where you can get away with it. But if you do a *Norma* like this in Italy there would be a revolution.

We want to hear Callas, Caballé, Scotto, Cerquetti, Sutherland, these big voices that are *soprano dramatico con agilità*, as we call them in Italy.[16] We know that Malibran was the first Norma, and Grisi, a soprano, was Adalgisa and they alternated the parts; one sang one night Norma and the other Adalgisa and then the other way around.[17] We have a tradition of playing this music of a Sicilian composer who came from the Neapolitan school full of energy. That is the way the musical bands in the south of Italy, the banda, still play this music, with great energy. When you take all the blood out of the Sicilians, this is not Bellini.

PATNER: To wrap up the season you have the four sacred pieces of Verdi, the *Magnificat* of Vivaldi and the *Ave verum corpus* of Mozart.

MUTI: Vivaldi wrote two versions of the Magnificat. The choral part is the same in both versions, but in the second version there are several arias instead of choral pieces, and every aria is dedicated to a different girl. You have the names of the girls. The red priest was a teacher. And so he gave this little gift. I don't know if he asked for something.

PATNER: Maybe he just liked their appearance.

MUTI: The introduction and these arias are really a masterpiece. It's not important if is Baroque or not Baroque. This is the Italian tradition. We play with a certain *virtuosi di Roma*. You remember *virtuosi di Roma* that Toscanini had in mind so much, the great energy in the way of making the music and the phrases.

The *Ave verum* of Mozart I have done many times and the best performance that I remember was with the Vienna Boys Choir because they sounded like angels. It's the way it should be done, with boys in the part of soprani and mezzo soprani. The *Ave verum* is only five minutes. It's music that I think that if there is a god somewhere, only God could write because it is the right expression of the transcendent. *Magnificat* is a beautiful piece, typical of Vivaldi, but more on the earth.

And the four sacred pieces of Verdi are the last compositions of Verdi. The *Stabat Mater* and *Te Deum* are with the orchestra, and the other two pieces only chorus. The *Ave Maria* is based on the enigmatic scale. Verdi invented this scale. It is not the normal scale, not the tonal scale, not the dodecaphonic scale, but a scale that Verdi invented with strange intervals, and because it doesn't belong to any of the scales that I've mentioned, he called it enigmatic. On this strange scale he wrote harmonically one of the most fantastic pieces. Very difficult for the chorus because if you lose the intonation, you are really in trouble. There is no exit. You start with Verdi and you end with some of the most avant-garde composers of today.

Then there is the *Laudi alla Vergine Maria* that Verdi originally wrote for four soloists. It's a tradition to do it with a small chorus of ladies. It sounds much better and Verdi approved.

Laudi alla Vergine Maria is on the text of Dante's "Paradiso" ["Vergine madre, figlia del tuo figlio, umile e alta più che creatura"]. It's one of the most complicated pieces, theologically speaking, because it underlines the contradiction of Mary, virgin mother. If you are a virgin, you cannot be a mother. But she is a virgin. She is also mother. "Figlia del tuo figlio." You are daughter of your son. It's another contradiction. And "umile e alta." You are humble but high, more than any other creature.

PATNER: Humble and to be worshiped.

MUTI: More than any other creature on the earth. And so how do you put music under this? It's impossible. Like when you want to put music under the text of [Giacomo] Leopardi. It's so elevated that music can only ruin the purity of the text. But Verdi succeeded because it's one of the most pure and untouchable pieces. Carlos Kleiber said to me there is some music that is so profound that you can only enjoy looking at the music on the page because as soon as you try to bring the music to life, you lose a lot of the intensity that you have in your mind and you cannot produce in a concrete way with the instruments.

PATNER: We have an artist of the highest level who spent his entire life working and working and then at the end is capable of creating exceptional things because of depth, experience, distillation. We know this from *Falstaff*, and we know this from the sacred pieces.

MUTI: Verdi was so critical in the last period of his life that he didn't want the *Four Sacred Pieces* to be performed. It started to be performed in Paris. But it is rarely performed because for the chorus it's extremely difficult. This program will be a challenge for the chorus because from Mozart to Vivaldi to the four sacred pieces, the entire evening is based on the chorus. There are three different ways of approaching the text. And the four Verdi pieces are completely different one from the other.

PATNER: When you, at this stage in your career, encounter, be it a conversation, a lecture, an article that raises some points that somehow had not yet been raised, and you have a piece that you have been working with for decades, do you find yourself saying, "I want to revisit how I think about this piece"?

MUTI: Always I revisit. For example, when I conduct Bruckner now, or Scriabin, every afternoon before the concert I go through the score, thinking and rethinking about what I have done, what I can make better, what I did wrong. The end in our profession, fortunately, doesn't exist.

Beautiful Singing and Deep Expression

Chicago Sun-Times, June 22, 2013 As he closes his third season as the
10th music director of the Chicago Symphony Orchestra, Riccardo
Muti appears more and more personal in his programming. Although he has an encyclopedic familiarity with the repertoire after
45 years as an international conductor, his preferences and emphases
have always been his own.

They start with the national composer of his native Italy, Giuseppe
Verdi; center around the literal sound of the human voice and the
vocal, singing sense ("cantabile" in Italian) of the musical line, and
hold always to the idea that a connection spanning centuries exists
between all the great composers and styles of Western art music.

All of these ideas are at work in Muti's presentation and preparation for his last CSO concerts of the season, which began Thursday at Symphony Center. The program of course leads to Verdi: his
Four Sacred Pieces, written, remarkably, between the ages of 75 and
84 (1889–1897), existing outside the composer's operatic catalog, and
never even intended to be grouped together or necessarily performed
in public.

Before that, Muti presented a small, delicate masterwork, Mozart's
own late *Ave verum corpus*, K. 618, written less than six months before
his death in 1791, and a much less known work, Antonio Vivaldi's
1715 *Magnificat*, in a 25-minute version revised in 1739 near the end
of that composer's life as well.

Oddly, the Mozart has never been performed in full before by the
CSO. The Vivaldi had a less surprising delayed premiere. But both
works were much less about the performance history of the CSO than
about an atmosphere and a context that Muti was creating as pro-
logue to the Verdi.

A reduced chorus for these first-half works sang from low risers
onstage rather than up on the choir terrace, even remaining seated
as they sang the Mozart. The effect, in a good way, was that of hearing music in a church. Not in an expansive cathedral with attending
pomp, but in a place of spiritual introspection, quiet and familiarity.

This was singing, along with strings and light organ and harp-sichord accompaniment, that sounded like that of meditative be-lievers more than professional performers, and the result was quite effective. In her CSO debut, Russian mezzo soprano Alisa Kolosova, who had sung with Muti before in Europe, showed a clear, vibratoless voice in the five solo arias, but lacked much color or variety.

These 18th century works laid the groundwork for the late 19th century Verdi pieces. The Muti pianissimos achieved with both chorus and orchestra in the earlier works are even more remarkable when heard in the ever changing and contrasting Verdi settings.

The CSO Chorus, prepared by director Duain Wolfe, with addi-tional coaching and shaping by Muti, a living legend as today's pre-eminent Verdi interpreter, was wholly involved, from the a-cappella, woman-only *Laude alla Vergine Maria* (the one piece not in Latin, but in Italian from Dante's "Paradiso") to the full scale and orchestrated expanded *Te Deum* (whose closing portions featured the appropri-ately innocent sound of chorus soprano Kimberly Gunderson).

The mysterious *Ave Maria*, for a cappella mixed chorus, was writ-ten as a response to a newspaper game proposing an "enigmatic scale." With Mozart still floating in listeners' heads, Verdi and Muti took us to a sound world almost like Debussy or the spiritual side of Wagner. The deeply personal *Stabat Mater*, the last piece Verdi ever wrote, seems to hold all of his *Otello*, and yet also silences and inward sentiments that exist nowhere else.

Like Verdi, Muti both belongs to no church or movement and yet is deeply spiritual. He shares here, from the public podium, quiet re-flections of three great composers that remind us, too, of who this very individual musician is.

He's back in September with programs including music from Verdi's *Nabucco*, *La forza del destino*, and the complete *Macbeth*, and then the *Requiem* in October to salute the composer's 200th birthday anniversary. Mark your calendars now.

Verdi's *Macbeth*

On a Unique Verdi Opera

WFMT Broadcast, **September 30, 2013**

PATNER: Is there a central message of Verdi's *Macbeth* for you?

MUTI: *Macbeth* is unique in Verdi's operas because it creates a work
of music that artistically we can call expressionism. It is an
opera of great psychology. Most of the opera is based on the
conflict of Macbeth and Lady Macbeth, the weakness of this
great general and the power of this lady, which is more terrifying than the real witches. Verdi wants to create something that
many times comes more from the mind of the personages. For
example, in *Macbeth* Verdi uses dynamic indications that he will
never use again in such a way in his operas. He asks the orchestra sometimes to play "con suono muto." As I explained to the
orchestra and to the chorus, "suono muto" is a contradiction
because if you have a sound, you cannot have a silence. "Muto"
doesn't mean muted, it means really without the possibility of
saying the words. So how to create suono muto?

PATNER: Silent sound.

MUTI: And then after that, diminuendo.

PATNER: You're starting at zero and then you must be quieter.

MUTI: You're nothing and then diminuendo on nothing. It's clear
that Verdi had in mind the use of the voice and the use of the
sound of the orchestra that was not known at that time. We are
long before the impressionists and before the dodecaphonic system and all the experiments of today. Verdi is much ahead, and
still today we imagine on paper what he wants, but how to produce it is almost impossible when you want to follow the indications of Verdi. Many times the singers ignore this, and they
shout, and instead of "con voce muta," you hear fortissimo in
the voice.

PATNER: And he's using these things for psychological and philosophical effect and commentary, not only for musical effect.

MUTI: Absolutely. In fact Verdi in one letter says that people don't imagine at all the concept of sound that he has in mind when he writes. For example, for the first chorus of the witches, la strega, Verdi writes, for the soprani and for the contralti, "non dimenti carsi que tratasi de strega que parla no." Don't forget that these are witches that speak. You have to find how it's possible to have the sound of witches. It can become comic, it can become exaggeration, it can become laughable, instead of being a dramatic effect that he wanted.

It's an opera that brings many question marks, like the idea of the band under the stage that is supposed to create a sound that comes from inferno or the voice of the apparitions. To do an opera like this you must know Shakespeare — and Verdi knew Shakespeare. He didn't speak English, but he had a fantastic translation that was in Italian of Shakespeare's works. In the beginning of Macbeth he tries to imitate the sound of a horrifying bagpipe. Clearly with the clarinet or oboe, he wants to create a sound that reminds us of an old instrument from Scotland. In the Brindisi, as I said to the chorus, it's not the Brindisi of *Traviata* but should be strong and heavy like rocks because Verdi had a great imagination about countries that he had never seen. Look at *Aida*. He was never in Egypt. But when you hear the beginning of *Aida* you feel immediately that you are near the Nile in a blue night with the moon and the stars and the water that shines. This is like Debussy when he writes "Les collines d'Anacapri." He was never in Capri, but he saw the image of Capri on a bottle of wine, and from there he understood the atmosphere. This is genius.

PATNER: So Verdi is creating for us orally and without words both the feeling of the characters and their ideas and also the geographic location.

·There are two versions of *Macbeth*, the original, which was done for Florence, and then the revision for Paris, after twenty or so years had gone by. You have, for the most part, played the second version. Philip Gossett,[18] with whom you have collaborated on Verdi, Rossini, other projects, makes the argument that even if some of the pieces, the four major changes and additions are quote, "better," unquote, they are written from a different musical period and a different musical style, and he doesn't see how that fits in.

MUTI: I studied both versions very deeply when I decided to do *Macbeth* in 1974 in Florence for the first time. I knew that Verdi had written *Macbeth* for Teatro de la Pergola and in the basement of the theater there is still the wooden chair that Verdi used when he conducted the premiere of *Macbeth*. When I did the recording, I added, as a bonus, some of the arias of the first version that are very difficult, but not at the level of "La luce langue" that he added, for example.

PATNER: They are difficult, but not at the artistic level of his later accomplishment.

MUTI: The aria of the baritone in the end is a very small aria and it's very touching, but Verdi took it away in the second version because he preferred a much more grand finale with the chorus singing for the victory and the freedom. The first version is much more crude. Raw. The second version is much more refined. After twenty years, Verdi became a much more refined composer. He wrote ballet music for Paris, although he generally didn't like to interrupt the dramatic action, to please the French people in Paris. When he did the Sicilian vespers for *Macbeth* he wrote music that in the end he liked and he knew that he had written something not second class quality. So I have done it always with the ballet and I have done always the second version.

Sometimes the stage director has asked me to do the aria of Macbeth from the first version, where Macbeth throws away the crown and says that for the desire of power he was a victim. The finale with the aria of Macbeth gives a soul to Macbeth. In the second version, he disappears. He dies in battle and is like a piece of meat that is killed. Stage directors like the first version

for the possibility of working on Macbeth that dies on stage cry-
ing, singing.

PATNER: If you're doing a concert version, you don't need to worry
about the stage director.

MUTI: But then, after the aria, the finale is too short and too abrupt.
We know that Verdi liked very much to end, boom, like this,
suddenly. It's like you are in an open ocean and suddenly you
find yourself in the port. So everybody's singing, and then
boom-bum-bum, finito. This is the style of Verdi in that period.
The second version has the chorus at the end. It's a little bit
pompous. A little bit rhetoric. But it has a meaning, it brings to
heroic and patriotic conclusion an opera like Macbeth.

PATNER: What do you look for in the singers for Macbeth?

MUTI: I need intelligent singers. We know that Verdi, for Macbeth
and Lady Macbeth, wanted singers with not some beautiful
voice. He had a concept of voice for this opera that was very special, very uncommon. The impresario wanted to have [Eugenia]
Tadolini, who was a very famous soprano at that time, and there
is a letter of Verdi that says Tadolini is not right for this part
because she has too beautiful a voice for this role. He considered
the part of Lady Macbeth extremely difficult, as it is, and he says
it is not easy like La Traviata.

PATNER: It's a different definition of easy.

MUTI: He meant that you need a woman and a singer that could
psychologically convey feelings that are almost not human.
So subtle, so evil. The finale, the scene of sleepwalking, the last
page of Lady Macbeth, is a sort of recitativo on a rhythmical element of the orchestra so that this movement is like Lady Macbeth is trying to take away the blood from her . . .

PATNER: "Out, damn spot."

MUTI: And the sort of recitative ends with a very high pianissimo
D-flat. Verdi very seldom went to that register of the voice, so
it means again that he wanted a sound not real, not natural,
unreal, unnatural. The baritone many times has con voce muta,

con voce so fogata, con voce perlata. He insists on indications
that have nothing to do with operas that were coming out of
the bel canto period.

PATNER: He is talking about a presentation that involves a speaking
sound or acting as opposed to making sounds as perfumed as
possible or as pretty as possible.

MUTI: He asks for all these things, but then in the end the baritone
has to sing an aria. And you cannot fake there. You have to sing:
"Pietà, rispetto, onore." The tradition changes it to pietà, rispetto, amore. But the original is pietà, rispetto, onore. Because
Macbeth, old and full of pains, asks for pietà, pity, mercy,
respect, and honor, not respect and love. Because rispetto,
onore, there are two O, one near the other, it's difficult—too
many Os—they say rispetto, amore, so it sounds beautiful.

PATNER: A Verdi opera also means in many cases a chorus, and the
chorus plays a key role, or choruses, really, because you have
witches, you have men, you have—

MUTI: Killers.

PATNER: You have killers. How does the chorus function within the
opera?

MUTI: Verdi said very clearly the three characters are Macbeth, Lady
Macbeth and the witches. So this says everything about the
chorus. The part of the witches is extremely difficult. The finale
of the first act and the second act, but especially the finale of the
first act, sounds like a big work of Michelangelo, it's so gigantic
and it's like the entire world is collapsing because of the death
of Duncan. So it's an opera that goes from nothing in sound to
a massive sound.

PATNER: It's very interesting that you say that about Michelangelo
because we think of Michelangelo and we think of these giant
works, but also, if you look at the sketches or if you look at even
the slaves, the delicacy and the intimacy, and the way this man
lived, beyond a monk, with no possessions and with no desire.
Verdi, too, has this sense of going to the very alone figure, and

also to the canvas of these choruses, and there's this sense of the artist expressing himself at the smallest and the biggest level.

MUTI: In the finale of the first act especially you have the little pieces, a capella parts, where the soloists have to sing pianissimissimus, and then the explosion of the entire orchestra and the entire chorus, so you go, like Michelangelo, from very tiny, delicate moment to St. Peter's.

PATNER: It is that breadth of humanity.

MUTI: And never for effect. Never for effect. This is one of the problems of Verdi interpretation because many times the performances are based musically on effects of soloist and orchestra, you know, bombastic. You can be very loud and not bombastic, and you can be mezzo forte and bombastic.

To play the music of Verdi well is extremely difficult. It's much more difficult to play well Verdi than to play well Wagner. Even if the impression of the public is the contrary that, you know, to play Wagner, there is so much going on that you think it's extremely difficult. It is difficult. But Verdi requires great precision because the music is many times vertical, and so intonation is very difficult. Every chord must have a different color, different effect, because every chord prepares a phrase or concludes a phrase, so there is not one forte, but there are a thousand different forte. And then you have to find the timbre, so you have to understand how to make the so-called complements that should not sound like the Germans accused Verdi, saying oompah-pah. That was a bad way of performing Verdi. There is a famous story that Tullio Serafin, the great Italian opera conductor, was conducting in Rome, and at a certain point the administration took away two rehearsals from him. He was heard in the corridor of the theater saying, in full voice, "They've taken away two rehearsals from me, but I am doing Bellini, not Wagner."

A Totally Alive Performance—Conversation with WFMT
Morning Program Host Carl Grapentine

WFMT *Broadcast*, **October 2, 2013**

PATNER: It's remarkable what happens when you have this 3-D
intensity and knowledge that Muti brings to Verdi. He takes
what he has lived with and studied forever and he brings the
gang of singers, chorus, children singers, and of course the
orchestra together with this idea that every single measure is
the point. And you're reminded how every measure leads to the
next measure—and how a fine but ordinary Italian conductor
with a feel of oom-pah can just carry us through or somebody
who sees it all as one long melody, as the Russians historically
did with Verdi, is missing the point, that this has to be grabbed
at every moment.

It's also a test of the works, of course, *Macbeth* being one
of the earliest of the works that can take that test and show you
that there's a real mind at work dramatically and musically, and
even spiritually. I think that's one of the things that came off
especially with the lead cast members of young singers, Luca
Salsi, Italian, and Tatiana Serjan, a Russian who has sung this
with Muti, and who has really come to connect strongly with
this part.

You had the sense, even without sets—maybe because of no
sets or costumes—that these were two people who were really
caught in something. They had an ability not to fake act on
stage, but somehow the combination of lust for power, terrible
neurosis, and sense of impending tragedy, all of this could be
communicated without any gimmickry.

GRAPENTINE: I'm told that Tatiana Serjan is actually a fairly delightful young lady, but you wouldn't know it by her stage demeanor.
She was so focused and intense, and I was scared to death of her.

PATNER: Interestingly, her much more casual, positive, warm side
was present when the maestro took the singers and some other
guests out to the girls' state detention facility in Warrenville

yesterday. These are young ladies who are incarcerated for a range of possible infractions. And although Miss Serjan was not performing because she has been singing with a cold, she was there mixing with the girls. You would have thought, oh, this is their folk singing instructor, just this kind of jolly hippie.

Of course we are leaving aside, and it's not an elephant in the room, but a set of brass angels in the room, that we win over the opera houses here because you've got the Chicago Symphony Orchestra on stage. The Metropolitan Opera has a wonderful orchestra, and we've heard them play wonderfully with operas. We don't hear them play an opera on stage. There were times where you sometimes had to come back, oh yes, there's somebody singing, even though they were singing so wonderfully, because of the total integration of soloists, chorus, and orchestra.

Verdi was a master of orchestration and here he's still working out certain ideas that he will develop. Muti likes to point out that there are many musical concepts in *Macbeth* that are not fully developed, but that he takes over the next decades and uses in the later operas. We have the offstage band here, which gives you that very regional Italian flavor.

GRAPENTINE: And *Macbeth*, in some ways, is a bit of a hybrid because he added several things and reworked some things for the Paris production that was eighteen years later. So it's early Verdi with a little bit of late Verdi in there, too.

PATNER: Whether *Macbeth* is your favorite opera of all time—it's not my favorite opera of all time—doesn't matter because this is really a textbook brought totally to life in how something should be performed and presented. It is one of the three great distillations of Shakespeare that Verdi did and that Verdi did better than any other opera composer. So you have the drama, and you have, across the board, casting, the voice qualities, everything is just right. And this wonderful, wonderful music. Of course Verdi is Muti's lowercase "g" god, and he has famously said that when he meets his betters, should Beethoven, should Brahms, should even Wagner say to him, "Riccardo, you disappointed me with what you did," he said he could survive, but if Verdi said, "Riccardo, you disappointed me," then his life would have been a failure because Verdi, he feels, is his master, and that all of his work comes together to try to achieve these things. And he just totally comes alive and totally directs you to the musical core and the musical concept of the work. It's something to see and hear.

What Makes a Composer Italian?

On Several Italians, including Schubert

WFMT *Broadcast*, January 29, 2014

MUTI: We do contemporary music because it's important. We have to go ahead. But really, in the last fifty years, what remains in the mind of people? At the time of Mozart, when he wrote "Là ci darem la mano," two days later the people in the street, they were singing "Là ci darem la mano," so Mozart was writing for the people. That was a direct message. With Beethoven already, the distance between composer and public was becoming more and more problematic. Robert Schumann said that at the time of Mozart the composer was like a shoemaker who made the shoes that everybody could wear. Schumann said today the composer makes shoes that only he can wear. And we are talking about Schumann. Can you imagine today?

PATNER: At the same time there are composers who are listening as well as writing, and try to be a part of their society. You have a composer working with the orchestra this week, Giovanni Sollima, who's also playing cello, so I guess with one hand he's writing and with one hand he's bowing.

MUTI: Sollima is a wonderful musician. He's very cultivated. This piece that he will perform together with Yo-Yo Ma is the result of his studies in the culture of the south of Italy, the rhythms and melodies that go back to the sixteenth century. The tarantella, generally we think is something happy, a sort of Neapolitan dance. But the original tarantella is very tragic, very dramatic, because the tarantella is the animal that, if it bites you, you die. This piece is very difficult for the two celli and also for the conductor and for the orchestra. But it brings memories and echoes from the Balkans, from the Middle East, and the Mediterranean. That is a way of writing music that can give you the feeling of the past, and music that tells you who you are, from where you come. I said one time that we all come from the Mediterranean. I remember when I was a guest conductor in Philadelphia and at the end of one of my first concerts with the orchestra a cellist of the orchestra who became a great friend, a huge man, came to see me in my room and with this voice like a basso profondo, he said, "Oh, Maestro, you are very good." Then a little silence. And then he said, "Are you sure that you are not Jewish?" I said, "You know, I don't know, but we all come from that area." In the music of Sollima, because he is Sicilian, there is all this flavor and this culture that in the music of today can come back and tell us a lot of things.

PATNER: The following week you have a new piece by Ennio Morricone, who most people know as a film composer.

MUTI: Morricone was a pupil of Goffredo Petrassi, one of the most important composers of the twentieth century in Italy. Giulini often conducted the music of Petrassi. Morricone studied composition with Petrassi. But when he writes music not for film, you don't have any idea that it is the same composer.

Rota was different. You could feel that was Rota in the music for movies and the serious music out of the movies. But nobody would think that this piece is Morricone that wrote music for the Westerns that made him famous. This music is very deep, very effective, and is against racism, against terrorism, and was written after the tragedy of the Twin Towers. The text is an English text. It's very moving because it says, "I am black, you are white, but we feel the same way." And there is a chorus that speaks about the "arcobaleno," the rainbow.

Morricone just got a Grammy, and he had also the Oscar, or

two or three, for his music. You become famous writing for what today is the most popular form of "art," in quotes. You can write the most important and interesting thing for the concert halls and nobody will know, and you don't even make money.

PATNER: For Schubert, particularly the lesser played symphonies, it seems that the rest of the world sometimes needs the Italians to open the door. You're playing the Third and Fourth Symphonies, and the last time the Third was played here it was a guy named Riccardo Muti. The last time the Fourth was played, it was a guy named Claudio Abbado. The recording with this orchestra of the Fourth is by Carlo Maria Giulini. These are the famous Viennese Schubert conductors, three great Schubert conductors, but you're all Italian.

MUTI: Schubert was very much influenced by Italian music. Salieri had a great influence on Schubert, and he was very much impressed by the operas, especially Rossini. Even Beethoven was angry about the fact that Rossini was more popular than Beethoven in Vienna.

I decided to do the entire Schubert cycle first because Schubert is extremely important to refine an orchestra. It's not that the Chicago Symphony needs to be refined, but generally the orchestras know how to play Brahms, they know more or less how to play Beethoven. How to play Schubert today remains, in a way, a mystery. Fortunately, we have, little by little, understood that Brahms comes also from Schubert. Many times in the tradition Brahms was played thick, and this was because he's German. But German doesn't mean heavy all the time.

PATNER: And Brahms moved south, and where did he vacation? Italy.

MUTI: When I did for the first time a symphony of Schubert with the Vienna Philharmonic, they asked me to record the entire cycle and then they invited me to conduct the New Year's concert because they said Schubert is the door to Johann Strauss and company.

Schubert's music reflected the soul of Vienna, but many of

his symphonies were performed only after his death. The entire cycle of symphonies gives the image of this really great composer that speaks not only about Vienna, about Austria, about the center of Europe, but has this melancholy. He was not interested in politics like Beethoven, who was open to social problems. Schubert was innocent. But in a way his music speaks to us, especially today, more than before because it gives us a certain comfort, with his melodies and with his incredible sense of harmony that is so Schubert.

PATNER: And if the audience and the orchestra sees how this developed over time, even if, in the end, maybe they'll still prefer the Great Symphony or the Unfinished Symphony, they'll understand where it's coming from and they'll also hear these pieces with the proper lightness.

MUTI: "Leggerezza" [lightness] is the word that I'm using with the orchestra. It doesn't mean that it is without bones, actually, because many times he tries to be the "little Beethoven." But "leggerezza"—it's purity, innocence.

PATNER: You're also going to play one of the Schubert masses that has never been played by this orchestra.

MUTI: One interesting thing about the masses of Schubert is that in the Credo he never uses the phrase "credo in unam sanctam catholicam et apostolicam ecclesiam." Nobody understands why. I don't think that was just because he didn't believe in the Catholic religion. But it is strange that in every mass he didn't put music under these words.

PATNER: He's not getting commissioned to write these. Sometimes they are suggested, but it's not like he's working for a pope, or a bishop or something. Credo means, "I believe," right? So maybe he couldn't put it after those words. He believed in rose petals.

MUTI: He didn't write this mass or the E-flat to please a cardinal or a bishop, or for liturgical reasons, but he wrote to express his feelings through the words of the Latin text. He didn't want to say, "I am Catholic, I am Christian, I am Jewish, or I am this."

PATNER: You mentioned the Vienna Philharmonic saying, "You

have done Schubert, now you can come and do Strauss." I was reading the reviews of your concerts with the orchestra in the Canary Islands, and you had one major critic, from the national paper, [Juan Ángel] Vela del Campo, who went to both performances of each program in the two capitals there and he was very complimentary. Then at the end he said, "But in many ways the greatest performance was the Strauss overture *Indigo and the Forty Thieves.*" He said the lightness and the excitement and the animation was like your old friend Kleiber.

MUTI: I learned with the four New Year's concerts that I did for the Vienna Philharmonic all this style and this lightness. But I was very impressed that the Chicago Symphony, the more we played this piece, the more they sounded like the Vienna Philharmonic—but it's still the Chicago Symphony.

PATNER: I remember a young conductor doing [Franz Lehár's] *Merry Widow* a few years ago at the opera here. I thought my goodness, this is much better music than I've heard played before. It was because someone was really passionate about it.

MUTI: The orchestration is so refined.

PATNER: If you look at the programs of the past decades, particularly in the years of the last century of Theodore Thomas, there would be overtures and encores all throughout the program. You have been bringing them back to us, and I think it's a wonderful thing.

MUTI: When I see the programs of Toscanini that he did as music director of the New York Philharmonic, they are very strange. Today you would kill me. Corelli Concerto Grosso, then Beethoven First Symphony, and then Albéniz. Sort of mixed salad. I would be interested to hear the answer of Toscanini if somebody asked him, "What is the concept of this program?"

Morricone and a Rare Schubert Mass

Chicago Sun-Times, **February 8, 2014** Part of Riccardo Muti's magic is his ability to take rarely played works and get full commitment from an orchestra and performers and total attention from an audi-

ence. For this week, the Chicago Symphony Orchestra music director assembled a program of three pieces having their CSO premieres,
including two works by Franz Schubert and a 2002 concert composition, "Voices from the Silence," by the beyond-prolific film scorer
Ennio Morricone.

Schubert is simultaneously beloved by musicians and listeners
and unknown beyond a number of important symphonies. Muti has
pulled out a fascinating and riveting great-sized A-Flat Major Mass of
1819–22 (revised 1825–26), and a rollicking *Overture in the Italian Style
in C Major* (1817) that might be subtitled, "Schubert Does Rossini."

Muti is a great campaigner not only for music of his Italian homeland, but also for the presence of Italian influences and spirit in other
music. The C Major overture, D. 591, certainly propels his case that
Schubert was captivated by the operatic output of Rossini. At once
tightly wound and filled with the leggerezza (lightness) that Muti
says characterizes Italian music, the overture received a thrilling performance.

The Mass, D. 678, clocks in at nearly 50 minutes, and needs four
soloists capable of great concentration—they have to hold their
pitches during an enormous orchestral and choral fugue—as well as
an idiomatic sense of each of the many changing styles. Three young
Italian soloists—soprano Rosa Feola, tenor Antonio Poli, and bass
Riccardo Zanellato—and Austrian mezzo Michaela Selinger were
absolutely matched and in sync with an ability to capture lightness
and even sweetness without the slightest touch of syrup. The Chorus,
prepared by Duain Wolfe, exhibited the same traits. The openings
of liturgical sections, while showing the influence of Handel and
Haydn, also foreshadowed the understanding of delicate musical
scene-setting that both Verdi and Wagner would use in their opera
later in the century. The expanded trombone section and other brass
created a lush bedding under Muti's direction. What a wonderful
work worthy of many more hearings.

In between came Morricone's *Voices of the Silence*. *Voices* uses a
text that at first seems simplistic—a poem by South-African writer
Richard Rive, intoned here beautifully by actress Ora Jones, and later

sung in Italian by the Chorus. Morricone combines a light touch of '60s avant-grade orchestration with recorded sounds of Middle Eastern chanting, wrapped up with the "Falls" theme from the 1986 movie *The Mission*. No great contribution but an offering of opportunities for meditation over its half-hour run time, the work was expertly played and sung.

A Musician's Retirement and a Conductor's Teacher

On Orchestras and on Learning to Conduct

WFMT Broadcast, June 16, 2014

MUTI: In the first concert we have the Mozart bassoon concerto played by David McGill, who is a great interpreter of the piece and also a great artist and a great musician.

PATNER: David McGill is taking an early retirement from the orchestra and is going to devote himself to teaching. Obviously, a big part of your job is to shepherd the new sheep and to help to select new members of the orchestra. Do you wish you could just turn a switch in your head or wave a wand and never have to think about these kinds of things?

MUTI: Of course a great orchestra is the result of work together of the several musicians. Life goes for all of us, and there is a moment where players have to retire or they feel tired of being every day in an orchestra, and to follow instructions from conductors, sometime intelligent, sometime musical, sometime nonmusical, not intelligent, and sometime conductors that could conduct very well a train or a truck. With all the respect for the truck drivers.

In the case of McGill, he is one of the stars of the Chicago Symphony, and is universally considered one of the greatest bassoon players in the world. The fact that he will leave the orchestra for his personal reasons is certainly very good for him, but it will be a big loss for the orchestra.

The woodwind section of the Chicago Symphony, speaking

about the principal players, is one of the best in the world. Especially in the woodwinds, like in the brass section, the quality
at a certain point is the result of players that play together all
the time, so everybody knows what the colleague does and
adjusts his playing to the playing of his colleague, it's a sort of
harmonic, *harmonico* atmosphere. When I was in Philadelphia
we had a group of woodwind players who had spent decades
together, so when they played together it was like one player
that was playing.

PATNER: I see that you have added a photograph on your wall, and
it looks like Maria Callas. And there's a story, I'm sure, behind it,
because I see she's with Antonino Votto, who was your teacher.

MUTI: I did research through our librarian about the concerts that
Antonino Votto did in Chicago with the Chicago Symphony in
the early sixties. And our librarian was kind enough to find the
reviews that he got. At that time the critic was this —

PATNER: Claudia Cassidy.

MUTI: Apparently she had the reputation to be extremely tough in
her judgment.

PATNER: She had strong opinions, which she expressed.[19]

MUTI: And she wrote the most fabulous reviews about the concerts
of Antonino Votto. Votto for a few years came to Chicago to conduct operas and one year he was here and Fritz Reiner got sick
suddenly, so they invited Votto to replace Fritz Reiner. I remember that when I was his student he spoke about this concert,
this fabulous orchestra. He said that when they asked him, he
sent immediately twelve possibilities of different programs. He
was the assistant of Toscanini and all these young conductors at
the time of Toscanini in the twenties were very strong and solid
musicians. So he did two programs with a pianist that played
a Mozart concerto, Weber *Oberon*, [Claude Debussy's] *La Mer*,
[Modest Mussorgsky's] *Pictures at an Exhibition*, a Haydn symphony. Cassidy wrote that it was one of the greatest concerts
in the season and praised Votto for his musicianship, elegance,
the way he was on the podium.

PATNER: She admired that.

MUTI: The old Italian way, very elegant and not so many circus movements. And for the third performance in the afternoon, Fritz Reiner, who was in the hospital, wanted to hear the performance. So they put a special microphone in the hall connected with the room of the hospital of Fritz Reiner, and Reiner was very impressed about the performance and he wrote a very beautiful message to Votto.

He came from a Neapolitan family. He brought us all the things that he had learned from Toscanini, including the need to prepare the operas, having the conductor playing the piano with all the singers around the piano.

PATNER: He doesn't arrive by helicopter for the dress rehearsal.

MUTI: And working, working, working, working. I learned this from him and still now I work many, many days. When I did *Otello* in 2001 in La Scala with Plácido Domingo and Plácido had already sung 300 performances of *Otello*, he stayed with me twenty-five days to re-study the opera. The same thing happened with Montserrat Caballé when Montserrat had a big triumph in La Scala with *Norma*. The year after we did *Norma* in Vienna and she studied the entire opera again, not because she had to learn the opera, but she was interested in a different approach. Of course these same singers with a conductor that didn't know what to say would not stay one second listening to nonsense.

Mozart for Bassoon and More Rare Schubert

Chicago Sun-Times, June 14, 2014 An orchestra is a living organism, its members much more than parts of a machine yet combining and interacting with one another to make something greater than their individual selves. No single player makes an ensemble and, try as some have, no one individual can break it.

Changes in personnel still have effects, though, and the Chicago Symphony Orchestra is preparing to say adieu to David McGill, principal bassoon since 1997 and a key figure in the Daniel Barenboim and Riccardo Muti eras in both concerts and recordings. McGill, whose sound and technique long ago made him a legend among wind players, is taking a very early retirement from the orchestra to focus on teaching, writing and solo work.

The solo voice of the bassoon is a signature in a number of pieces, most famously the opening of Stravinsky's *The Rite of Spring*. But normally it is an ensemble figure par excellence, and very few concertos for solo bassoon exist and fewer have entered the repertoire. So it was that McGill plays his last concerto as a member of the Chicago Symphony this week by returning to the greatest such work, Mozart's early B-Flat Major composition, K. 191, written when the composer was 18.

Playing his own cadenzas, in under 20 minutes Thursday night McGill offered pure beauty from the unusual-sounding instrument while offering a catalog of every sort of tongue flutter, breath control technique, articulation and pitch and volume leap and drop, all coming off as a wholly pleasurable unity. McGill has long said that the human voice is the absolute guide for the bassoon and the whole performance, not only the aria-like slow movement, was a sort of vocal communication, by turns playful, peaceful and poignant.

The ovation from the audience, Muti and other onstage colleagues was heartfelt.

Muti framed the Mozart with two symphonies by Schubert that are rarely played in concert: his Sixth, or "Little C Major," of 1817–18 and the First, in D, written four years earlier when Schubert was all of 16. Muti's spring survey of all eight of the repertoire symphonies has not been chronological ("Why?" he proposed jocularly to the audience at an open rehearsal Thursday morning, "Because I am original!") and that has been fine. The point is in hearing them all in a series and in the orchestra having the experience of learning and playing them: The Sixth has not been heard here since 1995 and the First was played by the CSO downtown for the first time in 1982 and never since.

Both works are beautiful, elegant and yet with a Schubertian restlessness and willingness to let musical ideas work themselves out as we listen. Even his first symphony, as Dvořák—one of the early public admirers of his orchestral works which were not known for decades after his early death in 1828—observed, could only be by Schubert. And in Muti's hands, of course, they are all about a vocal quality and line, too. And with the principal wind players all assembled, along with William Buchman taking the first bassoon chair, the combination of Muti and the CSO could do no wrong here.

Three Russians

Why the Story Inspires Composers

WFMT Broadcast, September 29, 2014

PATNER: You have a new record out, the *Romeo and Juliet* Suite of Prokofiev. People might say, "Oh, *Romeo and Juliet*, really, is this something that we need another record of?"

MUTI: That question is asked when a conductor makes programs: is it necessary to do this or to do that? It shocked me many years ago was when some critics asked, "Is it necessary to play the Beethoven symphonies or the Brahms symphonies because we have had so many historical performances and great conductors?" The bread of a symphonic orchestra is the symphonic repertoire. I believe it is a pity that Baroque music, Bach and composers of this period, going up to the classic period of Mozart and Haydn, now are more and more done by the so-called specialists. To take away from the big symphonic orchestras this repertoire, and to say that the symphonic orchestra should not play Bach, I think diminishes the possibility of an orchestra and the musicians of the orchestra to grow. Stokowski went too far because he made arrangements of Handel that were very beautiful according to the taste of that time, but today don't make any sense.

PATNER: Very plush.

MUTI: Sometimes Handel sounds like Rachmaninoff. But I recorded many years ago with the Berlin Philharmonic the *Water Music* of

Handel and I think it is still a good recording. For the so-called specialist today it would be considered not stylistically right. But who knows what's stylistically right at the time of Handel? This music was conceived to be played in the big boats that were on the Thames with 200 oboe players, in the open air and on the river. You couldn't hear anything. The king was eating apples, grapes, and doing something else, maybe. And they were out of tune playing this music. So that is the original.

PATNER: That's not to say that there shouldn't be different ways of playing things or experimenting with things.

MUTI: When I was a student at Conservatory Milano studying composition, I made a transcription of the *Sonata sopra Sancta Maria* of [Claudio] Monteverdi, and it was used a lot by some conductors at that time. I read many books about how to perform Baroque music. But still you have to interpret it like a man of today. I don't believe that we can be the ghosts that become again flesh and bones of a period. We don't have any documents. Nobody knows what was really, for example, the voice of Farinelli.[20] Today we have countertenors and some are very good. But what was the voice of Farinelli that made men and women cry?

PATNER: Back to Prokofiev, he had a busy association with Chicago, especially in the early years. Cyrus McCormick,[21] the president of International Harvester and a leader of the Chicago Symphony, found him in Russia and sent the music back. Stock said, "I like this." Prokofiev started coming here as performer, conductor, composer.

MUTI: I believe that *Romeo and Juliet* is the best thing that Prokofiev wrote. We know that in the Third Symphony he tried to express the real Prokofiev, but then Stalin stopped him. He wrote other symphonies, such as the Fifth Symphony that is extremely popular, where he goes back, harmonically speaking. Even going back he was able to express himself. But I think that *Romeo and Juliet* expresses the real heart of Prokofiev. He doesn't want to show, like in the Third Symphony, how avant-garde he is. In *Romeo and Juliet* he has the courage to express the melodic lines in a very open and direct way.

PATNER: I'm somebody that some listeners would say, "Oh, Patner, he doesn't like Prokofiev." I don't like some of Prokofiev as much as other things. But an argument for why he's important is that almost every serious conductor has at least one piece that he or she is connected to.

MUTI: You are not alone in having some reservations about the music of Prokofiev. Radu Lupu once told me that he heard that Claudio Arrau didn't like the Prokofiev piano concertos. He used to say that Prokofiev in the last part of his piano concertos always writes the word bravo. And Vitale my piano teacher told me that one time a friend of his went to see Prokofiev in Russia, and the daughter or the wife, I don't remember, said to him, "Wait here in the dining room a little because my father is busy putting the wrong chords in the normal music."

PATNER: One other positive side of Prokofiev, which he shares with his Russian and Soviet counterparts, is almost all of them were somehow naturally men of the theater, be it ballet, stage play, or opera.

MUTI: This story gave the possibility to many composers to write their best music. The *Romeo and Juliet* of Berlioz has the most beautiful love theme. The same in the short fantasy overture of Tchaikovsky. The love theme is a beautiful melody. And in Bellini, *I Capuleti ed i Montecchi*, the music of Juliet is so beautiful. Everybody has been touched by this spiritual, innocent love that ends in blood. And this story I think touched the heart of Prokofiev more than any other thing that he has written.

Why Play Them Together

WFMT Broadcast, January 19, 2015

PATNER: You're doing Scriabin symphonies here and then in New York.

MUTI: I became familiar with the music of Scriabin through Sviatoslav Richter. He was one of my first soloists and a great friend. As a pianist I was more familiar with the piano music and Richter was one of the greatest interpreters of Scriabin. But he suggested I take a look at the symphonies. The first Scriabin symphony that I conducted when I was in Philadelphia was the First Symphony that I'm doing here.

It is a symphony in six movements. The first five movements are among the best music that has been written not only by Scriabin, but in that period. You hear the influence of all European schools and also, Scriabin being a pianist, the influence of Chopin, but with a sense of harmony that is absolutely revolutionary and modern, with a lot of chromaticism, even if the basic element of the harmony is traditional. Many times, especially with the Third Symphony, his music has dissonances. The music is tortured because all these intervals give the impression that they have difficulty in finding the peace of a consonance. Not in the first movement but especially in the third movement of the first symphony is Scriabin in his best essence.

Unfortunately, the symphony ends with the sixth movement with a chorus and a soloist, and it's not a disaster, because I have to conduct the piece, but it's very academic. When a composer wants to be too philosophical, and to speak about all the metaphysic elements, all the statements become social and political, then the music suffers. We have to do the sixth movement anyway because the chorus is sitting there and the soloists are sitting there.

But the first movement and the third movement, the scherzo, are genial. Like the Tchaikovsky First Symphony, the third movement is genius. I think the fact that I put together Tchaikovsky and Scriabin, one in front of the other, will give an interesting view for the public and the critics and for the musicians.

PATNER: As different as they were, they had something in common, which is that they loved classical music. They were very familiar with what was going on in the West, but they wanted to create a Russian classical music. And they had to start almost de novo with those first symphonies.

MUTI: The difference between the two is that Tchaikovsky is clearly a composer that has roots in the Classical world. When I visited the house of Tchaikovsky outside Moscow, on the piano was the *Idomeneo* of Mozart. In fact when Tchaikovsky conducted the "Pathétique," the last symphony, in the first part of the program he conducted the ballet music of *Idomeneo*. In Tchaikovsky the scores are very Classical. The spirit, the music, it's Romantic, but the structure is Classical. We have to be careful not to put too much sugar in his music because it's always very noble.

In the Fifth Symphony, he writes at certain point "con noblezza." Composers always want to use Italian words. It is like the American Italian restaurants. You find in the menu a lot of dishes spelled wrong. "Noblezza" is the old Italian way to say it, but the word is "nobiltà," not "noblezza."

In Scriabin the score is much thicker than Tchaikovsky. The secret is to make this thick score sound clear, transparent. This is the work of the conductor, of course, when he works with the orchestra. In the way Scriabin uses all the woodwind instruments already you feel the influence of impressionistic music. The fact that he was in France shows clearly in his music.

He must have been a very strange person. In the pictures from his eyes you see that maybe it was not only his ideas but the entire personality was trying to reach the metaphysical world. He was also strange in his behavior. Radu Lupu told me that Artur Rubinstein told Radu that when he was very young, Rubinstein was invited to lunch by Scriabin in Paris. At a certain point Scriabin asked the young Rubinstein who was his favorite composer, and apparently Rubinstein told the truth and said Brahms. Scriabin was so upset and angry that he stood up and left the restaurant. So the poor Rubinstein, who was young and not rich, had to pay the bill.

PATNER: Just before he died he had a plan to bring world peace and he was preparing to present this in Geneva, but unfortunately then he died, so he wasn't able to save the entire world.

MUTI: Musicians are many times very strange. For example, Spontini was one of the greatest Italian composers in the classic, Romantic period, and he was very sure of himself. He thought that he was the incarnation of the music. When he was dying, he was on his bed and he was worried about the fact that "after me music will finish."

PATNER: At least he was concerned for us, for what would come afterwards. You mention Tchaikovsky's attempt at recreating maybe a medieval Italian instruction, but Scriabin has some very different instructions on his scores. He says that something should be mystical or it should be voluptuous. Are those messages to the conductor, to the orchestra players, or just to the audience to put them in a mystic mind?

MUTI: The audience will never know all these indications that are in the score. These are supposed to be for the conductor. But I don't believe so much in this. It's the music that speaks by itself.

PATNER: So if he is saying sublime, you think, well, if the pieces are sublime, they'll be sublime, if they're not, they won't be.

MUTI: Especially in the Third Symphony, in the "Divine Poem," every three, four bars he uses ludique, mystique, sublime, tenebroso, tempestoso. I mean, if you want to create all these changes of interior state you go crazy. Can you imagine explaining to the musicians how to do it? Now you have not enough tenebras. Your darkness is not quite . . . and now you have to be a little bit more lyric.

PATNER: But in two more measures, mystical.

MUTI: And then we are all in trouble because what is mystical? You have to go to St. Francis to ask him what is the mysticism. Certainly his brain was going in directions not normal.

PATNER: At least not known.

MUTI: But I'm sure that when he wrote these words, when he said lyrical, he felt in that moment that those notes should convey a certain lirismo, a certain delicatezza of the soul. We have said a few things smiling. But Scriabin was a great composer. Forget all this lack of control of his mind.

PATNER: You mentioned the exploration of sound.

MUTI: He created timbres completely new to Russian music, and completely different from Rimsky-Korsakov, who really was a painter of colors. In Scriabin the colors are never for themselves, the colors are for the colors, but convey a spiritual message.

Afterword

Riccardo Muti Remembers Andrew Patner

Conversation with David Polk, WFMT Program Director

WFMT Broadcast, **March 16, 2015**

POLK: I first of all would like to thank you for sharing so many of
your conversations between you and Andrew with our listeners.
How will you will remember Andrew?

MUTI: I have lost a great friend, a man of great integrity in his profession, great humanity, great culture, and great sense of humor.
You know, sometimes the way we Italians behave or make comments is so different from the American way. It's not that we are
better or the Americans are better, it's just different. We are a
different culture. But Andrew seemed easy with the American
attitude of life, of food, of culture, of making comments, and
with the European, especially the Italian. He was a Jew of Russian origin. I am a southern Italian. And southern Italian people
and Jewish people are very much alike because we belong to the
Mediterranean area. We are part of the same sea, and what I call
the land of olive trees.

　　He was a very important presence for me in Chicago, not
only because he was a wonderful music critic, but because I

don't have the opportunity to meet many people because of my profession. I have to spend most of my time at Symphony Center, so I don't have so much time to share with other people. With Andrew I felt so close that I could speak about Italy, about paintings.

I respected him deeply, even when we did not necessarily agree on something. Our friendship was independent—it didn't have a positive effect on his reviews. If he didn't agree, he said so, in a very civilized way. He made his comments. That didn't change or didn't touch our friendship because I knew that his comments were genuine.

When I saw him for the last time it was two days before we went to Carnegie Hall. I was going to New York to do our concerts. And then I was going to Italy for nine days and then back here. We left for New York on Monday and that Saturday—that was my last concert here—I said to my assistant, "Call Andrew and tell him that I would like to have dinner with him." I specified not as a critic, as a friend. And we had a wonderful dinner with Italian food and laughing.

POLK: The laughter came through in many of your interviews together.

MUTI: And that was the last time I saw Andrew. I wonder about the fact that I felt that I needed to see him—you know, I was going away, but I was coming back in ten days. But I needed to see him. He came, as I said, as a friend. And I'm so happy—happy is the wrong word—but the fact that I needed to see him, and then it was the last time. And a few days later I couldn't believe, and I still don't believe.

It's like I lost my brother a few months ago, and we are five brothers, and still now I say we are five. Then I think again and I say, "No, we were five." But my brother is still with me. And Andrew, in a way, was like my brother because he was a man of great soul. And if a man has a great soul, he's a brother with all the other people that feel in the same way.

It's a big loss for Chicago. Because his interviews were very thoughtful, he wrote very well, and you could feel his great culture. He knew everything. Everything. It was like having a great man of European culture. Every time a person like Andrew disappears, it will be very difficult to replace him. We know that nobody's indispensable in this world, but sometimes it is extremely difficult to find an equal person.

I used to read his reviews with great attention because sometimes in life you can learn from reviews—if you think about what you are reading, and if you respect the critic. If the critic knows what he is writing about, and is honest, then he can tell you certain things that can have a positive influence on your music making. This is not easy, and it doesn't happen very often.

Sometimes you don't agree with this or that person, but you receive ideas or concepts that make you think, and sometimes have a good influence on your music making. Andrew was this kind of critic.

When I was young, I made many concerts and recordings with Sviatoslav Richter, the great Russian pianist. He liked to read reviews. Being Russian, when he was in Italy, he didn't understand, so he had a lady that translated the review, and he would listen with great attention. And after every phrase he would say, "Mmm, oh yes, he's right," even if it was a criticism. And then, after another phrase, "No, no, I don't agree with him. Oh yes, I think that maybe . . . oh, this point I don't agree with you." It was very nice to see this giant of the piano criticizing the critic.

POLK: So is that how you read Andrew's reviews?

MUTI: Yes. Because first you need to have respect, admiration for the culture and the honesty of the other person. Andrew was the review that I was waiting for. In my hotel, when I did a concert, two days later I was waiting for the *Sun-Times* to read what Andrew wrote about my concert. I will miss him as a critic, but especially as a friend and as a man of culture. In the short period that we have lived together, seven years since I met him in Salzburg and all the five years in Chicago, certainly he's one of the

FIGURE 5.1. Andrew Patner (left) and Riccardo Muti, Salzburg, Austria.
Reproduced with permission of Tom Bachtell.

people who has enriched my life, and I will bring him with me forever.

POLK: When we play this interview on the radio, is there a piece of music or recording you would have us play?

MUTI: I would not choose one of the masterworks because Andrew was open to different kinds of music. It is not necessary to play the slow movement of the Beethoven Ninth symphony. I would recommend two little pieces. One is Martucci, the *Notturno* of Martucci that I played on tour as an encore and I played here. The *Notturno* is seven minutes — very tender, the kind of music that Andrew loved. It was a sort of Italian Mahler, this music that the orchestra played so wonderfully. And second from *Così fan tutte*, the famous trio in the first act, "Soave Sia il Vento." "Soave sia il vento, tranquila sia l'onda, ed ogni elemento benigno risponda ai nostri desir." That, of course, Andrew knew very well. We wish that the wind be soave, sweet, dolce, and the waves will be calm, and every element in the universe would smile in a benign way on our hopes. I want that it will be played also on the day of my departure because Mozart, with this trio, created this sense of voyage to somewhere where we all hope to find ourselves in a sort of blue sky.

POLK: Is there anything else you would want to say?

MUTI: I remember where he was seated, especially when he came to the rehearsals and the hall was empty. And always I liked to look at him, to see his expression. And if he smiled, it meant that I was doing something right. Sometime he had a face a little bit critical, you know, and then I was anxious to know from him what was wrong. Sometimes something was wrong but it had nothing to do with the music. The trousers were too short or, you know. So I want to say, "Andrew, thank you for everything you have given to me and to the orchestra, to the institution, to Chicago, to your friends."

Acknowledgments

John Schmidt thanks Tom Bachtell, Marc Geelhoed, David Polk (WFMT program director), and Laura Emerick (Andrew's editor at the *Sun-Times* and now digital content editor at the CSO) for early and continuing support for the whole project. WFMT, the *Chicago Sun-Times*, and the Patner family kindly granted the rights to bring this collection together. Alex Ross's offer to write a foreword was an invaluable step in gathering momentum for the project. Many thanks to CSO photographer Todd Rosenberg for providing excellent snapshots of each conductor, to Tom Bachtell for creating the frontispiece, and to CSO archivist Frank Villella for scouring the archives to find the historical photographs for the introduction. Thanks also to Marta Tonegutti at the University of Chicago Press for superb editorial guidance and support.

Douglas Shadle thanks his colleagues at Vanderbilt University, especially Melanie Lowe, Joy Calico, Gregory Melchor-Barz, Jim Lovensheimer, Ryan Middagh, and Dean Mark Wait, for their encouragement and support. Marc Geelhoed graciously provided key insights about the Haitink/Boulez era at the last minute. Thanks to Mark Evan Bonds, Jim Davis, Travis Stimeling, and the anonymous peer reviewers for sharing thoughts about possible directions and improvements for the book. And many thanks to John, Marta, and the University of Chicago Press for inviting him aboard this exciting project.

Notes

Introduction

1. Thomas, *Theodore Thomas*, 233.
2. Otis, *The Chicago Symphony*, 185.
3. Otis, *The Chicago Symphony*, 229.
4. Cassidy, "Defauw Makes Debut as Guest Conductor Here," *Chicago Tribune*, 8 Jan. 1943.
5. Cassidy, "Artur Rodziński Takes Over Chicago Symphony Orchestra in Deeply Satisfying Concert," *Chicago Tribune*, 10 Oct. 1947.
6. Cassidy, "Kubelik Makes American Debut as Conductor with Superficial Concert in Orchestra Hall," *Chicago Tribune*, 18 Nov. 1949.
7. Cassidy, "Harris' 5th Symphony Shares Concert with Dull Bach, Befuddled Brahms," *Chicago Tribune*, 19 Oct. 1951.
8. Cassidy, "Fritz Reiner Takes Over and Chicago Gets Its Orchestra Back," *Chicago Tribune*, 16 Oct. 1953.
9. Cassidy, "Reiner Is Back with His Orchestra and the Light Shines on Music," *Chicago Tribune*, 15 Feb. 1957.
10. Richard Orr, "Sees Symphony Rise, Decline of TV Comics," *Chicago Tribune*, 5 Dec. 1954.
11. Hart, *Fritz Reiner*, 168.
12. Solti, *Memoirs*, 108; Cassidy, "Lyric Suffers a Setback in First 'Figaro,'" *Chicago Tribune*, 10 Nov. 1957.
13. Cassidy, "Slashingly Powerful 'Sacre' Crests Rosbaud's Holiday Concert," *Chicago Tribune*, 23 Nov. 1962.

14. Cassidy, "Jean Martinon's Farewell Concert Lifts Esteem for Him to a New Level," *Chicago Tribune*, 16 Mar. 1962.

15. Cassidy, "Either Boston and Leinsdorf are Incompatible or They Need More Time to Make It Work," *Chicago Tribune*, 16 Apr. 1963; Cassidy, "Martinon's Brilliant Bartók Against Memory's Indelible Backdrop," *Chicago Tribune*, 25 Oct. 1963; Cassidy, "Inferior Concert Verges on Mayhem in the Gershwin Concerto," *Chicago Tribune*, 1 May 1964.

16. Willis, "Rafael Kubelik Back as Guest Conductor," *Chicago Tribune*, 4 Dec. 1966.

17. Gorner, "Solti Sound Exudes Drama, Lyric Vitality," *Chicago Tribune*, 19 Dec. 1969.

18. Von Rhein, "Acoustics Betray Solti's Bruckner 4th," 18 Oct. 1980.

Chapter 1

1. Gorner, "A Grand Night for Brucknerites," *Chicago Tribune*, 13 Nov. 1970; Willis, "Chicago Conductor Watchers Treated to the Cream of the New Young Breed," *Chicago Tribune*, 17 Jan. 1971.

2. Von Rhein, "Barenboim, Chicago Symphony Ring Out Old Year in Vigorous Style," 17 Dec. 1977; Von Rhein, "Chicago Will Miss You, Mr. Barenboim," *Chicago Tribune*, 27 Mar. 1981.

3. Von Rhein, "Barenboim Flirts with CSO Helm," *Chicago Tribune*, 21 Oct. 1988.

4. Lawrence Johnson, "CSO Stumbles Badly," *Chicago Tribune*, 31 May 1997.

5. Stephen Kinzer, "As Funds Disappear, So Do Orchestras," *New York Times*, 14 May 2003.

6. Ross, "Farewell Symphony," *New Yorker*, 3 July 2006.

7. Carl "Doc" Severinsen (1927–), jazz trumpeter and big band leader.

8. Franz Schubert's 1823 grand opera.

9. Artur Schnabel (1882–1952), Austrian pianist.

10. Ivan Galamian (1903–81), renowned violin pedagogue.

11. Allan Kozinn, "This is the Golden Age," *New York Times*, 28 May 2006.

12. Von Rhein, "Barenboim Shakes Down Thunder, Starts Farewell," *Chicago Tribune*, 27 May 2006.

Chapter 2

1. Giovanni Battista Pergolesi (1710–36), Italian composer; purported source of Stravinsky's *Pulcinella*.

2. Karol Szymanowski (1882–1937), Polish composer.

3. Gustav Klimt (1862–1918), Austrian painter.

4. Darmstadt International Summer Courses for New Music—new music fes-

tival that included performances, workshops, and classes and focused heavily on serial compositional techniques in the 1950s and 1960s.

5. Harrison Birtwistle (1934–), British composer.

6. Arthur Honegger (1892–1955), Swiss composer and member of "Les Six."

7. Boulez wrote two piano sonatas between 1946 and 1948, and a third from 1955 to 1957.

8. For example, Steve Reich (1936–) and Philip Glass (1937–).

9. "There are more things in heaven and earth, Horatio, than are dreamt of in your philosophy."

Chapter 3

1. Johnson, "CSO Stumbles Badly," *Chicago Tribune*, 31 May 1997; Von Rhein, "It's a Love Feast as CSO Realizes Haitink's Vision," *Chicago Tribune*, 18 Jan. 1997; Von Rhein, "Planning the CSO's Season: Hold the Cheese Sauce," *Chicago Tribune*, 20 Sep. 1998.

2. Von Rhein, "Conductor Haitink Takes Aging, Appreciation in Stride," *Chicago Tribune*, 7 Sep. 2008.

3. Felix Hupka (1896–1966), Austrian pianist and conductor.

4. Klemperer became partially paralyzed and began to behave erratically following a 1939 surgery to remove a benign brain tumor.

5. Eduard van Beinum (1901–59), Dutch conductor.

6. A small round brass instrument used to signal the arrival and departure of mail riders.

7. Witold Lutosławski (1913–94), Polish composer.

Chapter 4

1. Willis, "Unique Conducting Sustains an Asserted Command," *Chicago Tribune*, 26 July 1973; Willis, "Ready for a Musical Quiz?" *Chicago Tribune*, 21 Mar. 1975.

2. Joseph McLellan, "Philadelphia Orchestra," *Washington Post*, 12 Apr. 1983; Holland, "Riccardo Muti Makes Music His Way," *New York Times* 9 Oct. 1983; Kozinn, "Muti to Quit Philadelphia Orchestra," *New York Times*, 30 Mar. 1990.

3. Sandow, "Who Comes After Masur?" *Wall Street Journal*, 17 Feb. 2000.

4. Daniel J. Wakin, "At the Philharmonic, Musings about Muti," *New York Times*, 7 May 2008.

5. He is trying to translate the Italian expression "libero professionista" and confuses the words "sword" and "lance."

6. Nino Rota (1911–1979), Italian composer best known for writing the original music for the films of Federico Fellini and for *The Godfather* and *The Godfather Part II*.

7. A secondary school in Italy that leads to university training.

8. Saint Januaris I of Benevento—Saint in the Western and Eastern Christian Churches.

9. Outside of any shared passions, Mariani's introduction of Wagner's works in the 1870s stirred a lengthy controversy about opera and national identity. Verdi had retired by this time but was convinced to write *Otello* after discussing the possibility with his publisher, Giulio Ricordi, and the librettist, Arrigo Boito.

10. Predominantly African American church in Chicago's Woodlawn neighborhood. The CSO and Muti first performed there on September 22, 2011.

11. Muti had thrown out the first pitch at a Cubs game against the Detroit Tigers on June 13.

12. Night, whom in shape so sweet thou here may'st see / Sleeping, was by an Angel sculptured thus / In marble, and since she sleeps hath life like us: / Thou doubt'st? Awake her: she will speak to thee. (Translation: Algernon Charles Swinburne, 1889.)

13. Sleep likes me well, and better yet to know / I am but stone. While shame and grief must be, / Good hap is mine, to feel not, nor to see: / Take heed, then, lest thou wake me: ah, speak low. (Translation: Algernon Charles Swinburne, 1889.)

14. See p. 36 ["Lightning Strikes with Radu Lupu"].

15. Hermann Scherchen (1891–1966), German conductor

16. Sopranos Maria Callas (1923–77), Montserrat Caballé (1933–2018), Renata Scotto (1934–), Anita Cerquetti (1931–2014), and Joan Sutherland (1926–2010).

17. Sopranos Maria Malibran (1808–36) and Giulia Grisi (1811–69).

18. Philip Gossett (1941–2017), University of Chicago musicologist.

19. For more on Cassidy, see the introduction to this volume.

20. Farinelli (1705–82), notorious Italian castrato.

21. Cyrus McCormick, Jr. (1859–1936), president of International Harvester Company in Chicago.

Select Bibliography

Barenboim, Daniel. *A Life in Music*. New York: Arcade Publishing, 2013.

Furlong, William Barry. *Season with Solti: A Year in the Life of the Chicago Symphony*. New York: MacMillan Publishing Co., 1974.

Hart, Philip. *Fritz Reiner: A Biography*. Evanston, IL: Northwestern University Press, 1994.

Matheopolis, Helena. *Maestro: Encounters with Conductors of Today*. London: Hutchinson, 1982.

Morgan, Kenneth. *Fritz Reiner, Maestro and Martinet*. Urbana and Chicago: University of Illinois Press, 2005.

Muti, Riccardo. *Riccardo Muti: An Autobiography*. New York: Rizzoli Ex Libris, 2011.

Otis, Philo Adams. *The Chicago Symphony, Its Organization, Growth, and Development, 1891–1924*. Chicago: Clayton F. Summy Co., 1925.

Peck, Donald. *The Right Place, The Right Time! Tales of My Chicago Symphony Days*. Bloomington: Indiana University Press, 2007.

Robinson, Paul. *Solti*. Toronto: Lester and Orpen Limited, 1979.

Schabas, Ezra. *Theodore Thomas: America's Conductor and Builder of Orchestras, 1835–1905*. Urbana and Chicago: University of Illinois Press, 1989.

Solti, Sir Georg. *Memoirs*. New York: Alfred A. Knopf, 1997.

Spitzer, John, ed. *American Orchestras in the Nineteenth Century*. Chicago: University of Chicago Press, 2012.

Stewart, M. Dee, ed. *Philip Farkas: The Legacy of a Master*. Northfield, IL: Instrumentalist Publishing Company, 1990.

Thomas, Theodore. *Theodore Thomas: A Musical Autobiography*. Edited by George P. Upton. Chicago: A. C. McClurg and Co., 1905.

Index of Composers and Works